The 1930s

1933

• Hitler appointed German chancellor, gets dictatorial powers. Reichstag fire in Berlin; Nazi terror begins • Germany and Japan withdraw from League of Nations.
• Giuseppe Zangara executed for attempted assassination of president-elect Roosevelt in which Chicago mayor Cermak is fatally shot. Roosevelt inaugurated ("the only thing we have to fear is fear itself"); launches New Deal
• Prohibition repealed • USSR recognized by U.S • Glass-Steagall Act bans banks from dealing in stocks and bonds.
World Series: NY Giants d.Wash. (4-1)
Kentucky Derby Champion *Brokers Tip*
NCAA Football Champions Mich. (8-0-0)
• Edwin Armstrong introduces frequency modulation (FM), a static-free method of transmission • Esquire debuts as the first men's magazine • Laurens Hammond introduces his Hammond organ • Sally Rand's fan dance is a hit at the Chicago World's Fair • A.A. Michelson's work on the speed of light is completed posthumously.

The Game: 1933 GA.-14 UF -0

Undefeated UGA entered the UF showdown as the prime contender for the conference title, as well as national honors. Despite the Depression, a capacity crowd of 20,000 filled stadium in Jacksonville.

"We're crippled and we won't have our full power, but we are going to battle Georgia to the last ditch with the men on hand," said FLA coach D.K. "Dutch" Stanley, referring to having lost halfback Jack "Sonny" Henderson, Sr. center S.W. "Big Bill" Ferrazzi for this game, along with concerns about tackle Welcome Shearer and guard Tommy "Memory" Lane being able to play.

Homer Key slipped over left tackle and raced down the sidelines 33 yards before being knocked out of bounds on the UF 7 yard line. Next play Key scrambled in his backfield and lofted a "lazy flat pass" to Grant in the UF end zone. Grant PAT.

In the 3rd quarter, from the UF 36, Grant avoided numerous tacklers, and outran the rest into the end zone. He added the PAT. Orange and blue supporters sat in shocked silence while the Red and Black whooped it up.

1934

• Chancellor Dollfuss of Austria assassinated by Nazis, Hitler becomes Führer • USSR admitted to League of Nations • Mao Zedong begins the Long March north with 100,000 soldiers • Securities Exchange Act is passed, establishing the Securities and Exchange Commission.
• Federal Communications Commission is established to regulate communications.
• Dust storms ruin about 100 million acres and damage another 200 million acres of cropland in Kansas, Texas, Colorado, and Oklahoma ("Dust Bowl").
World Series
St. Louis Cardinals d. Detroit (4-3)
Kentucky Derby Champion *Cavalcade*
NCAA Football Champions Minn. (8-0-0)
Best Picture: Calvacade
• The Communications Act of 1934 creates the Federal Communications Commission, which regulates broadcasting • It Happened One Night sweeps the Academy Awards, winning Best Picture, Director, Actor, and Actress • Irene and Frederic Joliot-Curie create the first man-made radioactive substance by bombarding aluminum with alpha particles that create radioactive phosphorus • Henrik Dam discovers vitamin K.

The Game: 1934 GA.-14 UF-0

America was in the midst of Depression crime waves. This year John Dillinger, Bonnie Parker, Clyde Barrow, and "Pretty Boy" Floyd had been killed by lawmen. Members of the "Ma" Barker gang were hiding in a cottage just 100 miles south of Jacksonville on the day of this year's game.

"While neither team has had more than an average season, both have indicated potential power that brings to match two beaten, but eager elevens." **Sav. Morning News**

The long-range punting of GA's Maurice Green and John Bond kept UF backed up most of the game. Both defenses played ferociously.

Early in the 2nd quarter, GA back Johnny Jones sprinted 22 yards around right end downed inside the UF 10. After two rushes for no gain, Bond took the ball and headed again towards the line. He suddenly faded back and hit halfback Glenn Johnson who was clear in the end zone, with a perfect toss. Bond added the PAT and GA led 7-0.

"The Bulldog line became tenacious when the huskies felt the double stripes (of the end zone) drawing uncomfortably close to their backs." Associated Press

In the middle of the 4th quarter, Bond intercepted a Chase pass and ran it back 32 yards to the UF 42. After penalties and sizeable losses, Green faked a punt and ran 33 yards to the UF 30. Bond then hit Green with a TD pass. Bond again made the PAT and GA led 14-0.

John Bond was the GA star of the game with a TD pass, a TD catch, a 32-yard interception return, over 40 yards rushing, a 50-yard punting average, and two PATs.

1935

• Saar incorporated into Germany after plebiscite • Nazis repudiate Versailles Treaty, introduce compulsory military service • Mussolini invades Ethiopia; League of Nations invokes sanctions.
• Roosevelt opens second phase of New Deal in U.S., calling for social security, better housing, equitable taxation, and farm assistance • Huey Long assassinated in Louisiana • Persia becomes Iran under Reza Shah Pahlevi • Nazis enact Nuremberg Laws against Jews to prevent "racial pollution." Heinrich Himmler starts breeding program to produce "Aryan super race" • George H. Gallup begins the "Gallup Poll." In 1936 the poll will successfully predict outcome of the presidential election.
World Series Detroit d.Chi.Cubs (4-2)
Kentucky Derby Champion *Omaha*
NCAA Football Champions
Minnesota (CFRA, NCF, HF) (8-0-0)
& SMU (DS) (12-1-0)
Best Picture: It Happened One Night
•Although a primitive, two-color process was first used in 1922, audiences weren't impressed by Technicolor until a three-color system appeared in Becky Sharp.
• George Gershwin combines black folk idiom and Broadway musical techniques in Porgy and Bess • Allen Lane's Penguin Press, an English publishing house, reintroduces the paperback book.

The Game: 1935 GA.-7 UF-0

The nation was becoming weary of Hitler's actions against the Jewish population throughout Europe and had read about Mussolini's Italian army invading Ethiopia.

GA Coach Harry Mehre had said earlier that he would be giving SR. LHB and team co-captain John Bond and RHB Al Minot the afternoon off against UF, to rest up for the remainder of the season.

Throughout the game the UF offense was stymied, but their defense would not allow GA near their goal line.

The highlight of the day for UF fans was Billy Chase's 2nd half kick-off return of 65 yards.

"Home state fans were beginning to grow quite a little proud of the the scoreless dead lock they believed their team had in its grasp." **Florida Times Union.**

With the UF offense stopped again, Chase booted a quick-kick from his own 25. Bond caught the ball on the UF 40 and raced down to the 17 yard line. Al Minot then cracked off right tackle, knocking away several arm tackle attempts, and landed in the end zone. Bond made the PAT.

With less than a minute remaining, UF passed from their 45 down to GA's 20. After two five-yard gains, UF had the ball on the GA 10 with only seconds left to play. Anticipating the defense to play the pass, UF attempted to run for the score, but was stopped short of the goal.

1936

• Germans occupy Rhineland • Rome-Berlin Axis proclaimed (Japan to join in 1940) • Trotsky exiled to Mexico • King George V dies; succeeded by son, Edward VIII, who soon abdicates to marry an American-born divorcée, and is succeeded by brother, George VI • Spanish civil war egins. Hundreds of Americans join the Lincoln Brigades." (Franco's fascist forces defeat Loyalist forces by 1939, when Madrid falls.) • War between China and Japan begins, to continue through World War II • Japan and Germany sign anti-Comintern pact; joined by Italy in 1937

Gen. Anastasio Somoza leads a coup d'etat in Nicaragua ushering in Somoza family dictatorship for more than 4 decades • FDR is re-elected in a landslide. The Electoral Vote is 523-8. Dust Bowl problem continues in the midwest. World Series NY Yankees d. NY Giants (4-2) Kentucky Derby Champion *Bold Venture* NCAA Football Champions Minnesota (7-1-0) Best Picture: Mutiny on the Bounty The British Broadcasting Corporation (BBC) debuts the world's first television service with three hours of programming a day • Electric guitars debut • Margaret Mitchell's Gone with the Wind published.

The Game: 1936 GA.-26 UF-8

"If Josh Cody's Gators can maintain the pace they set against Maryland, they should be able to bowl over the Bulldogs." UPI dispatch.

The crowd was held to around 17,000 because of heavy rains in Jacksonville.

GA, behind great running by "Wild Bill" Hartman and Sanford Vandiver, surprised the strong UF line. One writer penned, *"After the first period the result never was in doubt as Georgia's set of fleet backs took to the air whenever their running attack bogged down."*

After a 50 yard drive, HB Alf Anderson passed to Vandiver in the end zone for GA's first score. The PAT was no good. UF answered when halfback Walter "Tiger" Mayberry spotted right end Watson Ramsey streaking across the GA goal line and hit him for the score. The PAT was missed, and the game tied.

GA scored again in short order. Hartman found FB Harry Stevens for a 25-yard gain. After two tough runs, Hartman crashed over from the one. Again, the PAT was no good.

In the 2nd half, GA HB Maurice Green lofted a 5-yard pass to E Otis Maffett for a TD. Green made the PAT and Ga. led 19-6. In the 4th quarter, Stevens rifled a pass to Maffett for another GA TD. The PAT made it 26-6. UF added a safety when Fonia Pennington blocked a GA punt out of the end zone for a safety. The solid GA defense and a mix of running and passing on offense had won the game.

"Florida was beaten by a machine which worked so perfectly for any player to stand out as a hero..." AP (This was the first time UF had scored on GA since the 1932 game.)

937

Hitler repudiates war guilt clause of Versailles Treaty; continues to build German power • Italy withdraws from League of Nations • U.S. gunboat *Panay* sunk by Japanese in Yangtze River. Japan invades China, conquers most of coastal area • Amelia Earhart lost somewhere in Pacific on round-the-world flight • Picasso's Guernica mural • Britain begins 999 emergency telephone number. The United States starts 911 service in New York in 1968 • The dirigible "Hindenburg" explodes at Lakehurst, N.J., killing 36.
World Series
NY Yankees d. NY Giants (4-1)

Kentucky Derby Champion *War Admiral* NCAA Football Champions Pittsburgh (9-0-1) Best Picture: The Great Ziegfeld • Edgar Bergen and his puppet Charlie McCarthy make their radio debut on NBC. • The Glenn Miller Band debuts in New York. • Walt Disney's first full-length animated feature, Snow White and the Seven Dwarfs, hits theaters and becomes an instant classic.

The Game: 1937 UF-6 GA-0

Before 22,000 fans, the game evolved into trench warfare with little offense and plenty of staunch defense.

Then came the "break" of the day. GA was punting from its own 44. As Bulldog HB Billy Mims took the snap, UF RT Charlie Kreijcier barreled through, "charging like a shot." The kicked ball hit him in the stomach and bounced backwards toward the GA goal. UF LE Clifford Whiddon scooped up the ball at the GA 25, broke away from two Bulldogs, and rambled into the end zone standing up. Clark Goff's PAT was no good.

In the 4th quarter GA twice threatened to break over the UF goal line.

After Mayberry punted 52 yards from behind his goal line, GA took over on their own 48. Hartman rambled wide around left end down to the UF 35. Mims passed to RE Carroll Thomas down to the 18. Mims again fired towards a Bulldog receiver at the goal line when Gator Jack Blalock stepped in front and intercepted the pass, sealing the win for Florida.

1938

• Hitler marches into Austria…Munich Pact— Britain, France, and Italy agree to let Germany partition Czechoslovakia • Douglas "Wrong-Way" Corrigan flies from New York to Dublin • Fair Labor Standards Act establishes minimum wage • Nazis destroy Jewish shops, homes, synagogues in Kristallnacht riots; 20,000-30,000 sent to concentration camps. • First oil strike in Kuwait transforms the emirate's economy • Orson Welles broadcasts his adaptation of H.G. Wells's War of the Worlds, creating a nationwide panic as listeners believe that aliens have landed in New Jersey (Oct. 30). World Series NY Yankees d. Chic. Cubs (4-0) Kentucky Derby Champion *Lawrin* NCAA Football Champions TCU (11-0-0) Best Picture: The Life of Emile Zola • Roy Acuff joins the Grand Ole Opry and brings national recognition to the Nashville-based radio program • Information Please quiz show debuts on radio.

The Game: 1938 GA-19 UF-13

UF Coach Cody transferred center and team captain Jimmy Oxford to blocking back in a move to bolster the offense. He was replaced in the line by John Berry, who would be pitted against Bulldog center and captain Quinton Lumpkin, a second-team All-SEC performer.

By Friday, Jacksonville's *"hotels were packed and jammed and most of the throng is expected to stay overnight (Saturday) either to celebrate or to forget."* **Florida Times Union**

A UF fumble gave GA the ball on the UF 24. After several attempts at breaking through the UF defensive line, Fordham ripped in for Georgia's first score. The PAT was wide. After

a short quick-kick by GA, UF moved 24 yards for the tying score. The PAT was wide right.

Early in the 4th quarter, GA G Ned Barbre intercepted a UF pass at the GA 33. HB Vassa Cate ran a reverse to the UF 49. GA QB Mims then whipped a pass to Cate who hauled it in on the dead run, flashed into the open and streaked into the Florida end zone. Barbre's PAT was good.

Mims finished off the Gators by passing to LE Alex McCaskill for 31 yards and a TD. The PAT was partially blocked.

"Neither team appeared up to the class for former Georgia and Florida combines, but the excessive heat may have had something to do with the listlessness that marked all but a few minutes of the affair. The teams could hardly be blamed for playing as if they were in the steam room of a Turkish bath." **Florida Times Union**

1939

• Germany invades Poland; occupies Bohemia and Moravia; renounces pact with England and concludes 10-year non-aggression pact with USSR • Russo-Finnish War begins; World War II begins • In U.S., Roosevelt submits $1,319-million defense budget, proclaims U.S. neutrality, and declares limited emergency • Einstein writes FDR about feasibility of atomic bomb • New York World's Fair opens •DAR refuses to allow Marian Anderson to perform • New York World's Fair opens • U.S. Department of Agriculture starts first food stamp program in Rochester, N.Y. World Series NY Yankees d. Cincinnati (4-0) Kentucky Derby Champion *Johnstown* NCAA Basketball Championship Oregon d. Ohio St. (46-33) NCAA Football Champions Texas A&M (11-0-0) Best Picture: You Can't Take It With You • The big-screen adaptation of Gone with the Wind premieres, and will go on to gross $192 million, making it one of the most profitable films of all time. It's also one of the longest films, clocking in at 231 minutes. • Robert Kane introduces the Batman cartoon.

The Game: 1939 GA-6 UF-2

The Armistice Day game in Jax was tempered by events in Europe. 20,000 fans crowded into the stadium for the 2:30pm kick-off. The game, as intense as any GA-UF game, was one of the sloppiest played so far in the series.The teams combined for 10 fumbles, four interceptions and 155 yards in penalties.UF FB Charlie Tate fumbled inside the UF 20. GA made a first down at the UF 5. On fourth down Kimsey tried to break the goal line but was stopped at the six inch line.

On a UF punt, Vassa Cate caught the ball on his own 48 and flashed down to the UF 31 before being stopped. Heyward Allen passed to LE Alex McCaskill for a nine yard gain. It was the only pass completion for the game, and carried GA down to the UF one. Fordham plunged through the Gator masses for the score. The PAT was no good.

Late in the game, UF back Bobby Johnson punted a perfect kick into the "coffin corner," and out of bounds at the GA one. Mims deliberately grounded the ball in the end zone, giving Florida a safety and two points.

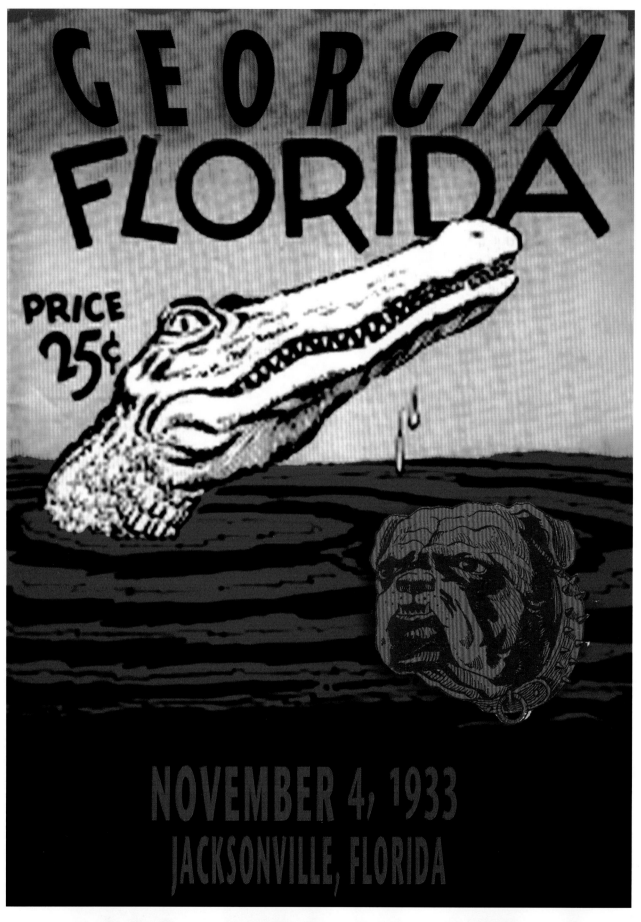

GEORGIA
FLORIDA

PRICE 25¢

NOVEMBER 4, 1933
JACKSONVILLE, FLORIDA

1933 · UGA 14   UFL 0

PROGRAM

Florida
FIGHTING GATORS
VS
Georgia
BULLDOGS

Sat. Nov. 3rd   Price 10¢

1934
UGA 14 UFL 0

1935
UGA 7 UFL 0

GEORGIA
VS
FLORIDA

GEORGIA vs. FLORIDA

1936 · UGA 26   UFL 8

GEORGIA

FLORIDA
1937 · UGA 0   UFL 6

FLORIDA vs GEORGIA
JACKSONVILLE, FLA   NOV. 5, 1938

1938 · UGA 19 UFL 13

GEORGIA VS. FLORIDA

JACKSONVILLE, FLA.   NOV. 11, 1939

1939 · UGA 6 UFL 2

The 1940s

1940

• Hitler invades Norway, Denmark, the Netherlands, Belgium, Luxembourg, and France • Churchill becomes Britain's prime minister • Trotsky assassinated in Mexico • U.S. trades 50 destroyers for leases on British bases in Western Hemisphere • Selective Service Act signed• The first official network television broadcast is put out by NBC
• Lascaux caves with Cro-Magnon art discovered by French schoolboy • The first Social Security benefit checks are paid out • The Pennsylvania Turnpike opens. It is the first multi-lane U.S. superhighway. The first Los Angeles freeway opens.
• The first McDonald's hamburger stand opens in Pasadena, Calif.
World Series Cincinnati d. Detroit (4-3)
Kentucky Derby Champion *Gallahadion*
NCAA Basketball Championship
 Indiana d. Kansas (60-42)
NCAA Football Champions Minn. (8-0-0)
Best Picture: Gone With the Wind
• CBS demonstrates color television in New York • WNBT, the first regularly operating television station, debuts in New York with an estimated 10,000 viewers • It's a bird! It's a plane! It's Superman! The radio show debuts • The first Bugs Bunny cartoon • Freeze drying is adapted for food preservation• Plasma is discovered to be a substitute for whole blood in transfusions • Karl Landsteiner and Alexander Weiner discover the Rh factor in blood.

The Game: 1940 UF-18 GA- 13

Coach Wally Butts outfitted his team in silver pants to complement their red jerseys. *"Silver Britches"* would become a GA Bulldog trademark. The Gators dazzled everyone with their orange jerseys, orange pants and navy stockings.
"The Gators may not be one of the best football teams in America, but certainly they are one of the best dressed," the Constitution said.
Frank Sinkwich had sprained his ankle in the Auburn game, and stories were flying that he would not be playing in today's game.
"We'll be in there-and so will they. They can't scare us with their bear stories," Florida Coach Thomas J. Lieb told the Atlanta Constitution.
UF and GA were the two most pass-oriented teams in the Southeastern

Conference in 1940.
After UF QB Tommy Harrison hit RHB Fondren Mitchell with a 36-yard pass to the GA 16, the defense stiffened and held UF. On fourth down, Paul Eller kicked a FG to give UF an early 3-0 lead.
After recovering a UF fumble, GA HB Jim Todd threw a 21-yard TD pass to Van Davis. Center Leo Costa booted the PAT and GA led 7-3.
UF end Fergie Ferguson blocked a Cliff Kimsey punt and FLA RE John Piombo scooped up the ball and ran 31 yards for a UF score. The PAT was no good. UF now led 9-7.
GA fumbled on a razzle-dazzle play at the end of the third quarter and FLA had the ball on the GA 40. Gator HB Bud Walton hit HB Fondren Mitchell with a long TD pass. Charlie Tate made the PAT, the score was now 16-7.
GA took the next kick-off and drove 80 yards, the score coming off a 45-yard pass from Jim Todd to George Poschner. The PAT was no good. UF now led 16-13.
A superb punt by UF skidded out of bounds on the GA six. With time running out, GA QB Todd drifted back in the end zone, looking deep for someone to pass to. He never saw UF LG Floyd Konesty break through the line, tackling him in the end zone for a safety, giving UF the victory score of 18-13.

1941

• Germany attacks the Balkans and Russia
• Japanese surprise attack on U.S. fleet at Pearl Harbor brings U.S. into World War II; U.S. and Britain declare war on Japan.
• Manhattan Project begins • Roosevelt enunciates "four freedoms," signs Lend-Lease Act, declares national emergency, promises aid to USSR • Congress passes the Lend-Lease Act, giving President the power to sell, lend, and lease war supplies to other nations.
World Series
 NY Yankees d. Brooklyn Dodgers (4-1)
Kentucky Derby Champion *Whirlaway*
NCAA Basketball Championship
Wisconsin d. Wash. St. (39-34)
NCAA Football Champions
Minnesota (8-0-0)
Best Picture: Rebecca
• In Citizen Kane, Orson Welles subordinates all previous technological and cinematic accomplishments to his own essentially cinematic vision. Using newly developed film stocks and a wider, faster lens, Welles pushes the boundaries of montage and mise-en-scène, as well as sound, redefining the medium.

• Actress Greta Garbo retires at age 36.
• Edward Hopper completes the painting Nighthawks • Glenn Seaborg and Edwin McMillan isolate plutonium, a fuel preferable to uranium for nuclear reactors
• RCA demonstrates a new simplified electron microscope that magnifies up to 100,000 times.

The Game: 1941 GA-19 UF-3

In less than a month America would be at war. As the fans cheered the '41 game, the Japanese were organizing a sneak attack on Pearl Harbor, forcing the US into World War II. But the attention at the moment was on GA's superback… Frank Sinkwich.
Sinkwich was back in action averaging more than 100 yards rushing per game. The GA tailback George Poschner would miss this game with a broken arm.
Underdog UF was paced by the passing combo of left halfback Tommy "the Red" Harrison to left end Forrest "Fergie" Ferguson.
"Sinkwich runs with more sheer power than any man to ever play on the local field. In addition, he has a deceptive style of starting that causes the opposition to lean the wrong way just long enough to give Fireball Frankie an opening," said the Florida Times Union.
UF scored first on a 17-yard Paul Eller field goal.
GA E Van Davis partially blocked Tommy Harrison's punt and GA had the ball on the UF 26. The Dogs drove to the UF 4-yard line before the drive stalled. UF regained possession.
UF QB Harrison rolled back into the end zone to pass, but was knocked down by Dick McPhee for a GA safety. GA trailed Florida 3-2.
In the middle of the 3rd quarter, Sinkwich took a handoff, wedged off tackle and dashed 23 yards for the go-ahead TD. Leo Costa added the PAT and GA led 9-3.
The next possession, GA drove to the UF 10 before being stopped. Sinkwich split the uprights for a 10 yard FG, giving GA. a 12-3 lead.
After a UF interception on their own 18, Sinkwich tore into the Gator line three times before scoring. The PAT made the score 19-3 in favor of GA.
UF attempted two fake punts and more razzle dazzle, but each time they drove towards the GA goal, an interception stopped them without any further scoring.

1942

• Declaration of United Nations signed in Washington • Nazi leaders attend Wannsee Conference to coordinate the "final solution to the Jewish question," the systematic genocide of Jews known as the Holocaust • Women's military services established • More than 120,000 Japanese and persons of Japanese ancestry living in western U.S. moved to "relocation centers," some for the duration of the war (Executive Order 9066) • Coconut Grove nightclub fire in Boston kills 492
• Women's military services established.
• Kaiser Foundation Health Plan, first health maintenance organization (HMO), begins in Oakland, Calif.
World Series
St. Louis Cardinals d. NY Yankees (4-1)
Kentucky Derby Champion *Shut Out*
NCAA Basketball Championship
Stanford d. Dartmouth (53-38)
NCAA Football Champions
University of Georgia 11-1-0
Best Picture: How Green Was My Valley
• Casablanca premieres in theaters • Bing Crosby releases "White Christmas," from the film Holiday Inn. The song goes on to be the all-time, top-selling song from a film • RCA Victor sprays gold over Glenn Miller's million-copy-seller Chattanooga Choo Choo, creating the first "gold record " • The first safe self-sustaining nuclear chain reaction is accomplished by Erico Fermi, Edward Teller and Leo Szilard at the University of Chicago • Harvard University chemist Louis F. Fieser invents napalm, a jelly-like mixture of gasoline and palm oils that sticks to its target until it burns out • Radar comes into operational use • The U.S. government establishes the Manhattan Project, led by Robert Oppenheimer, to coordinate ongoing American efforts to design and build the atomic bomb.

The Game: 1942 GA- 75 UF- 0

America was in its first year of war and the 22,000 fans in Jacksonville were keeping up with the progress of the Allies. Within hours of the game, news flashes reported that U.S. forces had invaded North Africa.

GA powered by the All–American running and passing of Sinkwich and a newcomer named Charley Trippi, came into the game unbeaten, untied and ranked number one in the nation. They soon lived up to their national ranking.

On UF's first series, HB Jack Jones threw a short pass that GA center Bill Godwin intercepted. Sinkwich, Lamar Davis, and Dick McPhee slammed into the UF line for sizeable gains. Sinkwich scored from seven yards out. Costa's kick was good, and in less than three minutes GA led 7-0.

On their next possession, Jones was again

intercepted by Godwin at the UF 24. Six plays later, Sinkwich scored from the 2. Costa's kick made it 14-0.

After stopping UF, Charley Trippi tossed a 59-yard bomb to left end George Poschner for the next score. Costa's kick made it 21-0.

Trippi picked off the next Jones' pass, which he returned 48 yards for the score. Costa added GA's 28th point. *All this happening in the 1st quarter.*

Sinkwich then fired a 62-yard pass to Poschner for another TD. Costa made it 35-0 as the half neared.

In the 3rd quarter, Sinkwich hit Poschner for another TD. Costa made it 42-0.

After picking off their fourth pass, GA drove down the field, culminated by Trippi's five yard TD. Costa missed his first PAT, but the scoreboard flashed 48 for GA and 0 for UF.

UF was stymied, and on GA's next possession, Trippi ran 40 yards for a TD. With Costa's PAT it was now 55-0, and GA's scoring was not over.

After a short UF punt, Mayfield "Sonny" Lloyd ran for a 6-yard TD. Costa made it 62-0.

It was now the reserves' turn to score. From the UF 41, Lafayette King caught reserve QB Jim Todd's pass for yet another TD. PAT no good. 68-0.

On their next possession UF QB Billy Mims retreated deep into his end zone to pass. Frank Riofski, a fourth-string center stepped in front of the receiver and ran the pass back 10 yards for the score. Costa's PAT made it 75-0.
"Indeed, the Bulldogs made everyone happy when the game was over," the Times-Union said.

Seven Bulldogs had scored, paced by Sinkwich, Poschner with three touchdown grabs, and Trippi's three TDs. Georgia defenders intercepted seven of UF's 21 throws, while only six of the 21 were received by their rightful targets.

1944

• Allies invade Normandy on D-Day • Bretton Woods Conference creates International Monetary Fund and World Bank • Dumbarton Oaks Conference—U.S., British Commonwealth, and USSR propose establishment of United Nations • Battle of the Bulge.
• Anne Frank and her family betrayed and sent to concentration camps. She will die in 1945.
• FDR is reelected, beating Republican challenger Thomas Dewey • GI Bill of Rights is passed, providing benefits for armed-service veterans.
World Series
St. Louis Cardinals d. St. Louis Browns (4-2)
Kentucky Derby Champion *Pensive*
NCAA Basketball Championship
Utah d. Dartmouth (42-40 OT)
NCAA Football Champions Army (9-0-0)
Best Picture: Casablanca
• The first instance of network censorship occurs. The sound is cut off on the Eddie Cantor and Nora Martin duet, "We're Having a

Baby, My Baby and Me" • The DuMont network goes on the air. Paramount Pictures backs the start-up enterprise, but its lack of affiliated radio networks leads to its early demise in 1956
• Scientists at Harvard University construct the first automatic, general-purpose digital computer • DNA is isolated by Oswald Avery • The Germans develop the V-2, the first true missile.

The Game: 1944 GA- 38 UF-12

Frank Sinkwich was gone, now playing for the Detroit Lions and Charley Trippi was in the service playing for the Third Air Force Gremlins.

UF right HB Ken McLean bolted for a 90 yard TD run. The PAT was no good. The Gators produced a trick play on their next possession. UF FB Jim Dyer passed to Rushing. As GA closed in on him, he suddenly lateralled to LHB Bobby Forbes who was flashing to the outside. The play caught the Bulldogs off-guard and Forbes ran untouched for 44 yards and a score. UF now led 12-0.

After blocking a UF punt, GA QB Billy Hodges hit Reid Moseley for a 6-yard TD. Bill Bryan's PAT was no good. FLA now led 12-6.

With less than a minute remaining in the half, Hodges again found Moseley open for a 44-yard TD pass. Bryan's kick was good, and GA led 13-12.

On the opening series of the third quarter, GA led by LHB and captain Billy Rutland, marched down the field and scored again, plunging over UF linemen. The PAT was wild.

GA. again held UF and when they got the ball, drove down towards the UF goal, with Hodges hitting E Sam Bailey in the end zone for a 16-yard TD pass. Bryan made the PAT. GA now led 26-12.

With reserves in the game, new life was brought into the GA offense, spelling defeat for the Gators. GA RHB Claude Hipps ripped 58 yards for a score. PAT no good, but GA now led 32-12.

Very late in the game, FLA fumbled and GA reserve QB Ken McCall, after several incomplete tions, connected with Moseley for Moseley's third TD catch of the game, making the final score 38-12.

1945

• Yalta Conference (Roosevelt, Churchill, Stalin) plans final defeat of Germany • Hitler commits suicide; Germany surrenders; May 8 is declared V-E Day • U.S. drops atomic bomb on Japanese cities of Hiroshima and Nagasaki
• Japan signs official surrender on V-J Day
• United Nations established. First electronic computer, ENIAC, builtm • Potsdam Conference (Truman, Churchill, Stalin) establishes basis of German reconstruction • FDR dies and Harry S. Truman becomes president.
• A B-25 bomber flies into the Empire State Building, damaging the 78th and 79th floors and killing 13.

World Series   Detroit d. Chicago Cubs (4-3)
Kentucky Derby Champion   *Hoop Jr*
NCAA Basketball Championship
Oklahoma A&M d. NYU (49-45)
NCAA Football Champions   Army (9-0-0)
Best Picture: Going My Way
• The FCC creates the commercial broadcasting spectrum of 13 channels, and receives 130 applications for broadcast licenses.
Movies: The Lost Weekend, Mildred Pierce, National Velvet, A Tree Grows in Brooklyn, Spellbound
• ENIAC (Electronic Numerical Integrator and Calculator), the first all-electronic computer, completed • Grand Rapids, Michigan becomes the first community to fluoridate its water supply • Raymond Libby develops oral penicillin. • American Cyanamid discovers folic acid, a vitamin abundant in green leafy vegetables, liver, kidney, and yeast.

The Game: 1945 GA-34 UF-0

Charley Trippi returned to Athens from the service and continued to pound opponents.

After exchanging blows with no one scoring in the 1st quarter, GA came to life. Trippi found an opening at left tackle and outran the entire UF team 50 yards into the end zone. George Jernigan's PAT made it 7-0.

GA drove, after receiving the second half kick-off, 61 yards, with John Donaldson scoring from the three. Jernigan made it 14-0.

UF fumbled on its next possession with Rauch coming up with the loose pigskin.

After several rushes, Rauch lateralled to Trippi, who scampered four yards for the score. Jernigan made it 21-0.

GA blocked the next UF punt, giving the Bulldogs a first down at the UF 48. Rauch passed 14 yards to Moseley on the first play. On the next, Rauch shot a lateral to Trippi who did not stop running till he was in the UF end zone. Jernigan missed the PAT, but GA still lead 27-0.

After a UF quick-kick, GA right halfback John Donaldson then passed to Moseley for the final Georgia TD.

Trippi scored three TDs and rushed for 239 yards out of a total 317 yards for the entire GA team.

946

First meeting of UN General Assembly opens in London • Winston Churchill's "Iron Curtain" speech warns of Soviet expansion • League of Nations dissolved • Italy abolishes monarchy. Verdict in Nuremberg war trial: 12 Nazi leaders (including 1 tried in absentia) sentenced to hang; 7 imprisoned; 3 acquitted • Goering commits suicide a few hours before 10 other Nazis are executed • Juan Perón becomes president of Argentina. Benjamin Spock's childcare classic published • The Philippines gains independ-

ence from the United States • US Atomic Energy Commission is established • Worst work stoppages since 1919, with coal, electrical, and steel industries hit hardest.
World Series
  St. Louis Cardinals d. Boston Red Sox (4-3)
Kentucky Derby Champion *Assault*
NCAA Basketball Championship
Okl. A&M d. No. Carolina (43-40)
NCAA Football Champions NotreDame(8-0-1)
Best Picture: The Lost Weekend
• The Cannes Film Festival debuts in France.
• The Best Years of Our Lives debuts, and is immediately recognized as a classic post-War film that accurately—and poignantly—portrays the readjustment families face when loved ones return from battle • Roberto Rossellini's Neorealist ode to the Italian Resistance, Rome, Open City, presents an alternative to Hollywood with its use of street cinematography, lyrically capturing the despair and confusion of post-World War II Europe.
Movies: It's a Wonderful Life, The Best Years of Our Lives, The Razor's Edge
Music "Dancing in the Dark "Chiquita Banana"   Coleman Hawkins, "Say It Isn't So" Frank Sinatra, "The Voice of Frank Sinatra" "Tenderly" "There's No Business Like Show Business" "Zip-a-Dee-Do-Dah"
• Vincent du Vigneaud (US) synthesizes penicillin • The US Army makes radar contact with the moon for the first time.

The Game: 1946 GA- 33 UF-14

GA came into this year's game undefeated, untied and ranked 3rd in the nation. UF was 0-5 under new Head Coach Raymond B. Wolf.

UF started the game pulling every trick play they could out of their hat, trying to keep the GA team off-balance. The first quarter was scoreless.   In the 2nd quarter GA tackle Jack Bush blocked Bill Gilmartin's punt and All-American candidate Herb St. John gathered in the ball and rumbled to the UF 8. Two plays later, Rauch fired to Trippi for a TD. Jernigan missed the PAT.

UF recovered a Geri fumble and drove 47 yards for the tying score. When George "Jock" Sutherland kicked the PAT, putting UF ahead, the crowd went crazy.

UF had a great chance to pad their lead, but their drives were stalled by the GA defensive line and by their own pass interceptions. After one interception by John Donaldson, GA drove into the UF end zone with the same Donaldson carrying the final seven yards. Jernigan's PAT was good, and GA led 13-7.

Another UF interception led to another GA TD via Rauch pass to Donaldson for 17 yards. Jernigan's kick was good, and GA now lead 20-7. After a lengthy drive by GA, Geri scored from the one. Jernigan's kick was good and now the lead was 27-7. After one of their best drives of the day, 92-yards to be exact, UF QB Buddy Carte raced around end ten yards for UF's second score. Sutherland's PAT made it 27-14.

A late GA drive, culminating with Trippi diving over from the one, and a missed PAT accounted for the final 33-14 score in the GA win.

1947

• Britain nationalizes coal mines • Peace treaties for Italy, Romania, Bulgaria, Hungary, Finland signed in Paris • Soviet Union rejects U.S. plan for UN atomic-energy control • Truman proposes Truman Doctrine, which was to aid Greece and Turkey in resisting communist expansion • Marshall Plan for European recovery proposed—a coordinated program to help European nations recover from ravages of war. (By the time it ended in 1951, this "European Recovery Program" had cost $13 billion.) India and Pakistan gain independence from Britain • U.S. Air Force pilot Chuck Yeager becomes first person to break the sound barrier. Jackie Robinson joins the Brooklyn Dodgers • Anne Frank's The Diary of a Young Girl published. • The Dead Sea Scrolls are discovered at Qumran • Hollywood "Black List" created by HUAC • Truman Doctrine proposes "containment" of communist expansion. • Taft-Hartley Act passed.
World Series
NY Yankees d. Brooklyn Dodgers (4-3)
NBA Championship
Phil.Warriors d.Chic.Stags (4-1)
Kentucky Derby Champion *Jet Pilot*
NCAA Basketball Championship
Holy Cross d. Okl. (58-47)
NCAA Football Champions
Notre Dame (9-0-0)
Best Picture: The Best Years of Our Lives
• The Yankees beat the Dodgers in seven games in the first televised World Series.
• Meet the Press debuts on NBC.

The Game: 1947 GA-34 UF- 6

"The Bulldogs have been up and down so much this year, they resemble a fisherman's cork on a summer afternoon. Florida couldn't be pleased more than to add the Georgia scalp," said an article in the Savannah Morning News. *"They're the martyr and we're the monster,"* Butts told the Atlanta Constitution. *"That's the way it is every year. I wouldn't mind if we just had a few monsters…I got to looking at those little old Georgia boys this morning at the breakfast table and it just nearly scared me to death to think about having to play them in a football game."*

A crowd of 23,000 watched the contest open with the "little old Georgia boys" overpowering UF's first offensive effort. Rauch, after faking the Gators defense out on numerous pass plays, sneaked into the end zone for the first GA TD. Joe Geri's PAT was good. GA 7 UF 0. Minutes later Rauch connected with Donaldson in the end zone for GA's second score. Geri made it 14-0.

UF twice marched inside the GA ten, but

came out empty both times. By the benefit of a controversial pass interference call, GA was given a first down on the UF 33, keeping their drive alive. Rauch called his own number in a QB sneak. Geri's kick was no good, GA now lead 20-0.

The teams exchanged the ball several times. GA's Geri punted to UF's Hal Griffin at the UF 32. Griffin cruised 68 yards for the score. The PAT by Laz Lewis was no good. On GA's next possession, Rauch hit Dan Edwards for a 21-yard TD. Geri made it 27-6.

Bulldog center Gene Chandler picked off Vic Vaccaro's pass at the UF 25 and chugged to the 15 before he was brought down. On the next play, Geri scored and his fourth PAT gave GA a 34-6 cushion and final score.

1948

• Gandhi assassinated in New Delhi by Hindu fanatic • Burma and Ceylon granted independence by Britain • Communists seize power in Czechoslovakia • Organization of American States Charter signed at Bogotá, Colombia.
• Nation of Israel proclaimed; British end mandate at midnight; Arab armies attack • Berlin blockade begins, prompting Allied airlift
• Stalin and Tito break. Independent Republic of Korea is proclaimed, following election supervised by UN • Verdict in Japanese war trial: 18 imprisoned; Tojo and six others hanged • United States of Indonesia established as Dutch and Indonesians settle conflict • Alger Hiss, former U.S. State Department official, indicted on perjury charges after denying passing secret documents to communist spy ring; convicted in second trial (1950) and sentenced to five-year prison term • Truman ends racial segregation in military • Alfred Kinsey publishes Sexual Behavior in the American Male • Tennessee Williams's A Streetcar Named Desire wins Pulitzer • Margaret Sanger founds the International Planned Parenthood Federation.
World Series Cleveland d. Boston Braves (4-2)
NBA Championship
Baltimore Bullets d. Philadelphia Warriors (4-2)
Kentucky Derby Champion *Citation*
NCAA Basketball Championship
Kentucky d. Baylor (58-42)
NCAA Football Champions
Michigan (9-0-0)
Best Picture: Gentleman's Agreement -
• The Hollywood Ten, a group of writers, producers and directors called as witnesses in the House Committee's Investigation of Un-American Activities, are jailed for contempt of Congress when they refuse to disclose if they were or were not Communists • Columbia Records introduces the 33 1/3 LP ("long playing") record at New York's Waldorf-Astoria Hotel. It allows listeners to enjoy an unprecedented 25 minutes of music per side, compared to the four minutes per side of the standard 78 rpm record • George A. Gamow (US) puts forth the "Big Bang" theory to explain the origin of the universe • Dennis Gabors of England devel-

ops the theoretical basis for holography • Edwin Land (US) invents the Polaroid Land camera • Physicist Richard Feynman and Julian Schwinger (US) develop a theory of quantum electrodynamics • The World Health Organization (WHO) is established under UN auspices.

The Game: 1948 GA-20 UF-12

The Jacksonville Stadium had been remodeled and was now called the "Gator Bowl."

GA and GA TECH were undefeated and tied for first place in the Southeast Conference. This game with UF was just a warm-up for GA.

34,000 fans filled the new stadium. GA marched 75 yards on a late 1st quarter drive with Rauch diving over the line for GA's first TD. Geri's PAT was Good. GA 7-0.

UF drove from their own 46 with backs John Cox, Loren Broadus, and Russ Godwin smashing into the GA line. Cox went the last yard. The PAT was fumbled and no good. GA-7 UF-6.

A roughing the kicker penalty negated a fine 56-yard punt return by UF's Chuck Hunsinger and gave GA the ball and a first down on the UF 27. Geri ran in the final 13 yards for GA's second TD. Geri added the PAT. GA-14 UF-6.

GA's LHB Billy Mixon scooted for runs of 30 and 21 yards, setting up Ga at the UF 5. Rauch pitched out to Reid who avoided tacklers for the TD. The PAT was no good. GA-20 UF-6.

Late in the game, UF's Chuck Hunsinger caught a GA punt at his own 36 and didn't stop running until he crossed GA's goal line.

The PAT was no good. Final score: GA-20 UF-12.

1949

• Cease fire in Palestine • Truman proposes Point Four Program to help world's less developed areas. Israel signs armistice with Egypt • Start of North Atlantic Treaty Organization (NATO)—treaty signed by 12 nations • Federal Republic of Germany (West Germany) established • First successful Soviet atomic test • Communist People's Republic of China formally proclaimed by Chairman Mao Zedong • German Democratic Republic (East Germany) established under Soviet rule. South Africa institutionalizes apartheid • Britain recognizes the independence of the Republic of Ireland • Northern Ireland remains a part of the United Kingdom • US recognizes the state of Israel.
World Series
NY Yankees d. Brooklyn Dodgers (4-1)
NBA Championship
Minneapolis Lakers d. Wash. Capitols (4-2)
Kentucky Derby Champion *Ponder*
NCAA Basketball Championship
Kentucky d. Oklahoma A&M (46-36)
NCAA Football Champions
Notre Dame (10-0-0)
Best Picture: Hamlet
• The first Emmy Awards are handed out on January 25, with Pantomime Quiz Time earning

top honor as the Most Popular Television Program • Cable television debuts, bringing better reception to rural areas where the conventional television signal is weak • Milton Berle hosts the first telethon, which benefits cancer research • 45 rpm records are sold in the U.S.
Movies: All the King's Men, Twelve O'Clock High, Sands of Iwo Jima, She Wore a Yellow Ribbon, The Third Man
Music: "Some Enchanted Evening"
"Ghost Riders in the Sky"
"Rudolph, the Red-Nosed Reindeer"
"Diamonds Are a Girl's Best Friend"
• Capt. James Gallagher and USAF crew make first round-the-world nonstop flight from Ft. Worth, Texas, and returning to same point: 23,452 miles in 94 hours, 1 minute • The antibiotics oxytetracycline and neomycin are developed.

The Game: 1949 UF -28 GA- 7

The Gator Bowl had been expanded again, and now could seat over 36,000. It would be th largest crowd to ever watch a GA-UF game.

"The teeming Gator Bowl was a mass of color under a bright sun. The variety of fall an winter clothing and a veritable forest of yellow and white chrysanthemums added to the Kaleidoscope of college banners and streamers." said the FLA Times Union.

In its second series, UF QB Williams hit LE Don Brown with a 27 yard completion. Hunsinger went 21 yards with a pitchout for UF's first TD. Laz Lewis made the PAT.

GA then drove from their own 47 down to th UF 7. QB Prosperi hit LE Walston for the TD. Walston's PAT was good, and the game was tied.

Just before the half was over, UF struck agai After a short GA punt, UF started at the GA 24 Hunsinger carried the ball down near the goal line. QB Williams called his own number and slipped around end for the UF TD. Lewis' PA put UF ahead 14-7.

With less than a minute left in the half UF's Broadus intercepted a Prosperi pass and ran back to the GA 29. Three plays later, Hunsinge plowed over for the TD. Lewis' PAT made it 21-7.

Early in the third quarter, Hunsinger scored his third TD from the 15. Lewis again made th PAT, and UF led 28-7.

"A roar such as never sounded before in the Gator Bowl went up from the sardined crowd. The band of hitherto hapless Gators administered a resounding smacking to the Bulldogs,' said the Fla. Times Union.

Hunsinger scored three TDs for UF. He outgained the entire GA team, running for 174 yards on 18 carries.

Florida-Georgia

Nov. 9 1940

25c

1940 • UGA 13 UFL 18

GEORGIA vs. FLORIDA

November 8, 1941

Price 25¢

1941 · UGA 19 UFL 3

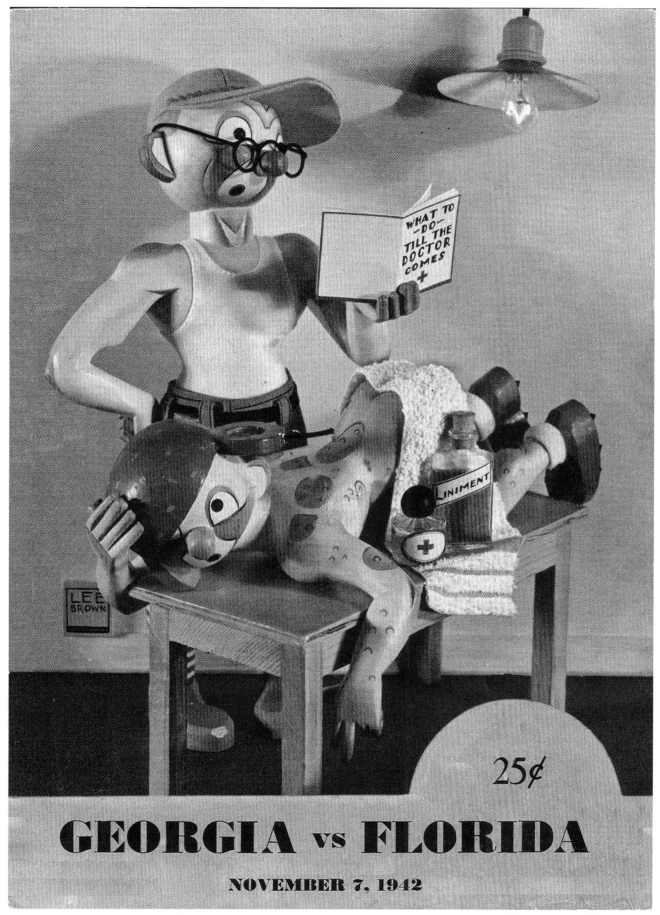

GEORGIA vs FLORIDA

NOVEMBER 7, 1942

1942 · UGA 75 UFL 0

Price
25¢

NOVEMBER 11, 1944
GEORGIA vs FLORIDA

1944 · UGA 38 UFL 12

NOVEMBER 10, 1945
GEORGIA vs FLORIDA

Price
25¢

1945 • UGA 34   UFL 0

GEORGIA vs FLORIDA

JACKSONVILLE, FLA.

NOVEMBER 9, 1946

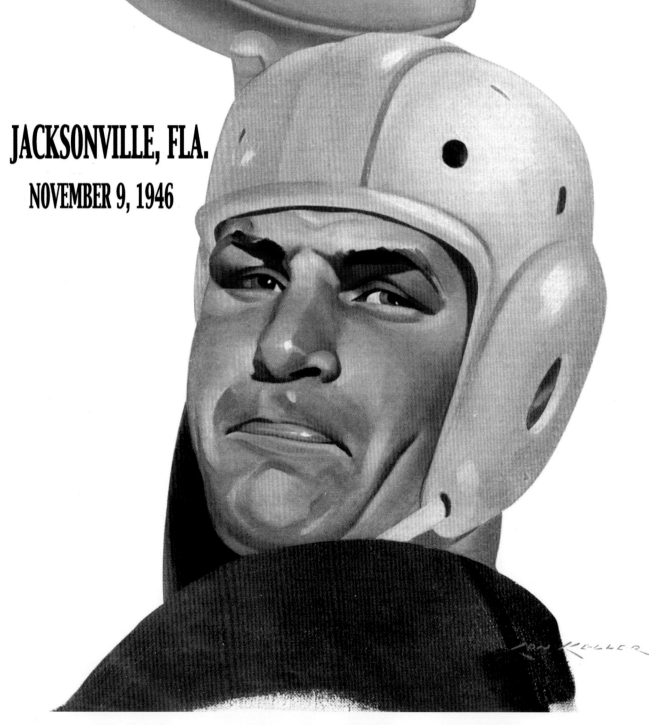

1946 • UGA 33 UFL 14

GEORGIA vs FLORIDA
NOVEMBER 8, 1947

Price
25¢

1947 · UGA 34   UFL 6

NOVEMBER 6, 1948

GEORGIA
vs
FLORIDA

Price
25¢

1948 · UGA 20   UFL 12

Georgia vs Florida

NOVEMBER 5, 1949

Price
25¢

1949 · UGA 28   UFL 7

The 1950s

1950

Brink's robbery in Boston; almost $3 million stolen. Truman orders development of hydrogen bomb. Korean War begins when North Korean Communist forces invade South Korea • McCarthyism begins.
World Series
NY Yankees d. Philadelphia Phillies (4-0)
NBA Championship
Minneapolis Lakers d. Syracuse (4-2)
Kentucky Derby Champion *Middleground*
NCAA Basketball Championship
CCNY d. Bradley (71-68)
NCAA Football Champions
Oklahoma (10-1-0)
Best Picture: All the King's Men
Sat. AM children's programming begins.
Charles Schulz's *Peanuts* strip begins.
Col. David C. Schilling (USAF) makes the first nonstop transatlantic jet flight in 10 hours and 1 minute.
The first Xerox machine is produced.
The first self-service elevator is installed by Otis Elevator in Dallas.

The Game: 1950 GA-6 UF-0

The 36,000+ fans entering the Gator Bowl in Jacksonville, had things other than the Red Chinese or the Red Scare on their minds. At least half of them wanted to see if UF could win two in a row… something not accomplished by a UF team since 1928-1929.

Sophomore QB Haywood Sullivan was UF's great hope. GA looked to "the Fitzgerald Phantom"… LHB Lauren Hargrove.

A very hard-hitting 1st quarter resulted in three fumbles, two recovered by UF and one by GA. The most potent weapon of the game, going into the 2nd quarter was GA punter Pat Field, whose deadly punts kept UF pinned deep in their own territory. In the middle of the 2nd quarter, UF punter Ted Monstdeoca, SEC Punting Champion of 1949, kicked one off the side of his foot, giving GA the ball on the UF 45. Here began "The Drive" of the 1950 game. GA QB Malcolm Cook headed around right end, then suddenly lateralled back to FB Billy Mixon, who darted forwards for yards. GA HB Gus Hlebovy gained 11 more yards in two rushes. Two more GA rushes placed the ball on the UF 5. On third and goal, GA QB Cook scrambled for his life, looking for an open receiver. GA E Bobby Walston found himself free in the end zone as the UF defense converged on Cook. Cook saw Walston and "lobbed" the ball over the defense wall into Walston's arms for a GA TD. Walston's PAT sailed wide left. GA led 6-0.

UF QB mixed his play-calling, trying to keep the GA defense off-guard. On one pass play UF E James French was so startled to be as wide-open as he was, that he dropped what would have likely been a scoring pass.

With just minutes left in the game, GA capt. and RE Mike Merola stepped in front of UF's Huggins and pulled down a Sullivan swing pass in UF's backfield and Merola wasn't pulled down until he was

caught by behind at the UF 25. GA was on the UF 2 yard line as the game ended.
"Georgia chewed just enough alligator hide off…for a traveling bag to carry home the victory," wrote the **Savannah Morning News.**

1951

-Julius and Ethel Rosenberg sentenced to death for passing atomic secrets to Russians.• Seoul falls first to Communist forces, then to US-led UN troops. Despite peace talks in July and October, the Korean War continues.• 22nd Amendment to the US Constitution, limiting the number of terms a president may serve, is ratified.
World Series
NY Yankees d. NY Giants (4-2)
NBA Championship
Rochester d. New York (4-3)
Kentucky Derby Champion *Count Turf*
NCAA Basketball Championship
Kentucky d. Kansas St. (68-58)
NCAA Football Champions
Tennessee (10-0-0)
Best Picture: All About Eve
• Yul Brynner makes his first appearance as the King of Siam in The King and I.
• Color television introduced in the U.S.
• In an effort to introduce rhythm and blues to a broader white audience, which was hesitant to embrace "black music," disc jockey Alan Freed uses the term rock 'n' roll to describe R&B.
• In the first broadcast of Edward R. Murrow's See It Now series, Murrow shows the split-screen image of the Golden Gate and Brooklyn bridges and tells viewers it is the first time to see the Atlantic and Pacific oceans simultaneously.
• UNIVAC (Universal Automatic Computer), the first business computer to handle both numeric and alphabetical data, is introduced.
• The first nuclear power plant is built by the US Atomic Energy Commission.

The Game: 1951 GA-7 UF-6

A brisk wind blew in from the north over the packed Gator Bowl. The wind would factor into the outcome of today's game. UF won the toss and chose to go with the wind in the opening quarter. UF crossed up GA by grinding out yardage through the GA line. UF's ran Billy Reddell, Floyd Huggins, Rick Casares, and Sam Oosterhoudt at GA. When UF QB Sullivan did pass deep in GA territory, GA's Bob West intercepted.

UF drove again deep in GA territory only to have Marion Campbell break through the UF line, dropping Sullivan for a loss. At this point UF's Casares missed a short FG attempt.

The 2nd quarter, with the wind at their backs, GA's offense showed some signs of life. GA's "Zippy" Morocco fielded a UF punt, lateralled to Conrad Manisera at the GA 17. Manisera went 33 yards to the midfield stripe before being stopped. Morocco ran for 13 yards. Bratkowski hit White at the UF 28. Bratkowski hit Roberts at the goal line, but he couldn't hold on. Bratkowski went right back to the air again, hitting Morocco at the six. Two UF lineman tried to keep him out of the end zone, but Morocco "zipped" right by them. GA's Sam Mrvos made the PAT, and

GA led 7-0.

In the 4th quarter UF Long intercepted a Bratkowski pass at the GA 41, running it back to the GA 29. ON a fourth down deep in GA's territory, UF's Sullivan tossed a pass towards Oosterhoudt, but the wind carried the ball high over the intended receiver's hands. UF fans were very disappointed until they noticed the referee's flag on the ground. GA was called for pass interference, giving UF a first and goal at the GA 7. On 3rd down, after two no gains into the GA line, Long ran around the left side into GA's end zone. Casares' PAT veered wide right.

For the day, Bratkowski threw for 115 yards compared to Sullivan's 94. Sullivan had three big interceptions. And even though GA had been out-rushed 213 yards to 79, the 7-6 score would be all GA needed.

1952

-George VI dies; his daughter becomes Elizabeth II • King Farouk of Egypt is ousted by a military coup • Britain announces its development of atomic weapons • Greece and Turkey join NATO. • US explodes first thermonuclear bomb at Enewetak Island • President-elect Dwight Eisenhower follows through with his campaign promise to visit Korea • 56 million watch Richard Nixon's "Checker's speech" on TV.
World Series
NY Yankees d. Brooklyn Dodgers (4-3)
NBA Championship
Minneapolis Lakers d. New York (4-3)
Kentucky Derby Champion *Hill Gail*
NCAA Basketball Championship
Kansas d. St. John's (80-63)
NCAA Football Champions
Michigan St. (AP, UP) (9-0-0)
& Georgia Tech (INS) (12-0-0)
Best Picture: An American in Paris
• Jose Quintero's revival of Tennessee Williams's Summer and Smoke premieres at Broadway's Circle in the Square Theatre and is the first major Off-Broadway success.
• Television's first magazine-format program, the Today Show, debuts on NBC with Dave Garroway hosting.
• The Jackie Gleason Show (The Honeymooners) debuts on CBS.
• Jonas E. Salk (US) develops the first experimentally safe dead-virus polio vaccine.
• The first plastic artificial heart valve is developed at Georgetown Medical Center.

The Game: 1952 UF-30 GA-0

"A temporary truce was called as the two schools' bands joined in playing 'The Star Spangled Banner' prior to the kickoff. Immediately afterwards, the War Between the States was in full force again…" The Florida Times Union reported.

Two minutes into the game, a fight broke out between GA E Harry Babcock (Bratkowski's favorite target) and UF's Arlen Jumper. Both were ejected.

UF drew first blood with a 33-yard FG by Casares. UF then intercepted a Bratkowski pass on their own 25 and started a six-first down drive culminating with QB Doug

Dickey sneaking in from the one. Casares made it 10-0 with the PAT.

In the 3rd quarter, UF recovered a GA fumble at the GA 28 and successfully drove GA backwards on the ground. The final three yards were covered by Casares for another UF score. With his PAT good, the score was now UF 17 GA 0. In the 4th quarter, UF's Dickey handed off to Long who danced over left tackle, spun to his left, reversed the field and found 77 yards of open space in front of him, all the way to the GA end zone. Casares PAT was good and UF now led 24-0.

UF Reserve QB Fred Robinson drilled a 19 yard TD pass to Leonard Balas in the waning seconds of the game. The PAT was missed. But the final score wasn't... UF 30 GA 0. Casares rushed for 108 yards on 27 attempts, and scored 12 points.

1953

-Gen. Dwight D. Eisenhower inaugurated President.
-Stalin dies. Malenkov becomes Soviet premier; Beria, minister of interior; Molotov, foreign minister. James Watson and Francis Crick publish their discovery of the molecular model of DNA. Edmund Hillary of New Zealand and Tenzing Norgay of Nepal reach top of Mt. Everest. East Berliners rise against Communist rule; quelled by tanks. Egypt becomes republic ruled by military junta. Julius and Ethel Rosenberg executed in Sing Sing prison. Korean armistice signed. Moscow announces explosion of hydrogen bomb. Tito becomes president of Yugoslavia. James Watson, Francis Crick, and Rosalind Franklin discover structure of DNA. Ernest Hemingway wins Pulitzer for The Old Man and the Sea. Alleged Communist Charlie Chaplin leaves U.S.
World Series NY Yankees d. Brklyn Dodgers (4-2)
NBA Championship
Minneapolis Lakers d. New York (4-1)
Kentucky Derby Champion *Dark Star*
NCAA Basketball Championship
Ind. d. Kansas (69-68)
NCAA Football Champions Maryland (10-1-0)
Best Picture: The Greatest Show on Earth
• The first issue of TV Guide magazine hits the newsstands in 10 cities with a circulation of 1.56mil.
• Lucille Ball gives birth to Desi Arnaz, Jr. on same day the fictional Little Ricky is born on I Love Lucy.
• Playboy magazine hits newsstands. A nude Marilyn Monroe graces the cover.
• First successful open-heart surgery is performed in Philadelphia.

The Game: 1953 UF-21 GA-7

The Gator Bowl was filled to capacity, and so was every sofa in southeast America, as the game was being televised regionally. UF had a bevy of running backs, but Joe Brodsky, at 215 pounds, was the most effective at driving into the GA line.

After a long drive by GA, UF sent in Doug Dickey at QB, replacing Harry Spears. Dearing, Simpson, Haddock, and Cason riddled the GA line for sizeable runs. From the GA 21, Dickey went back to pass. He found UF team captain Jack O'Brien alone in the end zone and UF took a 6-0 lead. Spears' PAT made it 7-0.

On GA's next drive, Bratkowski moved his team down the field towards the UF goal. With seconds left in the first half, "Brat" found his RE Gene White open in the end zone. The ball hit White in the numbers and fell to the ground. After two more dropped passes, Bratkowski saw his end Cleve Clark break open over the middle. The GA QB put the ball right in his arms, but Clark was hit, high and low by two Gators and couldn't hold onto the ball, and the half ended.

In the 3rd period, Bratkowski was intercepted by UF's Spears at the GA 35. He was finally brought down at the GA 8. After two rushing attempts netted six yards, UF's Brodsky finally landed in the end zone. Spears' PAT made it 14-0. Bratkowski, working with a shortened field after a botched kick-off, passed to his end White for the final nine yards and a GA TD. Joe Graff kicked the PAT. Score 14-7 UF. Bratkowski left the field in the third quarter with an injury. UF took advantage of this and in the fact that they could shuffle in and out their supply of QBs. Starting from their own 44. Florida backs cracked the GA line for gains, moving the team down near the GA goal. With GA expecting another push by one of the UF backs, they loaded up the middle of their line.Instead HB Scott took a handoff from Dickey on a fake to the FB and ran around end to the GA 2. Dickey drove it in on a QB sneak. Spears made it 21-7.

A reporter wrote that UF defenders were covering GA's star receiver John Carson the way bobby soxers surrounded Frankie Sinatra. Harry Mehre wrote in the Atlanta Journal-Constitution, "The Bulldogs lack speed in the backfield and heft in the line. Florida showed more speed, more depth, and more versatility. You can't overcome all three with a lone weapon."

1954

-First atomic submarine Nautilus launched. Soviet Union grants sovereignty to East Germany. Army v. McCarthy inquiry—Senate subcommittee report blames both sides. Dien Bien Phu, French military outpost in Vietnam, falls to Vietminh army. U.S. Supreme Court (in Brown v. Board of Education of Topeka) unanimously bans racial segregation in public schools. Dr. Jonas Salk starts inoculating children against polio. Algerian War of Independence against France begins; France struggles to maintain colonial rule until 1962 when it agrees to Algeria's independence • William Faulkner's A Fable wins Pulitzer.
• Nasser becomes premier of Egypt.
• Geneva Conference is convened to bring peace to Vietnam (April to July). The country is divided at the 17th parallel, pending democratic elections.
World Series NY Giants d. Cleveland (4-0)
NBA Championship
Minneapolis Lakers d. Syracuse (4-3)
Kentucky Derby Champion *Determine*
NCAA Basketball Championship
La Salle d. Bradley (92-76)
NCAA Football Champions
Ohio St. (AP, INS) (10-0-0) &
 UCLA (UP, FW) (9-0-0)
Best Picture: From Here to Eternity
•The World Series is broadcast in color for the first time • Bill Haley and the Comets begin writing hit songs. As a white band using black-derived forms, they venture into rock 'n' roll • The USS Nautilus, the first atomic submarine, is commissioned at Groton, Connecticut.
• Boeing tests the 707, the first jet-powered transport plane.

The Game:1954 GA-14 UF-13

GA entered this game in first place in the SEC with UF and Mississippi tied for second. After seven games, GA's defense had allowed the opponents but 28 points. Their one loss came to Texas A&M (0-6). Dickey's UF was 4-3 but his "flaming sophomores" were unpredictable and could beat any team on any Saturday.

The Gators were led by center Steve DeLaTorre, Fullback Big Joe Brodsky, and a trio of quarterbacks, Bobby Lance, Dick Allen, and Fred Robinson. The Bulldogs strong point was their front wall with Guard Don Shea and end Joe O'Malley as the mainstays. On offense GA looked to Fullbacks Bobby Garrard and Bob "Foots" Clemens to carry the load.

Prior to the game UF held a pep rally at Hemming Park in Jacksonville. The UF rally was infiltrated by GA band members who starting screaming "*Dog Food! Dog Food!*" The UF band responded with screams of "*Gator Bait! Gator Bait!*"

On UF's first possession, HB Bob Davis fumbled the ball and GA's John Bell fell on it at the UF 40. GA, following QB Jimmy Harper's passing and Garrard's running punched over the game's first score. Charles Madison kicked the PAT. GA led 7-

Late in the 1st quarter, UF had the ball on the GA 44, when Joe Brodsky fumbled the ball towards the GA goal. A Gator finally dove on the ball at the GA 26. QB Allen passed to Don Chandler at the GA15. A couple of runs brought UF to the GA 6 as the 1st quarter ended. Starting the 2nd quarter, UF HB Jackie Simpson circled right end and sliced into the endzone. Allen's PAT tied the game.

GA's Madison rumbled 40 yards to the UF 28. After runs by Madison, Clemens and HB Wendell Tarleton gave GA a 1st down on the UF 5, Clemens took the ball into the endzone. Madison's PAT made it GA14 UF 7.

UF was held and had to punt from deep in their own territory. GA started their series at the UF 40. Harper swing pass was picked off by UF's Chandler at the UF 26. With Chandler streaking towards the GA goal, the only Bulldog in position to stop him was QB Harper. After a 67 yard return, Harper pushed Chandler out of bounds on the GA 7.

Two plays later UF FB Davis ran 7 yards around end for the UF score. On the PAT attempt, GA End Roy Wilkins blocked the kick and GA still lead, 14-13.

The third period saw both teams driving towards scores, only to be stopped by defensive stands. GA Garrard got off the punt of the day when he kicked ball that rolled dead on the UF 1. UF's Robinson went to the air to move downfield, but one of his passes was picked by GA's Bill Saye at the UF 22, killing UF's final attempt to gain the lead.

GA's Bill Saye was the defensive standout, intercepting two passes, recovering two fumbles and deflecting several pass attempts.

1955

-Nikolai A. Bulganin becomes Soviet premier, replacing Malenkov • Churchill resigns; Anthony Eden succeeds him. West Germany becomes a sovereign state. Warsaw Pact, east European mutual defense agreement, signed. Argentina ousts Perón. President Eisenhower suffers coronary thrombosis Denver. Rosa Parks refuses to sit at the back of the bus. Martin Luther King, Jr., leads black boycott of Montgomery, Ala., bus system; desegregated service begins Dec. 21, 1956. AFL and CIO become one organization—AFL-CIO. Tennessee Williams's Cat on a Hot Tin Roof wins Pulitzer.
• US starts sending $216 million in aid to Vietnam
World Series Brklyn Dodgers d. NY Yankees (4-3)
NBA Championship
Syracuse d. Ft. Wayne Pistons (4-3)
Kentucky Derby Champion *Swaps*
NCAA Basketball Championship
San Francisco d. La Salle (77-63)
NCAA Football Champions Oklahoma (11-0-0)
Best Picture: On the Waterfront
• On the Waterfront nearly sweeps the 1954 Academy Awards, winning Best Picture, Best Actor (Marlon Brando), Best Supporting Actress (Eva Maria Saint), and Best Director (Elia Kazan).
• Gunsmoke debuts on CBS, and will go on to be television's longest-running western.

mes Dean dies in a car accident at age 26.
arinder Kapany (England) develops fiber optics.

The Game: UF-19 GA-13

ach Butts was employing the dual quarterback
tem, rotating Jimmy Harper as his rushing direc-
and Dick Young behind center for passing situa-
s. UF Coach Woodruff declared he would be
ting three quarterbacks...Jon May, Dick Allen,
Bobby Lance. UF had two speedy running
ks in Jackie Simpson and Jim Roundtree. The UF
s defense was strong and had a number two rat-
in the SEC, and Don Chandler, the UF punter,
s averaging 47 yards per kick, which lead the
on.

fter exchanging punts in their first two series, a
leton run of 30 yards gave GA the ball deep in
territory. After losing a yard, trying to sneak into
endzone, Tarleton finally broke the plain, fum-
g after he had crossed the goal line. Ken Cooper
ked the PAT and GA led 7-0.

A's John Bell recovered one fumble on the GA
GA then drove 68 yards on the legs of Harper,
rard, Jefferson Davis and Henry Dukes. GA's
rard went the final five yards for the score.
per's PAT was partially blocked, but GA now
113-0.

F's Roundtree caught the second half kickoff at
UF 15 running up the middle through the entire
team, not stopping till he crossed the goal line
UF's first score. Chandler's PAT was wide right,
UF was now on the board. After stopping GA,
's Simpson grabbed a punt and returned it 33
ds to the GA 40. UF pushed GA back to their
n six as the quarter ended. Woodruff sent in all
h offensive players to start off the 4th quarter.
stopped May on first down for no gain at the six.
indtree took the second down hand-off and ran
und end into the end zone. Allen's PAT tied the
ne at 13-13.

ensing a shift in momentum, GA suddenly
ved to the air in an attempt to move against the
ors. Harper went back and threw towards end
l Roberts. Before the ball arrived in Roberts'
ds, a UF defender deflected the ball and UF's
en, playing defensive back, caught the ball at his
n 48 and started running down the sideline. Hit at
GA10, Allend kept his feet and continued into
end zone. Allen's PAT was blocked, but the
ors now led for the first time, 19-13. UF's 19-
nt rally was the greatest comeback in the rivalry's
ory.

Roundtree's run set the UF team afire and they
k it from there," said Coach Butts.

956

kita Khrushchev, First Secretary of USSR
mmunist Party, denounces Stalin's excesses. First
al H-bomb tested over Namu islet, Bikini Atoll—
million tons TNT equivalent. Egypt takes control
Suez Canal. Hungarian rebellion forces Soviet
ps to withdraw from Budapest. Israel launches
ck on Egypt's Sinai peninsula and drives toward
z Canal. British and French invade Port Said on
Suez Canal. Cease-fire forced by U.S. pressure
s British, French, and Israeli advance. Morocco
ns independence • Workers' uprising against
mmunist rule in Poland is crushed • Autherine
ey, the first black student at the University of
bama, is suspended after riots.
rld Series NY Yankees d. Brklyn Dodgers (4-3)
A Championship
ladelphia Warriors d. Ft. Wayne Pistons (4-1)
ntucky Derby Champion *Needles*

NCAA Basketball Championship
San Francisco d. Iowa (83-71)
NCAA Football Champions Oklahoma (10-0-0)
Best Picture: Marty
• With many hit singles (including "Heartbreak
Hotel"), Elvis Presley emerges as one of the world's
first rock stars. The gyrating rocker enjoys fame on
the stages of the Milton Berle, Steve Allen and Ed
Sullivan shows, as well as in the first of his many
movies, Love Me Tender.
• Grace Metalious's steamy Peyton Place is a best-
seller.
• The Wizard of Oz has its first airing on TV.
• Felix Wankel (Germany) develops the rotary inter-
nal combustion engine.
• The DNA molecule is first photographed.

The Game: 1956 UF-28 GA-0

All through the stands, the fans wore either GA,
UF or "I Like Ike" buttons on their coats. President
Dwight D. Eisenhower had just won a landslide re-
election over Adlai Stevenson just four days earlier.

UF was ranked 13th in national ratings and were
14-point favorites over GA this year. UF was lead by
guard and team captain John Barrow. They also had
swift halfbacks in Jim Roundtree and Jackie
Simpson, along with a battering fullback in Joe
Brodsky, not to mention a great quarterback in
Jimmy Dunn and Harry Spears as their kicking spe-
cialist. These players had given UF a 5-1-1 record so
far this year.

The 3-3-1 Bulldogs would have to play without
their star receiver Jimmy Orr. They would have to
rely on a flock of sophomores, who so far had a pretty lackluster year.

On UF's second series, Woodruff sent in all fresh
players, including a new backfield. Uf quarterback
Spears hit FB Sears for 15. HBs Symank and Parrish
rushed for two first downs, taking UF down to the
GA 17. After two more rushes, Parrish rambled into
the endzone. Spears PAT was good and UF led 7-0.

Watching the listless Bulldogs as long as they
could, fans began yelling derogatory comments
about Coach Butts. Nancy Butts, the coach's daughter and GA cheerleader, yelled back, "He's all right
'cause he's my little fat daddy."

In the second half, UF gave GA two opportunities
to get back in the game with fumbles, but the UF
defense was too much for the dogs.
On one occasion, UF's Simpson fumbled and GA
guard Tony Cushenberry recovered inside the UF 25.
QB Hearn was intercepted by UF's Brodsky, who
ran the ball back to the GA 36. On the next play,
Roundtree ran against the flow of the GA defense,
and into the GA end zone. Spears' PAT made it 14-0
with about ten minutes left in the 3rd quarter.

Early in the 4th quarter, GA HB George Whitton
fumbled a punt with UF's Simpson falling on the
ball at the GA 25. Dunn then threw to Roundtree
who ran over several Dogs on his way into the endzone. Spears kick the PAT and UF now led 21-0.
GA again tried to start an air attack. Under pressure,
Hearn passed long but Brodsky again intercepted,
running the ball back to the GA 24. Four plays later
Simpson ran around right end for 13 yards and UF's
final score. Spears PAT made it 28-0.
The Gators outrushed GA 225 to 88. UF's Brodsky
was voted the player of the game.

1957

-Eisenhower Doctrine calls for aid to Mideast coun-
tries which resist armed aggression from
Communist-controlled nations. The "Little Rock
Nine" integrate Arkansas high school. Eisenhower

sends troops to quell mob and protect school integra-
tion. Russians launch Sputnik I, first Earth-orbiting
satellite—the Space Age begins. Anthony Eden
resigns; MacMillan becomes British Prime Minister.
The USSR tests its first successful ICBM.
World Series Mil. Braves d. NY Yankees (4-3)
NBA Championship
Boston d. St. Louis Hawks (4-3)
Kentucky Derby Champion *Iron Liege*
NCAA Basketball Championship
North Carolina d. Kansas (54-53 3OT)
NCAA Football Champions
Auburn (AP) (10-0-0)
& Ohio St. (UP, FW, INS) (9-1-0)
Best Picture: Around the World in 80 Days
• Leonard Bernstein's West Side Story debuts on
Broadway and brings violence to the stage.
• Eugene O'Neill's A Long Day's Journey Into Night
is produced posthumously and wins both the Tony
Award and Pulitzer Prize.
• Columbia University professor Charles Van Doren
becomes a media sensation by winning $129,000 on
the quiz show Twenty One.
• Leave It to Beaver premieres on CBS, ushering in
an era of television shows that depict the ideal
American.
• Temporary artificial heart invented by Willem
Kolff.
• Interferon invented by Alick Isaacs and Jean
Lindemann (England and Switzerland).
• Clarence W. Lillehie and Earl Bakk (US) invent the
internal pacemaker.
• Bardeen, Cooper, and Scheiffer (US) propose a the-
ory of superconductivity.
• First round-the-world nonstop jet plane flight. Maj.
Gen. Archie J. Old, Jr. (USAF) led a flight of three
Boeing B-52 bombers around the world in 45 hours,
19 minutes (completed Jan. 18).

The Game: 1957 UF-22 GA-0

The Soviet Union had announced that it had
launched a second orbital satellite in a month. The
Gator Bowl had been enlarged to make it possible
for 42,000 fans to attend games. UF was going for
an unprecedented third win in a row over GA.

UF's passing defense was stout and ranked 4th in
the nation. They looked to QB Jimmy Dunn and
runners Bernie Parrish, Ed Sears, and Charlie
Roberts to propel the UF Offense. GA FB Theron
Sapp was the SEC's leading rusher and at QB
Charley Britt, who Butts was sure would be an All-
American. Speaking of Coach Butts…Butts was in
hot water with the GA alumni and supporters. 1954
had been his last winning season. He had a losing
record against UF during the 50s, and to top it off, he
had lost eight in a row to archrival Ga. Tech.

After a stand-off in each opening possession, UF's
offensive line began tearing holes in the GA defense,
allowing Roundtree, Parrish and Dunn to ram the
ball towards the GA end zone on a 47 yard drive.
The last nine yards came on Dunn's first pass of the
day, a TD pass to Don Fleming. Parrish kicked the
PAT and UF led 7-0, late in the 1st period.

In the 2nd period, GA was pinned deep in their
own territory by a long kick by UF's Dunn. Failing
to get a first down, GA had to punt from their end
zone. The snap went over the head of GA punter
Ken Cooper for a UF safety. UF led now 9-0 with
almost nine minutes left in the first half.

GA was rattled. Twice on the safety kick-off, the
GA kicker kicked the ball out of bounds, and by the
time the kick stayed fair UF got the ball on the GA
30. After driving towards the GA goal, UF's
Newburn fumbled the ball and GA held. Then GA
fumbled to UF on their own 13, another chance for

UF to score. GA held and UF turned the ball over to GA, but not for long. On the second play, GA QB Charley Britt fumbled and UF fell on the ball on the GA 18. UF QB Mickey Ellenburg lofted a spiral to Parrish, who dragged a bulldog with him into the end zone. Parrish's PAT gave UF a 16-0 lead at the half.

In the 3rd period both teams drove and both teams stalled. Early in the 4th quarter GA's Davis fumbled and UF took over on the GA 31. UF had their third and fourth string players in the game now. One of them, QB Jim Rhyne. After several rushing attempts, Rhyne saw that Newbern had gotten behind GA defenders and hit him with a 20 yard TD pass. UF's Roundtree rushed for 73 yards and 10 carries and was voted player of the game. He was also noted for his tough blocking. "I've always thought he was one of the most dangerous runners in the conference," Butts said. " A great back can do a lot of things on his own, and Roundtree did just that."

For this year, GA had failed to score for the second straight year.

1958

-European Economic Community (Common Market) becomes effective. Army's Jupiter-C rocket fires first U.S. Earth satellite, Explorer I, into orbit. Egypt and Syria merge into United Arab Republic. Khrushchev becomes premier of Soviet Union as Bulganin resigns. Gen. Charles de Gaulle becomes French premier, remaining in power until 1969. Eisenhower orders U.S. Marines into Lebanon at request of President Chamoun, who fears overthrow. New French constitution adopted, de Gaulle elected president of 5th Republic. The US Supreme Court rules unanimously that Little Rock, Ark., schools must integrate
World Series   NY Yankees d. Mil. Braves (4-3)
NBA Championship St. L. Hawks d. Boston (4-2)
Kentucky Derby Champion *Tim Tam*
NCAA Basketball Championship
Kentucky d. Seattle (84-72)
NCAA Football Champions
LSU (AP, UPI) (11-0-0) & Iowa (FW) (8-1-1)
Best Picture: The Bridge on the River Kwai
• Billboard debuts its Hot 100 chart. Ricky Nelson's "Poor Little Fool" boasts the first No. 1 record.
• Alvin Ailey establishes the American Dance Theatre • Elvis Presley is inducted into the U.S. Army.
Movies: Vertigo, Gigi, Cat on a Hot Tin Roof, The Defiant Ones
• First transatlantic jet passenger service started by BOAC, with a New York to London route.
• The existence of the Van Allen Belt, a radiation belt surrounding the Earth, is confirmed by the Explorer I satellite.
• NASA initiates Project Mercury, aimed at putting a man in space within two years.

The Game: 1958 UF-7 GA-6

It was a typical Florida football Saturday…heavy rains throughout the week had turned the Gator Bowl field into a mud pit, and unusual gusty winds would play havoc with lofted footballs. Regardless of the weather, 40,000 fans turned out to see the '58 game.

UF was looking to beat GA for the fourth straight year. It would also be the first year that UF was to play cross-state rivals FSU. The Dogs were hoping UF had their mind more on the Seminoles than on them. GA was relying on an Athens Minister's son, Francis Tarkenton, their sophomore quarterback. Tarkenton was responsible for the lone touchdown drive in their loss against Texas after replacing Charley Britt. Dog fans wanted Butts to give Tarkenton more snaps.

In this game, the Dye brothers started side-by-side, Nat at left tackle and Pat at left guard. The Gators would rely on the passing and sly ball-handling of their senior QB Jimmy Dunn and his favorite target, Capt. Don Fleming.

GA made the first scoring threat, moving the ball down to the UF 6 before running out of gas and downs. After stopping the Gators, GA again drove down to the UF 10, where a Britt pass on fourth down fell incomplete. GA held again, and again drove downfield to the UF 12 before a holding penalty killed any scoring opportunity. Next series, same results. GA held UF, got the ball back, drove to the UF 4, but was unable to score.

With UF lining up for fourth down inside their own 15, it appeared GA would once again get great field position. UF punter Bobby Joe Green had other ideas. His punt almost left the Gator Bowl. Hanging in the wind, Green's spiral traveled 82 yards, rolling dead at the GA 6. It was the longest punt in the rivalry's history.

The fist half ended in a scoreless tie. The GA offense had blown six chances to score. The GA defense had held the Gators outside the GA 40, and without a first down for the entire first half.

Late in the third period, GA's Britt returned a punt to the UF 17. Tarkenton came in to QB the Dogs. After driving to the UF 5, Tarkenton hit Fred Brown in the end zone for the first score of the game. On the PAT attempt, Gator HB Russell Dilts blocked the kick. UF made its first first down with around two minutes left in the third period. But, that was it. The Gators punted and GA got the ball back.This time it was the UF defense who held. On fourth down, GA's Bobby Walden punted 51 yards to the UF 24. On their first play, UF QB Jimmy Dunn rolled left and sliced upfield. Suddenly, he was in the clear and distancing himself between the remaining Bulldogs' dives to drop him. 76 yards later, he gave the ball to a referee, who was signaling, touchdown. Billy Booker's PAT was good and UF led 7-6.

Butts brought Britt back in the game at QB. The crowd boo'd their disapproval. Britt was unable to move the team. The GA defense again held UF's offense in check. On GA's next series Tarkenton was back in charge.The drive started on the GA 6. Tarkenton hit Norman King with a 46-yard pass. Then completed a 16-yarder to Bill Herron. With only seconds left in the game, GA had the ball, once again, deep in UF territory. The scoreboard clock had quit in the 3rd quarter. Tarkenton was not sure how much time was remaining. In the confusion, the GA QB, instead of kicking a FG for the win, attempted one last pass that Gator HB Jack Westbrook intercepted, sealing the win for UF. After the game, Butts said that GA kicker Carl Manning was in the game when the pass was intercepted, and could have tried to kick the winning field goal. "We just didn't know what time it was," Butts told the Atlanta Constitution.

1959

Cuban President Batista resigns and flees—Castro takes over. Tibet's Dalai Lama escapes to India. St. Lawrence Seaway opens, allowing ocean ships to reach Midwest. Alaska and Hawaii become states. Leakeys discover hominid fossils. Soviet Premier Nikita Khrushchev tours the United States, meeting with Eisenhower at Camp David. Britain recognizes the independence of Cyprus.
World Series LA Dodgers d. Chi. White Sox (4-2)
NBA Championship Boston d. Minn. Lakers (4-0)
Kentucky Derby Champion *Tomy Lee*
NCAA Basketball Championship
California d. West Virginia (71-70)
NCAA Football Champions Syracuse (11-0-0)

Best Picture: Gigi
Record of the Year: "Nel Blu Dipinto di Blu" (Volare), Domenico Modugno Album of the Year: The Music From Peter Gunn, Henry Mancini Song of the Year: "Nel Blu Dipinto di Blu," Domenico Modugno, songwriter
• The National Academy of Recording Arts and Sciences sponsors the first Grammy Award ceremony for music recorded in 1958.
• Frank Sinatra wins his first Grammy Award -- Best Album for Come Dance with Me.
• Rumors of cheating on quiz shows erupt into a national scandal.
Movies: Some Like It Hot, North by Northwest, Ben-Hur, Anatomy of a Murder, Room at the Top
• Jack S. Kilby of Texas Instruments (US) supervise the development of the first integrated circuit.
• The US Navy launches the Vanguard satellite.
• The Lunik II probe (USSR) reaches the moon; photographs the dark side of the moon for the first time.

The Game: 1959 GA -21 UF -10

It was another cloudy, cold and rainy day for the 37th renewal of this rivalry. 42,000 had filled the Gator Bowl.

This season GA was the surprise team of the SEC with a 6-1 record, coming into the yearly bout with UF. Tarkenton was leading the SEC in passing and was second in total offense. UF's team had been hit with many injuries and added a lot of poor playing to their woes. This game would be a duel between the two top punters in the nation: Florida's Bobby Joe Green and GA's Bobby "The Toe from Cairo" Walden.

GA got the ball for the first time on the UF 48. O three plays, GA moved the ball eight yards. Three more plays moved the ball down to the Gator 14. From the 14, Britt pitched out to Walden, who appeared to be making a sweep around end. Walden suddenly pulled back and tossed the ball to Gordon Kelley in the end zone. Durwood Pennington kicke the PAT and GA led 7-0. GA held UF on their next series, and UF quick-kicked. Britt caught the ball o the GA 36 and returned it to the UF 37. Two plays later, Britt hit Towns for a second quick GA score. Pennington's kick made it 14-0.

UF started one possession on its own 28. UF QB Dick Allen hit Bobby Joe Green with a pass, and th fleet back streaked towards the GA goal line. The only Dog fast enough to catch him was Charley Britt. Britt pulled down Green on the GA 2, after a play of 70 yards. Four times UF tried to penetrate GA's goal line. The GA defensive wall consisted o Dye, Roland, Thompson and end Jimmy Vickers, / the Savannah Morning News said of the stand of a collision between a UF runner and two GA defenders, *"It reminded you of someone diving into a poo in which there is not water."*

GA took over, but the UF defense held the Dogs right there for three plays. On fourth down, Bobby Walden, set up to punt from deep in his own end zone. The soggy ball hit Walden's hands and slippe away. By the time UF End Dave Hudson fell on th ball, it had traveled out of bounds, thus giving the Gators their two points of the game.

Late in the third quarter, after a wobbly Walden punt, UF drove the ball down to the GA 9. Allen spied an open receiver in the end zone and set the ball towards him. GA's Britt stepped in front of the receiver and sprinted 100 yards with the intercepti for a GA score. Pennington's kick made it 21-2.

In the fourth quarter Britt threw from midfield to slanting end, Jack Westbrook, a UF defender, stepped in and intercepted the pass, returning it 54 yards for UF's first TD of the game. QB Allen ran around end for the two-point conversion, making th score GA 21, UF 10. UF's four game winning stre was over.

Price
25¢

GEORGIA VS FLORIDA
NOVEMBER 11, 1950

1950 · UGA 6 UFL 0

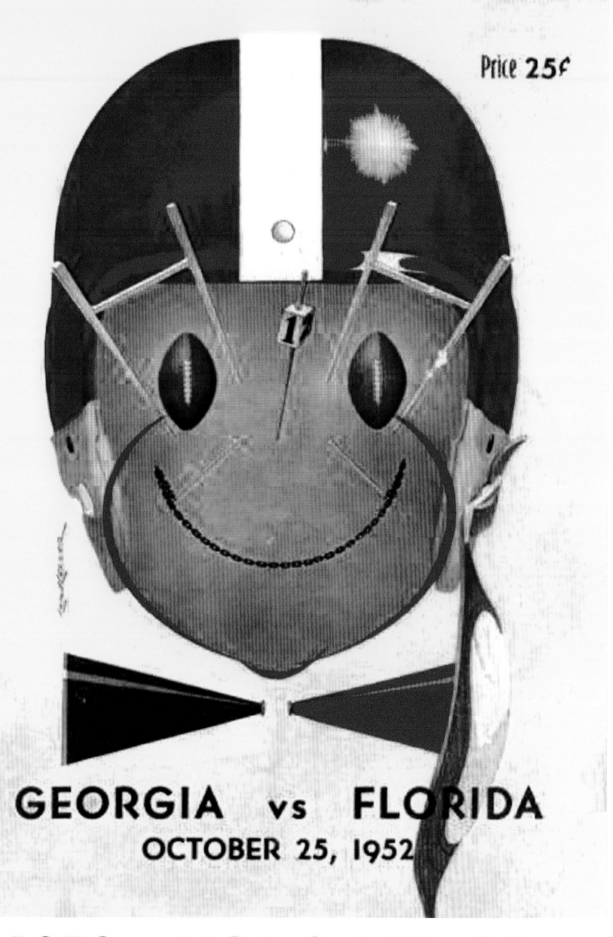

Price 25¢

GEORGIA vs FLORIDA
OCTOBER 25, 1952

1952 · UGA 0 UFL 30

GEORGIA vs FLORIDA
NOVEMBER 7, 1953

Price 35c

1953 · UGA 7 UFL 21

GEORGIA vs FLORIDA

NOVEMBER 6, 1954

PRICE 35¢

1954 · UGA 14 UFL 13

GEORGIA VS FLORIDA
NOVEMBER 5, 1955

1955 · UGA 13 UFL 19

Georgia vs Florida
November 10, 1956

Price **50c**

1956 · UGA 0 UFL 28

Georgia vs Florida
November 9, 1957
Price 50c

1957 · UGA 0 UFL 22

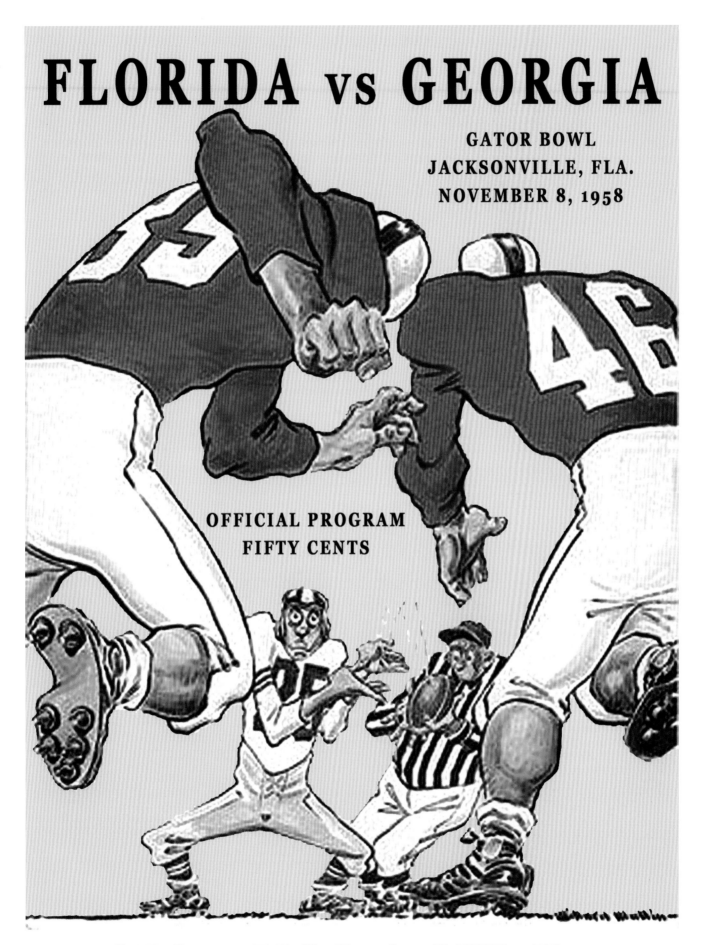

FLORIDA vs GEORGIA

GATOR BOWL
JACKSONVILLE, FLA.
NOVEMBER 8, 1958

OFFICIAL PROGRAM
FIFTY CENTS

1958 · UGA 6 UFL 7

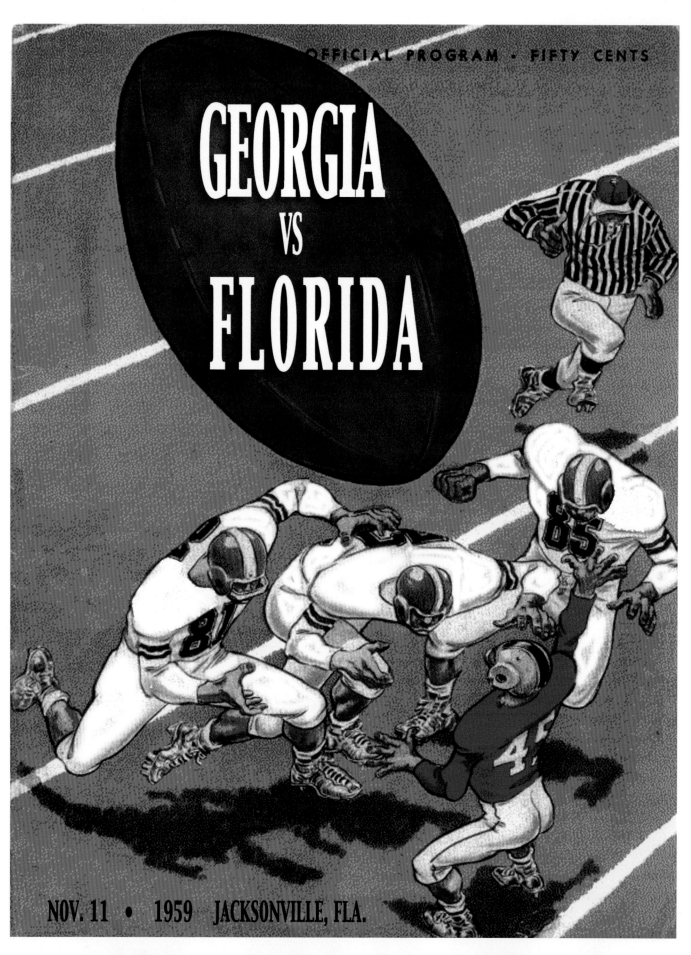

OFFICIAL PROGRAM · FIFTY CENTS

GEORGIA VS FLORIDA

NOV. 11 · 1959 JACKSONVILLE, FLA.

1959 · UGA 21 UFL 10

The 1960s

1960

American U-2 spy plane, piloted by Francis Gary Powers, shot down over Russia. Khrushchev kills Paris summit conference because of U-2.

Top Nazi murderer of Jews, Adolf Eichmann, captured by Israelis in Argentina—executed in Israel in 1962.

Communist China and Soviet Union split in conflict over Communist ideology. Senegal, Ghana, Nigeria, Madagascar, and Zaire (Belgian Congo) gain independence.

• There are 900 US military advisers in South Vietnam.

• John F. Kennedy defeats Richard Nixon in a closely-fought presidential race.

• Black sit-in at Greensboro, N.C., diner receives national attention. Background: Civil Rights • Cost of a first-class stamp: $0.04

World Series
Pittsburgh d. NY Yankees (4-3)
NBA Championship
Boston d. St. Louis Hawks (4-3)
Kentucky Derby Champion *Venetian Way*
NCAA Basketball Championship
Ohio St. d. California (75-55)
NCAA Football Champions
Minnesota (AP, UPI, NFF) (8-2-0) &
Mississippi (FW) (10-0-1)
Best Picture: Ben-Hur
Record of the Year: "Mack the Knife."
Bobby Darin Album of the Year: Come Dance With Me, Frank Sinatra
Song of the Year: "The Battle of New Orleans," Jimmy Driftwood

• Seventy million people watch the presidential debate between Sen. John F. Kennedy and Vice President Richard Nixon.

• John Coltrane forms his own quartet and becomes the voice of jazz's New Wave movement.

• Ninety percent of U.S. homes have a television set.

• Alfred Hitchcock's Psycho terrifies movie-goers and becomes one of the year's most successful films, as well as one of the most memorable psychological thrillers.

Movies: Psycho, The Apartment, The Sundowners, Sons and Lovers

• The first working laser is built by T. H. Maiman (US).

• Echo I, the first communications satellite, is launched.

• NASA launches Tiros I, the first weather satellite. Background: Space Exploration

The Game: 1960 UF -22 GA -14

Closer to home, the Ray Graves era had begun at UF, and the Butts era was drawing to a close.

GA, the defending SEC champions (5-2) came into the game a 3-point favorite, riding on the passing arm and scrambling of Francis Tarkenton and the blocking and defense of guard Pat Dye. GA also featured a pack of running backs including Fred Brown, Bill McKenny and Billy Jackson. Leading UF was tiny QB Larry Libertore and a power fullback named Don Goodman. Libertore was second in the SEC in rushing.

It was observed that the overflow crowd showed more Kennedy buttons on their jackets and coats than did they Nixon buttons. The winner of the game would no doubt receive a bid to play in the Gator Bowl in December.

UF wasted no time, behind Libertore's and Goodman's running ground out a 77-yard drive. Goodman scored the TD from the 1. Bill Cash kicked the PAT and UF led 7-0. GA's Don Tomberlin fumbled the kick-off and UF fell on the ball on the GA 28. Libertore went airborne in this drive. He hit Tommy Kelley with an 18-yard pass. From there Goodman and Libertore rushed the next five plays, driving down to the GA 1 where Goodman, once again plunged the final yard into the end zone. Cash kicked the PAT and UF now led 14-0.

After trading possessions, GA's Tarkenton hit HB McKenney with a 21-yard pass. GA FB Wayne Taylor ran twice, getting GA down to the UF 22. GA turned the ball over on a Tarkenton interception by Gene Page on the UF 12.

Near the end of the first half, Libertore was injured returning a punt. In the second half, UF sent in their second string QB, Bobby Dodd, Jr. and their offense didn't miss a beat. Dodd directed a 10-play drive to the GA goal line, where Dodd scored on a QB keeper. With Dodd holding, Cash lined up for the PAT. Instead of placing the ball down for the kicker, Dodd circled the end for a two-point conversion. UF now led 22-0.

Tarkenton earned his nickname "The Scrambler" on GA's next series. GA drove from their own 40 down to the UF 7. Tarkenton had a fourth and goal when he faded back to pass. He faded all the way back to the UF 30, looking for an open receiver. Seeing none, Tarkenton tucked the ball in and eluded all UF defenders as he ran along the sidelines for the TD. GA's Walden passed to Fred Brown for a 2-point conversion for GA. The score was now UF 22, GA 8.

On the next series, UF's Deal fumbled and GA's Pete Case fell on the ball. GA drove to the UF 26. Billy Jackson took a pitchout from Tarkenton and lofted a pass to Walden, who made a terrific one-hand catch in the end zone. GA went for another 2-point conversion with Jackson again hitting Walden in the end zone, but the GA end could not hold onto the ball. The score was now UF 22, GA 14.

Tarkenton had injured his hip in GA's last scoring drive, so Jackson was taking pitchouts from Tarkenton and then throwing downfield. On their final drive of the game, GA rolled down to the UF 39 where they were stopped as the game ended.

Butts told reporters that Tarkenton had suffered an asthma attack the night before and had not slept, so even before his injury, he was not at full speed.

This was the first time since 1940 that a UF team had beaten both GA and Ga. Tech in the same season. The Gators finished behind Ole Miss in the SEC. It would be the last game that Butts would coach his dogs against UF. In 21 games against UF, Butts had won 12 and lost 9. Seven of those losses had come in the past ten years.

1961

• US breaks diplomatic relations with Cuba • 1,200 US-sponsored anti-Castro exiles invade Cuba at the Bay of Pigs; the attackers are all killed or captured by Cuban forces • East Germany erects the Berlin Wall between East and West Berlin to halt flood of refugees • USSR detonate 50-megaton hydrogen bomb in the largest man-made explosion in history

• There are 2,000 US military advisers in South Vietnam • OPEC (Organization of Petroleum Exporting Countries) formally constituted.

• First US astronaut, Navy Cmdr. Alan B Shepard, Jr., rockets 116.5 miles up in 302-mile trip • Virgil Grissom becomes second American astronaut, making 118-mile-high, 303-mile-long rocket flight over Atlantic

World Series
NY Yankees d. Cincinnati (4-1)
NBA Championship
Boston d. St. Louis Hawks (4-1)
Kentucky Derby Champion *Carry Back*
NCAA Basketball Championship
Cincinnati d. Ohio St. (70-65 OT)
NCAA Football Champions
Alabama (AP, UPI, NFF) (11-0-0) &
Ohio St. (FW) (8-0-1)
Best Picture: The Apartment
Record of the Year: "Theme From A Summer Place," Percy Faith
Album of the Year: Button Down Mind, Bob Newhart
Song of the Year: "Theme From Exodus, Ernest Gold, songwriter

• Patsy Cline releases "I Fall to Pieces" and "Crazy." The success of the songs help her cross over from country to pop.

• West Side Story is adapted for the big screen, and will go on to win Oscars for Best Picture, Supporting Actor, Supporting Actress, and Directing .

• Audrey Hepburn delights as Holly Golightly in Breakfast at Tiffany's, but Henry Mancini emerges as the real star. He won two Oscars and four Grammy Awards for the score, which included the hit "Moon River."

Movies: West Side Story, The Hustler, Judgment at Nuremberg, La Dolce Vita

• Moscow announces putting first man in orbit around earth. Major Yuri A. Gagari

• Gherman Stepanovich Titov is launched in Soviet spaceship Vostok II: makes 17 1/2 orbits in 25 hours, covering 434,960 miles before landing safely

1961 UF 21 GA 14

Johnny Griffith was in his first year coaching the Dogs and Ray Graves was starting his second. GA had lost four of seven games, while UF was a mediocre

1. UF's QB Larry Libertore was one of the
EC's best, while GA's QB Larry Rakestraw was
ll learning the ropes.
The 47,000 fans that crammed the Gator Bowl
ere welcomed by a warm and cloudy day.
A fumbled on its own 16. After gaining a few
rds, UF found themselves with a fourth down
the GA 15. UF QB Batten hit Lindy Infante in
corner of the end zone for UF's first score. Cash
cked the PAT and UF led 7-0.
Midway through the second quarter, GA's Bill
cKenny fumbled a punt on GA's 14 where
F's Anton Peters recovered it. GA pushed UF
ck to the 29, where Cash missed a FG.
UF held and got the ball back near the midfield
ipe. On first down, Batten hit Bob Hoover at
GA 20. He didn't stop till he had crossed the
al line. Cash missed the PAT, but UF lead was
w 13-0.
In the third quarter, GA recovered a fumble
ar midfield. On second down, Rakestraw hit
hn Landry with a 47 yard pass and a GA TD.
nnington's kick was good. The score was now
-7 with plenty of time remaining in the game.
The Dogs held on the next UF series. Starting
m their own 20, Rakestraw came out firing. In
elve plays, GA was sitting on the UF 17. After
o rushes, GA was three feet away from tying
e game. Rakestraw took the snap and just fol-
wed his blockers into the end zone.
nnington's PAT put GA ahead 14-13.
UF drove and missed a field goal. GA could
t move and punted to the UF 37. Batten hit on
sses of 10 and 30 yards. After losing a yard on
attempted rush, Batten hit Ron Stoner for a
. A penalty forced the Gators to go for the
T from the 8-yard line. Instead of kicking,
tten faded back and hit Russ Brown for the
o-point conversion. UF now led 21-14.
A drove down the field, and with seconds left,
kestraw attempted to hit an open end, but once
ain UF's safety Paul White intercepted and
led the UF victory.
"The truth of the matter is, the Gators didn't
ve to be very smart Saturday for in Tom Batten
y had a quarterback who performed magic
ry time he stepped back to throw," said the
anta Constitution.

962

rance transfers sovereignty to new republic of
geria • Cuban Missile Crisis: USSR to build
ssile bases in Cuba; Kennedy orders Cuban
ockade, lifts blockade after Russia backs down.
ope John XXIII opens Second Vatican Council
uba releases 1,113 prisoners of 1961 invasion
empt. • Burundi, Jamaica, Western Samoa,
anda, and Trinidad and Tobago become inde-
ndent • James H. Meredith, escorted by federal
rshals, registers at University of Mississippi •
Brown defeats Richard Nixon in the
lifornia gubernatorial race.
rld Series NY Yankees d. S F Giants (4-3)
A Championship Boston d. LA Lakers (4-3)
ntucky Derby Champion *Decidedly*
AA Basketball Championship
cinnati d. Ohio St. (71-59)
st Picture: West Side Story
cord of the Year: "Moon River," Henry
ncini Album of the Year: Judy at Carnegie
ll, Judy Garland (Capitol)
ng of the Year: "Moon River," Henry Mancini
Johnny Mercer • Marilyn Monroe dies of a
g overdose at age 36. • The first transatlantic
vision transmission occurs via the Telstar
ellite, making worldwide television and cable

networks a reality. • Government regulations
force studios out of the talent agency business.
• Johnny Carson takes over hosting duties of The
Tonight Show.
Movies: Lawrence of Arabia, To Kill a
Mockingbird, The Manchurian Candidate,
Divorce-Italian Style
• Lt. Col. John H. Glenn, Jr., is first American to
orbit Earth — three times in 4 hours 55 minutes
(Feb. 20). Background: US Staffed Space Flights
• Mariner II, the first interplanetary probe, reach-
es Venus • Unimation introduces the first industri-
al robot • The commercially sponsored Telstar
communications satellite is launched.

The Game: 1962 UF -23 GA- 15

The 45,000 fans filling the Gator Bowl this
year were fired up about the game, even with the
country in the midst of the Cuban Missile Crisis.
The world seemed to be on the verge of a nuclear
war. The only "war" on the minds of fans in
Jacksonville was between "Dogs" and "Gators."
Larry "Long Gone" Dupree was proving to be
one of UF's finest running backs of all time. At
QB UF had Tom Shannon who running at 57%
completions of all passes he had thrown. GA had
the third rated QB in the SEC in Larry Rakestraw
and they had FB Leon Armbrester who was the
SEC's top rusher, averaging 4.7 yards a carry.
Early in the game, UF's Hoover fumbled a
pitchout. GA recovered on the UF 23. Armbrester
rumbled for six yards. Rakestraw tossed to end
Mickey Babb on the UF 3. Porterfield crashed
through the line for GA's first TD. Bill
McCullough's PAT made it 7-0.
UF didn't start moving until the middle of the
second quarter. After several rushing plays, UF's
Dupree took a handoff and found a seam and
scored. Shannon hit Newcomer in the end zone
for the 2-point conversion. UF now lead 8-7.
Late in the first half, GA's Jake Saye's punt got
caught in the wind and rolled dead on the GA 41
after traveling only 21 yards. Between FB Jim
O'Donnell's running and Shannon's passing, UF
was sitting on the GA 11 after nine offensive
downs. Dupree took the next hand-off and squirt-
ed through the hole in the line at right tackle for
his second score. Hall kicked the PAT and UF
now lead 15-7 just before halftime.
UF's "Big Blue Line" was successfully stopping GA's rushing attack, while the stiff winds at
the Gator Bowl blew Rakestraw's tosses off-
course.
UF took the second half kick-off and rushed
seven times at the GA line. O'Donnell, Dupree,
and Shannon found holes and moved the ball
down to the GA 5. Two plays later, UF's Hoover
banged over from two yards out. Shannon skirted
around the end for a two-point conversion. UF
now led 23-7.
GA's Rakestraw seemed to defy the breeze on
GA's next and most impressive drive of the
game. Starting at the GA 27, Rakestraw completed five of nine passes moving GA to the UF 7.
On the 13th snap of GA's drive, Rakestraw hit
Barry Wilson with a TD pass.
GA also went for two, with Rakestraw hitting
Don Blackburn with a strike. It was now UF 23,
GA 15.
The UF defense consisting of Peters, Pettee,
Travis, Richbourg, and Brown closed down the
GA offense for the rest of the game, keeping GA
near their own goal and far away from UF's. GA
ended up with a grand total of 30 yards rushing
for the game. UF's Dupree had rushed for 111
yards, while O'Donnell added another 80 to go
with UF's total offensive yards of 298.
the PAT.
In the 3rd quarter, UF recovered a GA fumble
at the GA 28 and successfully drove GA back-

wards on the ground. The final three yards were
covered by Casares for another UF score. With
his PAT good, the score was now UF 17 GA 0. In
the 4th quarter, UF's Dickey handed off to Long
who danced over left tackle, spun to his left,
reversed the field and found 77 yards of open
space in front of him, all the way to the GA end
zone. Casares PAT was good and UF now led 24-
0.
UF Reserve QB Fred Robinson drilled a 19
yard TD pass to Leonard Balas in the waning
seconds of the game. The PAT was missed. But
the final score wasn't… UF 30 GA 0. Casares
rushed for 108 yards on 27 attempts, and scored
12 points.

1963

• France and West Germany sign treaty of cooperation ending four centuries of conflict • Pope
John XXIII dies, and is succeeded June 21 by
Cardinal Montini, who becomes Paul VI.
• British Secretary of War John Profumo resigns
in the wake of an affair with Christine Keeler, a
teenage showgirl who was also involved with the
Soviet naval attaché • Washington-to-Moscow
"hot line" communications link opens, designed
to reduce risk of accidental war • Kenya achieves
independence • There are 15,000 US military
advisers in South Vietnam • 32 independent
African nations establish the Organization for
African Unity • Michael E. De Bakey implants
artificial heart in human for first time at Houston
hospital • US Supreme Court rules no locality
may require recitation of Lord's Prayer or Bible
verses in public schools • "March on
Washington," civil rights rally held by 200,000
blacks and whites in Washington, D.C.; Martin
Luther King delivers "I have a dream" speech.
• President Kennedy shot and killed in Dallas,
Tex. Lyndon B. Johnson becomes President same
day • Lee Harvey Oswald, accused Kennedy
assassin, is shot and killed by Jack Ruby.
World Series LA Dodgers d. NY Yankees (4-0)
NBA Championship Boston d. LA Lakers (4-2)
Kentucky Derby Champion *Chateaugay*
NCAA Basketball Championship
Loyola-IL d. Cincinnati (60-58 OT)
NCAA Football Champions Texas (11-0-0)
Record of the Year: "I Left My Heart in San
Francisco," Tony Bennett Album of the Year: The
First Family, Vaughn Meader Song of the Year:
"What Kind of Fool Am I" • Viewers tuned into
NBC witness Jack Ruby shoot Lee Harvey
Oswald on camera – the first live telecast of a
murder • Beatlemania hits the U.K. The Beatles,
a British band composed of John Lennon, George
Harrison, Ringo Starr and Paul McCartney, take
Britain by storm • The Rolling Stones emerge as
the anti-Beatles, with an aggressive, blues-
derived style • The French Chef with Julia Child
debuts on educational television.
Movies: Tom Jones, Lilies of the Field, America,
America
• Quasars are discovered by Marten Schmidt
(US) • The first liver transplant is performed by
F.D. Moore and T.E. Starzl. Background: Health
& Nutrition • The first commercial nuclear reac-
tor goes online at the Jersey Central Power
Company • The sedative Valium (chlordiazepox-
ide) is developed by Roche labs.

The Game: 1963 UF -21 GA -14

In Jacksonville, everyone was rating this year's
game between UF and GA pretty much a toss-up. UF
fanatics were dishing up "Bulldog Stew" just before
48,000 of their closest friends filled the Gator Bowl.

The game was just a little over two minutes old when a Rakestraw pass found its way to the wrong receiver. UF Safety Bruce Bennett ran the interception back 43 yards for the score. Hall kicked the PAT and UF had a quick 7-0 lead. UF Coach Ray Graves then caught the GA team napping, as he called for an on-sides kick. UF's Russell landed on the ball on the GA 45. UF QB Shannon mixed his passing and moved the Gators right down the field. The first quarter wasn't even half way through and the Gators were back on the GA 4 yard line. Dupree changed that. Shannon handed off to him and watched him run through the GA line for UF's second score. With Hall's PAT, it was now UF 14, GA 0.

But UF was keeping one of its traits it had established throughout the 1963 season. They were prone to fumble. UF's Newcomer coughed up the ball on the UF 21 with Armbresteer landing on it. GA went to the UF 10 in three plays. HB Bob Taylor rushed nine yards, almost getting into the endzone. On the next play he did. GA's Bill "The Machine" McCullough kicked the PAT. It was now UF 14, GA 7.

On it's next series, GA returned the favor with Rakestraw dropping the ball on his own 5 yard line. On the first play, Dupree pushed towards the end zone. The ball popped out of his hands and rolled into the endzone. Everybody on the field went for the ball. Gator end Lynn Matthews ended up with the bouncing ball for a TD. Hall made it 21-7.

UF held Rakestraw in check for the first half. He had two interceptions (one going for a score), a fumble, just one completion in six attempts, and had generaled GA to only 29 yards of total offense in the first half. GA's defense kept them in the game for the third quarter, not allowing UF to score. UF's defense did the same to GA. Late in the third period UF's Dick Kirk fumbled a GA punt and the Bulldogs were in business at the UF 24. Rakestraw hit Pat Hodgson for 14 yards, and a rush later, GA was on the UF 5. Rakestraw then threw to Mickey Babb for the score. McCullough's kick made it 21-14 with plenty of time left in the game.

After a heated defensive battle, GA had one last chance to even the score. A long Rakestraw pass was again intercepted by Bruce Bennett. Time ran out for the Dogs. Rakestraw, GA's best runner lost 19 yards on 12 rushes and was intercepted four times. UF's Shannon was not a lot better. He hit nine of 19 passes for 107 yards and three interceptions

1964
• Nelson Mandela sentenced to life imprisonment in South Africa • Congress approves Gulf of Tonkin Resolution after North Vietnamese torpedo boats allegedly attack US destroyers • Khrushchev is deposed; Kosygin becomes premier and Brezhnev becomes first secretary of the Communist Party • China detonates its first atomic bomb • US Supreme Court rules that Congressional districts should be roughly equal in population • Three civil rights workers-Schwerner, Goodman, and Cheney—murdered in Mississippi • President's Commission on the Assassination of President Kennedy issues Warren Report concluding that Lee Harvey Oswald acted alone • Jack Ruby convicted of murder in slaying of Lee Harvey Oswald.
World Series St.L Cardinals d. NY Yankees (4-3)
NBA Championship Boston d. SF Warriors (4-1)
Kentucky Derby Champion *Northern Dancer*
NCAA Basketball Championship
UCLA d. Duke (98-83)
NCAA Football Champions Alabama (AP, UPI), (10-1-0); Arkansas (FW), (11-0-0) & Notre Dame (NFF), (9-1-0)
Best Picture: Tom Jones, Tony Richardson, producer (United Artists-Lopert Pictures)
Record of the Year: "The Days of Wine and

Roses," Henry Mancini Album of the Year: The Barbra Streisand Album, Barbra Streisand
Song of the Year: "The Days of Wine and Roses,"
• Folk musician Bob Dylan becomes increasingly popular during this time of social protest with songs expressing objection to the condition of American society • Psychedelic bands such as The Grateful Dead and Jefferson Airplane enjoy great success with songs celebrating the counter-culture of the '60s • Peyton Place premieres on ABC and is the first prime-time soap opera. Color television makes its way into U.S. homes.• The Beatles appear on The Ed Sullivan Show.
Movies : Red Desert, Dr. Strangelove, My Fair Lady, Mary Poppins, Zorba the Greek, Becket
• Ranger VII takes 4,316 high-resolution pictures of the moon. • US Surgeon General Luther Terry affirms that cigarette smoking causes cancer.

The Game: 1964 GA -14 UF- 7
Names that would play heavy in the football history of both schools were introduced this season. GA Coach Johnny Griffith had disappointed many GA fans and alumni and was replaced this year by first year Coach Vince Dooley, who came to GA from Auburn after Griffith and AD Butts were dismissed from GA. UF's Coach Graves had a new leader at QB for this year's team. A lanky and accurate Steve Spurrier was hitting on 58% of his passes, most to E Charles Casey, who led the SEC in receptions. This duo gave the Gators a #9 ranking the AP polls. GA at this point in the season had the SEC's worst pass defense, so UF was an early favorite to win his 5th straight game over GA.

Dooley abandoned the "silver britches" and had his team wear white pants. On the sunny field, in front of 48,000 fans, "UGA" GA's cheerleaders' mascot, a white English Bulldog dressed in a red sweater. On the opposite side of the field "Sam," the Boxer, was clad in orange and blue.

The first score did not come until the second period, even though UF had gobbled up massive yardage in the first period. Spurrier mixed his running and passing and led the Gators from their own 17 down to the GA 7. Dupree took the next handoff and didn't stop until he had crossed the goal line. Hall kicked the PAT and UF led 7-0.

Spurrier again marched the UF offense down the field the next time UF got the ball. When the drive faltered on the GA 7, Hall missed an attempted FG. This score remained until the third period.

Three minutes into the third period UF HB Allen Trammell was rammed by GA's Ray Rissmiller and fumbled the ball over to GA at the UF 39. The hit was so hard that Rissmiller dislocated his right elbow and was lost for the season. GA drove to the UF 17 where Barber fumbled the ball back over to UF. On the next series, Spurrier returned the favor, being hit behind the line by GA's George Patton and losing the ball to GA's Vance Evans. GA had the ball on the UF 11. Any thought of GA scoring on this series was snapped when GA QB Preston Ridlehuber was intercepted on the UF goal line by Jimmy Berhardt. GA held UF and Spurrier punted out to GA's Wayne Swinford, who returned the ball to the UF 30. GA rushed the UF line six times, getting down to the UF 2 just as the game entered the fourth quarter. Barber ran over from there and Etter kicked the PAT. Game tied.

Just two plays later, UF QB Shannon miffed a pitchout to FB John Feiber and the ball ended up in the possession of GA's Douglas McFalls at the UF 21. GA's Barber and Lankewicz rushed the Dogs to the UF 5. On fourth down, Dooley sent in Etter to kick a FG and give GA the lead. A high snap got away from Wilson the holder, and Etter found himself with the ball, desparately trying to score. GA

holder Wilson leveled one Gator defensiveman honing in on Etter, allowing the panicked kicker to get into the endzone untouched. Etter then did kick the PAT and GA led 14-7 with a little over nine minutes left in the game.

The GA defense held. The UF defense held. A GA punt rolled dead at the UF 1 with a minute left in the game. On came Spurrier. He tossed one pass to Casey for 12 yards. Then he heaved a 44-yarder to Jimmy Jordan. GA fans started yelling for their defense to show up. Spurrier tried the same long pass again, but this time three GA defensive backs surrounded the ball, with McFalls intercepting it on the GA10 as the game ended.

Of Etter's run, Furman Bisher of the Atlanta Journal said, "It was the first time in his whole life he had ever carried a football, except to get it pumped up."

1965
• The first US combat troops arrive in Vietnam. By the end of the year, 190,000 American soldiers are in Vietnam. • US marines land in the Dominican Republic as fighting persists between rebels and Dominican army • France withdraws its Atlantic fleet from NATO • Rhodesia unilaterally declares its independence from Britain • Rev. Dr. Martin Luther King, Jr., and more than 2,600 others arrested in Selma, Ala., during demonstrations against voter-registration rules • Malcolm X, black-nationalist leader, shot to death at Harlem rally • Blacks riot for six days in Watts section of Los Angeles: 34 dead, over 1,000 injured, nearly 4,000 arrested.
World Series LA Dodgers d. Minnesota (4-3)
NBA Championship Boston d. LA Lakers (4-1)
Kentucky Derby Champion *Lucky Debonair*
NCAA Basketball Championship
UCLA d. Michigan (91-80)
NCAA Football Champions Alabama (AP, FW-tie) (9-1-1) & Michigan St. (UPI, NFF, FW-tie) (10-1-0)
Best Picture: My Fair Lady Record of the Year: "The Girl From Ipanema" Album of the Year: Getz/Gilberto, Stan Getz and Joao Gilberto
Song of the Year: "Hello, Dolly!"
• The Sound of Music premieres. An instant hit, the film was one of the top grossing films of 1965 and remains one of film's most popular musicals • ABC pays an unprecedented $32 million for a four-year contract with the NCAA to broadcast football games on Saturday afternoons • Bill Cosby, starring in I Spy, becomes the first African American to headline a television show.
Movies: Dr. Zhivago, The Sound of Music, A Thousand Clowns, Darling
• Arno A. Penzias and Robert W. Wilson's (US) discovery of cosmic background radiation confirms the "Big Bang" theory • Early Bird, the first commercial communications satellite, is launched • Wally Schirra and Thomas Stafford aboard Gemini VI perform the first rendezvous with another spacecraft, Gemini VII with Frank Borman and James Lovell • Soviet cosmonaut Aleksei Leonov performs the first space-walk. Edward White II becomes the first American to walk in space.

The Game: 1965 UF-14 GA-10
It was windy and rain drizzled, off and on, over the 61,500 fans filled the newly enlarged Gator Bowl. President Lyndon Johnson was trying to negotiate a peace by Christmas in Vietnam, where the war had intensified. In Athens, Coach Dooley had suspended three players for disciplinary reasons…one starter and two back-ups. Spurrier and Casey were lighting up the scoreboard every game, and GA's weak defense was considered to be UF's next victim.

The first quarter was a punting duel between GA'

...irby Moore and UF's Steve Spurrier. UF recovered ...GA fumble and drove to the GA 1, but fumbled the ...all back to GA in the end zone.

Three minutes before halftime, Spurrier marched ...e Gators 46 for their first score. The big play in ...e drive was a screen pass from Spurrier to Harper ...r 28 yards. Poe scored from six yards out and ...ayne Barfield kicked the PAT to make it 7-0, UF. ...the third quarter, UF fumbled and GA's George ...atton recovered on the UF 41. Kirby Moore led the ...ogs down to the UF8, but on fourth down, Dooley ...ose for Etter to come in and boot a FG. Now the ...ore was UF 7, GA 3.

After taking a UF punt in the fourth quarter, GA ...oduced it's best drive of the day. From the UF 45, ...idlehuber ran for 21 yards, the longest GA run of ...e day. GA drove down to the UF 8, where Dooley ...mbled on a fourth and five. Moore went back to ...ass, saw Hodgson breaking free in the end zone and ...t him with a high pass. Hodgson made a fingertip ...tch and held onto the ball as he slid across the ...uddy field. Etter's PAT was good. Now GA led 10-...

With just over four minutes left in the game, and ...under rolling in from the east, Spurrier made one ... his legendary border war drives. Spurrier hit ...asey for a 45 yarder. On the next play, Spurrier hit ...arper diving across the goal line. Dog fans feel that ... defensiveman Lynn Hughes had not stumbled, he ...ould have intercepted the ball. But, hey, that's why ...ey call it football. Harper caught the pass and ...arfield kicked the PAT. UF led 14-10 with three ...d a half minutes remaining in the game. UF had ...ly used 30 seconds for their score. The UF defense ...ffed GA one more time and the game was over.

966

France withdraws its forces from NATO. ...resident De Gaulle visits the USSR • Sukarno ...aves office in Indonesia; Suharto assumes power. ...Botswana, Lesotho, and Guyana become inde-...ndent states within the British Commonwealth • ...dia suffers the worst famine in 20 years; Lyndon ...hnson asks for $1 billion in aid to the country • ...edicare begins.

...upreme Court decides Miranda v. Arizona, pro-...ting rights of the accused • Stokeley Carmichael ...ected president of Student Nonviolent ...oordinating Committee (SNCC).
...orld Series Baltimore d. LA Dodgers (4-0)
...BA Championship Boston d. LA Lakers (4-3)
...entucky Derby Champion *Kauai King*
...CAA Basketball Championship
...xas Western d. Kentucky (72-65)
...CAA Football Champions
...tre Dame (AP, UPI, FW, NFF-tie) (9-0-1) &
...ichigan St. (NFF-tie) (9-0-1)
...st Picture: The Sound of Music
...cord of the Year: "A Taste of Honey" Herb ...pert and the Tijuana Brass Album of the Year: ...ptember of My Years, Frank Sinatra Song of the ...ar: "The Shadow of Your Smile" (Love Theme ...om The Sandpiper).
...he first Star Trek episode, "The Man Trap," is ...oadcast on September 8. The plot concerns a ...ature that sucks salt from human bodies. • CBS ...cks out of plans to broadcast Psycho, deeming ... movie too violent for at-home viewing.
...ovies: A Man for All Seasons, Who's Afraid of ...rginia Woolf?, Alfie. A Man and a Woman
...he Food and Drug Administration declares "the ...l" safe for human use

1966 GA-27 UF-10

...his was the showdown for the SEC champi-...ship. GA was 6-1, while UF was 7-0 and ranked ...mber seven in the nation. Spurrier had become the ...ion's premier passer. He was completing 66% of ... passes, had thrown for 14 touchdowns and 1400 ...ds. The Bulldogs secondary had 17 interceptions

on the year to lead the SEC. The Ga defense was headed by Terry Sellers and All-SEC safety Lynn Hughes. They also had a very strong pass rush fea-turing George Patton, an All-American and Bill Stanfill. UF's FB Larry Smith and GA's Ronnie Jenkins were battling for conference lead in rushing. There would be over 62,000 in the stands to watch this year's match-up.

UF took the opening kick-off and just ate the Dogs' defense with Spurrier's passing and McKeel's running. With a little over five minutes gone in the first quarter, McKeel scored for UF. Barfield's PAT was good. UF 7 GA 0.

GA behind QB Kirby Moore drove from their 45 to the UF 13 before bogging down. Etter kicked a 29-yard FG. UF 7 GA 3.

On the kick-off, UF's Harmon Wages ran from his goal line to GA's 28. The Ga defense stiffened, Spurrier threw two incompletions and was sacked by Stanfill for a six-yard loss. Barfield hit a 26-yard FG and with a little under 14 minutes remaining in the second quarter UF led 10-3.

GA drove towards the UF goal line following the kick-off. Moore passed to Frank Richter for 56 yards. Moore passed to Richter for 19 more. Moore's next pass was intercepted in the end zone by George Grandy.

Dooley and Erk Russell of GA decided to change strategies at half time. They would come out running at UF, instead of trying to keep up with Spurrier's passing. Randy Wheeler and Kirby Moore, along with Kent Lawrence did most of the running on this drive. Jenkins scored from the four. Etter kicked the PAT and the game was tied at 10.

GA's defense crush caused Spurrier to start to rush his passes. His first interception led to a missed Etter FG. The second interception fared much better for the Dogs. Ga's Lynn Hughes had stepped in front of the intended UF receiver and had then run 39 yards for the score. Etter's PAT was good and now GA led 17-10.

UF could not move on the next possession and kicked to GA. Behind runs by Jenkins, Lawrence and reserve fullback Brad Johnson, GA drove to the UF 17 where Etter kicked another FG. Now the score was GA 20 UF 10.

UF, in the next series, had a fourth and short deep in their own territory. Spurrier threw short and GA took over. GA drove to the UF 3 were Moore took the ball over. Etter's kick was good. GA27 UF10.

GA held UF to a single first down in the second half. Ga ended up tying Alabama for the SEC Crown, beating SMU in the Cotton Bowl and end-ing up with a 10-1 record and ranked fourth in the nation.

1967

• Israeli and Arab forces battle; Six-Day War ends with Israel occupying Sinai Peninsula, Golan Heights, Gaza Strip and West Bank • Right-wing military coup deposes King Constantine II of Greece • Communist China announces explosion of its first hydrogen bomb • The US and USSR propose a nuclear nonproliferation treaty. • Racial violence in Detroit; 7,000 National Guardsmen aid police after night of rioting. Similar outbreaks in New York City's Spanish Harlem, Rochester, N.Y., Birmingham, Ala., and New Britain, Conn. .

• Thurgood Marshall sworn in as first black US Supreme Court justice • Astronauts Col. Virgil I. Grissom, Col. Edward White II, and Lt. Cmdr. Roger B. Chaffee killed in fire during test launch.
Super Bowl Green Bay d. Kansas City (35-10)
World Series St.L. Cardinals d. Bo. Red Sox (4-3)
NBA Championship Phil. 76ers d. SF Warriors (4-2)
Kentucky Derby Champion *Proud Clarion*
NCAA Basketball Championship
UCLA d. Dayton (79-64)
NCAA Football Champions USC (10-1-0)
Best Picture: A Man for All Seasons
Record of the Year: "Strangers in the Night," Frank Sinatra Album of the Year: Sinatra: A Man and

His Music, Frank Sinatra Song of the Year: "Michelle," John Lennon and Paul McCartney.
• Congress creates PBS • Rolling Stone and New York Magazine debut, spawning the popularity of special-interest and regional magazines.
Movies: The Graduate, Bonnie and Clyde, Guess Who's Coming to Dinner?, In the Heat of the Night, Cool Hand Luke
Music: The Beatles, Sergeant Pepper's Lonely Hearts Club Band
• Antony Hewish and Jocelyn Bell Burnel (UK) discover pulsars. • Jerome Friedman, Henry Kendall, Richard Taylor (US) discover protons and neutrons to be composed of even smaller particles called quarks. • The MIRV (Multiple Indepenently Targetable Reetry Vehicle), which allows one mis-sile to carry several nuclear warheads, is developed • Dr. Christiaan N. Barnard and team of South African surgeons perform world's first successful human heart transplant. The patient dies 18 days later.

The Game: 1967 UF-17 GA-16

This Saturday in November gave those interested, a break from the serious side of life. ABC, for the first time in the series' history, would televise the game from one side of the nation to the other. 70,000 sun drenched fans in the Gator Bowl all hammed it up for the TV cameras. GA was 5-2 and a serious contender to repeat as SEC champion. UF was 2-2 in the conference and 4-2 overall. Spurrier was gone, in his place UF looked to All-SEC rusher, Larry Smith. The QB position had been taken over by Larry Rentz. GA's strong point was their defense. Days before the game, the Bulldogs were informed that UGA I, the mascot for the team the last eleven years had died. UGA I had retired the year before, and had been replaced by his son, UGA II. Bad news for all dogs.GA linebacker and defensive star, Tommy Lawhorne went down early in the game with an ankle injury and would be gone for the day.

GA safety Jake Scott returned a UF punt to the UF 29. Kent Lawrence rushed for 11 yards on a third down play. After five plays, the Dogs were on the Gators' 1. Ronnie Jenkins banged the ball over for the first score of the game. UF's safety Paul Maliska got a hand on the PAT and knocked it off to the side. GA 6, UF 0.

UF fumbled on their own 44. GA QB Kirby Moore threw for 16 yards to Ronnie Jenkins, who ran another 28 yards to the Gators' 16. UF stiffened and held GA to just another three yards. McCullough hit a 33-yard FG and GA led 9-0.

UF marched from their own 35 to the GA 20 on the next drive. UF's Richard Trapp caught passes for 8 and 18 yards. Larry Smith caught one for 13 yards. At GA's 20, UF fumbled and a wild scramble ensued. UF finally retained possession, but in the process had lost 13 yards to the GA 33. On the next play, Rentz hit flanker Mike McCann for a 33-yard TD. Barfield's PAT closed the score to 9-7.

Early in the third period, GA's Jake Scott intercept-ed a Rentz pass and ran 32 yards for the score. McCullough kicked the PAT and GA led 16-7.

The score remained the same until mid-way through the fourth quarter. With the ball on their own 37, Rentz hit Trapp at the GA 40. From there Trapp's moves kept the Dogs off-balance, especially a reverse spin he made on three tacklers zeroing in on him. He went 52 yards untouched into the GA end-zone. Barfield kicked the PAT and the score was now 16-14.

UF held the Dogs' offense and took over on their own 47 with a little less than four minutes left in the game. Rentz hit Trapp for a 24-yard gain. McKeel rushed to the GA 14. On fourth and one, Graves decided, very late in the game, to go for the first down instead of the field goal. Smith made the first down, but the UF offense brought Rentz to the turf for a six-yard loss with a minute left. Smith attempt-ed one more run at the Dogs and got the ball down to the GA 14. Graves then decided to bring in his kicker and kick the field goal. Spotting the ball at the GA 31, Barfield kicked the ball. He wasn't sure if it was going to be long enough, but he felt it was straight. The ball split the uprights and UF had upset the Dogs. Fans swarmed onto the field and mobbed the Gators, especially Barfield. Barfield, who was from Albany, Georgia, said that before he went into kick the FG, Coach Graves had told him "that the ball had better go right through the uprights if he ever wanted to go back home to Albany."

1968

• North Korea seizes US Navy ship Pueblo; holds 83 on board as spies • North Vietnamese launch the Tet Offensive, a turning point in the Vietnam War • American soldiers massacre 347 civilians at My Lai • Czechoslovakia is invaded by Russians and Warsaw Pact forces to crush liberal regime.
• President Johnson announces he will not seek or accept presidential renomination • Martin Luther King, Jr., civil rights leader, is slain in Memphis.
• James Earl Ray, indicted in King murder, is sentenced to 99 years • Sen. Robert F. Kennedy is shot and critically wounded in Los Angeles hotel after winning California primary and dies next day.
Super Bowl Green Bay d. Oakland (33-14)
World Series Detroit d. St. Louis Cardinals (4-3)
NBA Championship Boston d. LA Lakers (4-2)
Kentucky Derby Champion *Forward Pass*
NCAA Basketball Championship
UCLA d. North Carolina (78-55)
NCAA Football Champions Ohio St. (10-0-0)
Best Picture: In the Heat of the Night
Record of the Year: "Up, Up and Away," 5th Dimension Album of the Year: Sgt. Pepper's Lonely Hearts Club Band, The Beatles
Song of the Year: "Up, Up and Away"
• 60 Minutes airs on CBS, beginning its reign as the longest-running prime-time newsmagazine • The motion picture rating system debuts with G, PG, R and X • The rock musical Hair opens on Broadway.
Movies: 2001: A Space Odyssey, Romeo and Juliet, Funny Girl, The Lion in Winter, Oliver!
• Prototype of world's first supersonic airliner. The Soviet-designed Tupolev Tu-144 made its first flight, Dec. 31. It first achieved supersonic speed on June 5, 1969. • The largest reservoir of American petroleum north of Mexico is discovered in Alaska. • Amniocentesis is developed.

The Game: 1968 GA-51 UF-0

For this year's game, the sun was a no-show. A driving rainstorm blanketed the 70,000 packed into the Gator Bowl. GA was 5-0-2 and the Gators were 4-2-1. UF had All-SEC Fullback Larry Smith, while GA featured the SEC's leading rusher, Bruce Kemp, who, because of injury, was expected to see very limited play. GA would be lead by Soph. QB Mike Cavan on the offense and by Jake Scott and Bill Stanfill on the defense. With a little over nine minutes gone in the the first quarter, Scott sloshed 59 yards with a punt return to the UF 5. Kemp scored two plays later. McCullough kicked the PAT and GA led 7-0.

On GA's next possession Cavan went to the air, regardless of how wet that air was. He hit Bill Brice with a 17 yard completion. Then hit Kent Lawrence for 27-yards down to the UF 21. Cavan ran for 13 to the UF 7. On fourth down, Farnsworth lumbered into the endzone. McCollugh's PAT made it 14-0, with the game still in the first quarter.

GA's third drive of the day started on the UF 37. Cavan passed for nine yards to Charles Whittemore. Then to Dennis Hughes for a first down at the UF 9. As the second period started, Cavan hit Huges in the endzone for GA's third score. McCullough made it

21-0.

On UF's next possession Gator Brian Hipp gave the ball back to GA on a fumble near midfield. Cavan went to work, hitting Whittemore for 16 yards, and a few plays later, hit a sliding Whittemore for a 26-yard TD. McCullough made it 28-0.

Late in the first half, with GA starting on their own 41, Cavan hit Hughes for 41 yards to the UF 18. He then hit Farnsworth with a pass down to the UF 7. Cavan then faked a hand-off into the line and skirted around end for the score. With a little over two minutes left in the half, McCullough made it 35-0.

In the third period, the first time UF got the wet ball, they once again lost their grip. UF's Rentz was bashed by Stanfill at the UF 20 and GA's Terry Osbolt recovered the ball on the UF 5. Brad Johnson scored two plays later. McCullough then missed his first PAT of the year, but with a 41-0 lead, who was complaining.

Dooley loaded up the field with replacements. Even with the second and third-stringers, the Dogs marched on. QB Donnie Hampton led the team on a 14 play drive, with Farnsworth carrying the ball the final eight yards into the Gator endzone. Soccer-styled kicker, Pete Rajecki kicked the PAT and the score was 48-0. GA's final score was another FG by Rajecki from the UF 22 with a little over five minutes remaining in the game.

Said Ray Graves, after the game, "When you play a rivalry like this you don't ever have enough points. They just beat us every way you can get beat. All I can do is congratulate them on a great victory."

GA won its second consecutive SEC crown this year, losing on New Year's Day to Arkansas in the Sugar Bowl, 16-2.

1969

• Nixon begins "Vietnamization" in Southeast Asia.
• The United States, USSR, and about 100 other countries sign the nuclear nonproliferation treaty (NPT). • Russian and Chinese troops clash along the Ussuri River. • 27-year-old Colonel Muammar al-Qaddafi deposes King Idris of Libya and establishes a pro-Arabic, anti-Western, Islamic republic.
• Richard M. Nixon is inaugurated 37th President of the US • Stonewall riot in New York City marks beginning of gay rights movement • Sen. Edward M. Kennedy pleads guilty to leaving scene of fatal accident at Chappaquiddick, Mass. in which Mary Jo Kopechne was drowned—gets two-month suspended sentence • Apollo 11 astronauts—Neil A. Armstrong and Edwin E. Aldrin, Jr.,—take first walk on the Moon
Super Bowl NY Jets d. Baltimore (16-7)
World Series NY Mets d. Baltimore (4-1)
NBA Championship Boston d. LA Lakers (4-3)
Kentucky Derby Champion *Majestic Prince*
NCAA Basketball Championship
UCLA d. Purdue (92-72)
NCAA Football Champions Texas (11-0-0)
Best Picture: Oliver!
Record of the Year: "Mrs. Robinson," Simon and Garfunkel Album of the Year: By the Time I Get to Phoenix, Glen Campbell Song of the Year: "Little Green Apples," Bobby Russell,
• Midnight Cowboy wins the Best Picture Oscar, the first and only time an X-rated movie received the honor • In August, more than half a million people gather in the small, upstate New York town of Bethel (near Woodstock, N.Y.) for four days of rain, sex, drugs and rock 'n' roll. Performers include Janis Joplin, Jimi Hendrix, The Who, Joan Baez, Crosby, Stills, Nash and Young, Jefferson Airplane and Sly and the Family Stone.
• A Rolling Stones fan is killed at the group's Altamont, California, concert by members of Hell's Angels • The FCC bans all cigarette advertising on television and radio • Children's Television Workshop introduces Sesame Street.

Movies: Midnight Cowboy, Butch Cassidy & The Sundance Kid, Easy Rider, Anne of 1000 Days
• The first in vitro fertilization of a human egg is performed in Cambridge, England • ARPA (Advanced Research Projects Agency) goes online in December connecting four major US universities. Designed for research, education, and government organizations, is the foundation upon which the Internet will eventually be built • The scanning electron microscope is developed • The use of DDT is banned in residential areas.

The Game: 1969 GA-13 UF-13

More than 71,000 fans would fill the Gator Bowl this year to watch two nationally ranked teams. It would be Ray Graves last year coaching the Gators. He would finish up being the winningest coach in UF history. The 69' Gators were led by Soph Phenom John Reaves. UF was 6-0 and ranked number seven, before falling to Auburn the week before this game. The Dogs at 5-2 had slipped in the rankings to number 16. UF's Reaves was about to break the SEC total offense record for a season, a mark originally set by GA's own Frank Sinkwich in 1942 Carlos Alvarez was Reaves' favorite target. GA's defense plan called for the blanketing of Alvarez and the pressuring of Reaves.

Early GA drives actually made it to deep in Gator country. GA had a TD run called back and they missed a fairly simple FG. It turned out that GA QB Hampton had dislocated his shoulder early in the first quarter, but played painfully on.

Early in the second period GA's Smiley fumbled on his own 33. UF's Tommy Durrance and Mike Rich pounded out ground yardage for the Gators, down to the GA 12. Reaves handed off to Rich who pounded defenders along his 12 yard TD run. Richard Franco kicked the PAT, and UF led 7-0. GA behind Hampton, drove to the UF 10, but there the Gators intercepted the next pass, and started driving on their own. Reaves hit split end Cheney for some 36-yards on two plays, before going back to his steady, Alvarez for 12 down to the GA 20. The drive stalled there. Graves called for a fake kick, to see if he could surprise GA. The UF kicker botched the snap and was thrown down trying to pass. An official ruled that because of several officials having to clear photographers out of the end zone and evidently whistling a time-out that neither team heard, the play would be run again. This time Graves chose to let Franco come in and actually kick the FG, which he did. UF led 10-0 with just over a minute left in the half. Georgia fans considered this "the fifth down play."

In the second half, Dooley again brought in Cavan to replace a hurting Hampton. He seemed to step right in as if it were 1968, instead of 1969. Cavan hit tight end Green for passes of 11, 6, and 8 yards. Smiley gained 8 yards on three carries, and Cavan ran for seven. The ball nosed the UF 6 yard line. Farnsworth ran in from there and McCullogh missed the PAT, making the score 10-6. After a short UF punt, Cavan handed off to RB Paine who rushed in the secondary and past all Gator defenders into the end zone. McCullough made the PAT this time and GA moved ahead 13-10.

IN the final quarter, UF drove from their own 16 to the GA 21, where Graves called Franco into the game to tie it with a FG. With five minutes left to play, the game was tied at 13-13.

Reaves drove the Gators with completions of 8, 12, and 15 yards. UF was sitting on the GA 15 with less than 15 seconds left. Graves called Franco in to ice the game. The center's snap was low and the ball was bobbled by the holder, unable to hold it still before Franco kicked. The ball sailed off to the left of the goalposts. The tie was set.

After halftime, someone broke into the UF locker room and stole all the players' money, watches, rings and other valuables. The Atlanta Constitution quoted Florida Governor Claude Kirk, "Only someone from Georgia would do a thing like that."

Georgia vs Florida
November 5, 1960

Price 50c

1960 · UFL 22 UGA 14

Georgia vs Florida
November 11, 1961

Price **50c**

1961 · UGA 14 UFL 21

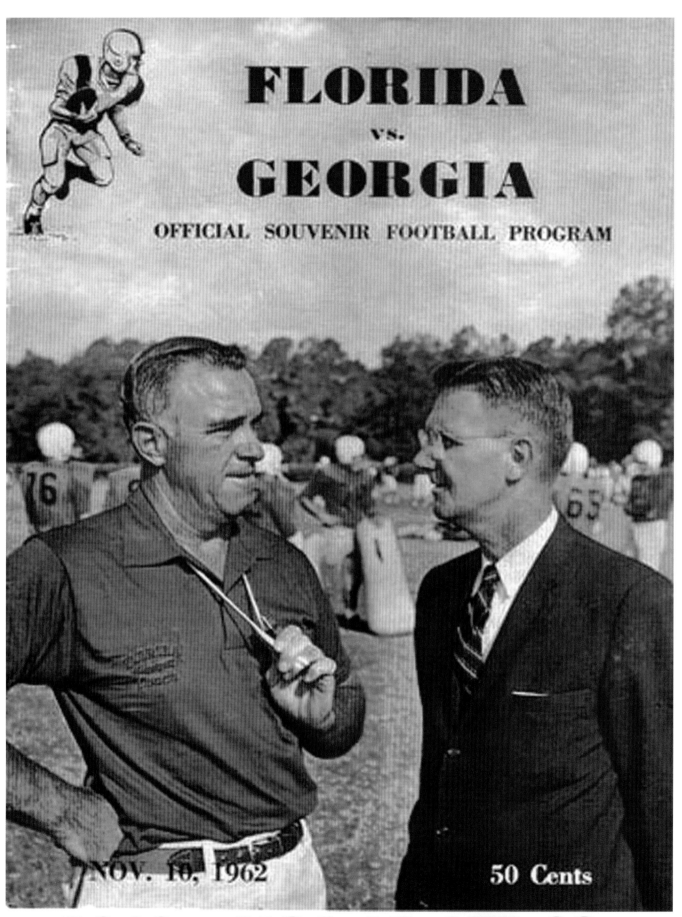

FLORIDA
vs.
GEORGIA

OFFICIAL SOUVENIR FOOTBALL PROGRAM

NOV. 10, 1962

50 Cents

1962 · UGA 15 UFL 23

OFFICIAL SOUVENIR FOOTBALL PROGRAM
50 CENTS

FLORIDA vs. GEORGIA
NOV. 9th, 1963

1963 · UFL 21 UGA 14

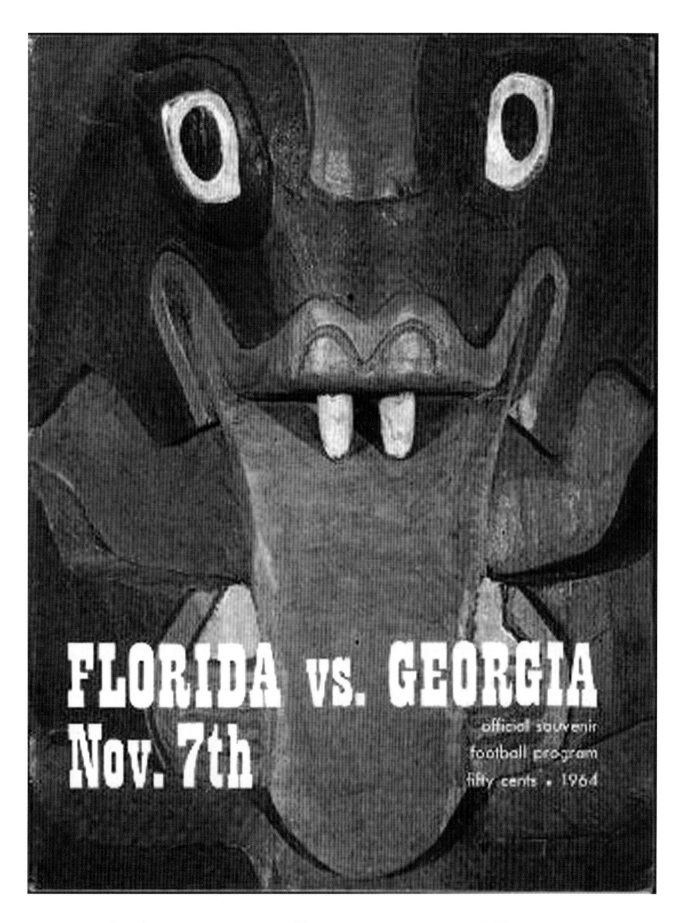

FLORIDA vs. GEORGIA
Nov. 7th

official souvenir
football program
fifty cents · 1964

1964 · UGA 14 UFL 7

FLORIDA
VS.
GEORGIA

Nov. 6th

official souvenir football program • fifty cents • 1965

1965 · UFL 14 UGA 10

FLORIDA vs GEORGIA

NOV. 5, 1966

Official Souvenir
Football Program
Fifty Cents

1966 · UGA 27 UFL 10

FLORIDA GATORS

UNIVERSITY OF FLORIDA, GAINESVILLE | OFFICIAL FOOTBALL MAGAZINE $1.00

THE GEORGIA GAME

NOV. 11, 1967

1967 • UGA 16 UFL 17

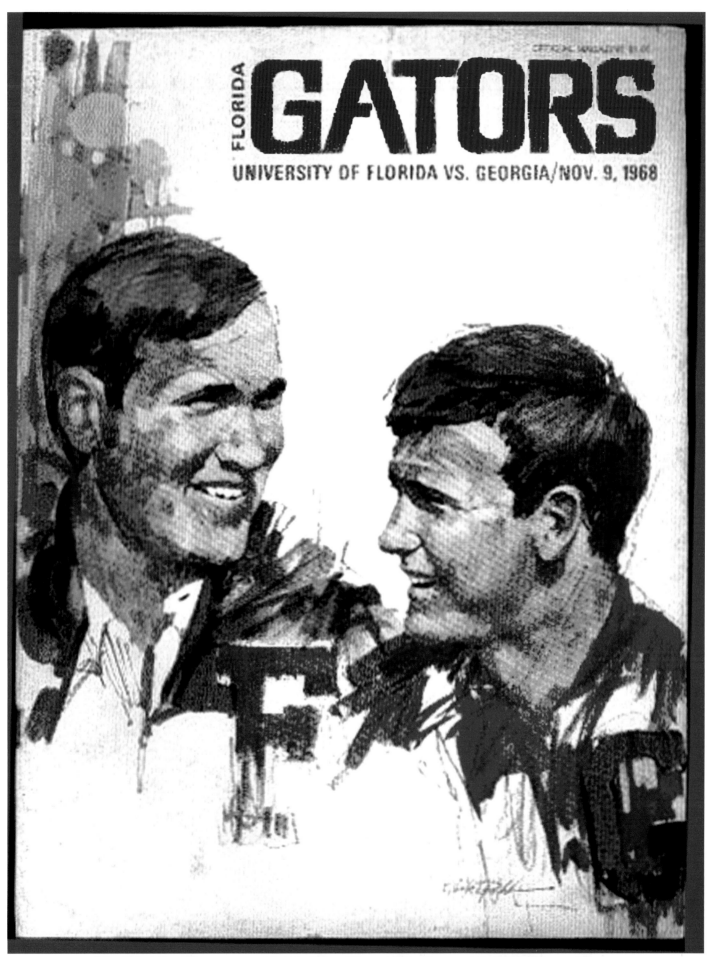

FLORIDA **GATORS**

UNIVERSITY OF FLORIDA VS. GEORGIA/NOV. 9, 1968

1968 · UGA 51 UFL 0

GEORGIA VS FLORIDA

THE GATOR BOWL NOVEMBER 8, 1969 ONE DOLLAR

1969 · UGA 13 UFL 13

The 1970s

1970

• Biafra surrenders after 32-month fight for independence from Nigeria • Rhodesia severs last tie with British Crown and declares itself a racially segregated republic • US troops invade Cambodia • A Palestinian revolt erupts in Jordan. Forces loyal to King Hussein suppress the revolt and expel the PLO from the country • Earthquake kills more than 50,000 in Peru • Egyptian President Nasser dies and is replaced by Anwar el-Sadat • Four students at Kent State University in Ohio slain by National Guardsmen at demonstration protesting incursion into Cambodia • Senate repeals Gulf of Tonkin resolution
Super Bowl KC d. Minnesota (23-7)
World Series Baltimore d. Cincinnati (4-1)
NBA Championship N Y d. LA Lakers (4-3)
Kentucky Derby Champion *Dust Commander*
NCAA Basketball Championship
UCLA d. Jacksonville (80-69)
NCAA Football Champions
Nebraska (AP, FW) (11-0-1); Texas (UPI, NFF-tie), (10-1-0) & Ohio St. (NFF-tie), (9-1-0)
Best Picture: Midnight Cowboy Record of the Year: "Aquarius/Let the Sunshine In," 5th Dimension Album of the Year: Blood, Sweat and Tears, Blood, Sweat and Tears Song of the Year: "Games People Play," Joe South
• The Beatles break up. By the end of the year, each member had released a solo album.
• George C. Scott gives one of film's most memorable performances in Patton. He won the Best Actor Oscar for his turn as the title character, but refused the gold statuette • Jimi Hendrix and Janis Joplin both die drug-related deaths at age 27 • FCC regulations require separate ownership of television networks and studios •Monday Night Football debuts on ABC, with Howard Cosell, Frank Gifford, and Don Meredith giving play-by-play.
Movies: M*A*S*H, Patton, Love Story, Airport
• IBM introduces the floppy disk • Bar codes (computer-scanned binary signal code) are introduced for retail and industrial use in England • The LCD (liquid crystal display) is invented by Hoffmann-La Roche •The Food and Drug Administration warns that birth control pills may cause blood clots • Lithium is approved by the FDA for the treatment of manic-depression.

The Game: 1970 UF-24 GA-17

President Nixon was promising to bring at least 40,000 troops home from Vietnam by Christmas…just a little over a month away….over 70,000 fans would show up at this years' Gator Bowl batttle. Doug Dickey was brand new at coaching at UF. Reaves was leading the SEC in passing, but the Gators were mysteries every week as to who would show up on the field. The 1970 Gators had enrolled their first two black athletes as Willie Jackson and Leonard George were roster players this year.
GA had gotten off to a horrible start in 1970, by the weekend of the UF game, they were 4-3. Paul Gilbert had replaced the injured Mike Cavan at QB. This would be Gilbert's first start of the year.

On GA's opening drive of the game, Dooley relied on his runners, Ricky Lake and Robert Hunneycutt to move the dogs moving towards the Gators' goal line. Gilbert threw in a 15-yard completion to Rex Putnal to keep Florida guessing. After 11 plays, GA was on the UF 2. In 12 the score was 6-0. Kim Braswell made it 7-0 in favor of GA. UF tried to cross GA with a running game, but had little effect. The game turned into a defensive battle with both offenses being kept out of the scoring range.
In the second quarter, UF drove to the GA 12 before having to settle on a Jim Getzen 29-yard FG, making the score 7-3 in GA's favor. The score remained through the half. In the third quarter GA rushed down to the UF's 4 yard line, but the drive was thwarted and Braswell kicked a 20-yard FG. Georgia now lead 10-3. After GA's kick-off, UF went to the air on Reaves' arm. Reaves hit Alvarez for 20 yards on one play, then hit him for 22 yards on the next. One more pass to Alvarez put the Gators on the GA 7. FB Mike Rich smashed it over from there. With Getzen's PAT, the game was tied at 10.
GA kept to the ground on their next drive. In five plays the Dogs were on the UF 39. GA's Hunneycutt got the ball next, tearing away from several Gator defenders, being stopped just short of the goal line after a 38 yard run. Gilbert dove over on the next play, and with Braswell's PAT, GA led again 17-10.
Reaves almost gave the game away when he fumbled to GA on the UF 37. GA drove to the UF 2 before Hunneycutt returned the favor and the ball to UF's Jack Youngblood. Youngblood later stating, " I just snatched the ball away from him. Heck, I see the pros do that all the time."
After swapping punts, Reaves began passing on every down. In three passes, UF was on the GA 32. On the next play, Reaves hit the "Cuban Comet" on the GA 7, from there Alvarez ran right through the defenders. Getzen's PAT made it 17, all.
On the next series, GA drove to the UF 38. The drive stalled and Dooley gambled for the first down, instead of going for the FG. UF stiffened and knocked the Dogs back. With only two minutes remaining, Reaves went back to work. A screen pass to Tommy Durrance went for 14 yards down to the GA 48. Next play, Alvarez caught Reaves' pass at full stride, and getting a great reverse block from Willie Jackson went all the way in for the score.Getzen's PAT made it UF 24 GA17.

1971

• A military junta led by Major General Idi Amin siezes power in Uganda • Mao Zedong invites the US ping-pong team to visit Beijing • Nixon ends the US trade embargo against China • Erich Honecker assumes leadership of the East German Communist Party after Walter Ulbricht's resignation • US Supreme Court rules unanimously that busing of students may be ordered to achieve racial desegregation • Anti-war militants attempt to disrupt government business in Washington — police and military units arrest as many as 12,000; most are later released • Pentagon Papers published • Twenty-sixth Amendment to US Constitution lowers voting age to 18.

Super Bowl Baltimore d. Dallas (16-13)
World Series Pittsburgh d. Baltimore (4-3)
NBA Championship Mil. d. Balt.Bullets (4-0
Kentucky Derby Champion *Canonero II*
NCAA Basketball Championship
UCLA d. Villanova (68-62)
NCAA Football Champions Nebraska (13-0-0)
Best Picture: Patton Record of the Year: "Bridge Over Troubled Water," Simon and Garfunkel Album of the Year: Bridge Over Troubled Water, Simon and Garfunkel Song of the Year: "Bridge Over Troubled Water," Paul Simon
• All in the Family debuts on CBS and introduces a trend in socially conscious programming • Jim Morrison dies in Paris at age 27 • The Allman Brothers' Duane Allman dies in a motorcycle accident at age 24
Movies : A Clockwork Orange, The French Connection, The Last Picture Show, Fiddler on the Roof, McCabe & Mrs. Miller
• Intel introduces the microprocessor • Cho Hao Li synthesizes the growth hormone somatotropin • Mariner IX, orbiting Mars, takes revealing pictures of the planet's surface.

The Game: 1971 GA 49 UF 7

Once again ABC was on hand to broadcas the regional showdown, and their cameras panned over the 70,000 fans ready for the day's action. Dooley's Dogs came into this game 8-0 and ranked 6th in the nation. Much to the Gators' dismay, the Dogs have not eve allowed an opponent to score in the last three games. GA was a 21-point favorite in this year's game. UF had to go up against the country's second rated defense.
Countering GA's success, UF entered the game with a 2-6 record, losing their first five games of the season. Reaves and Alvarez were still in Gator uniforms, but they had ye to become as much a threat as they had bee in the past.
Both defenses were unpenetrable in early series by both teams. GA punter kicked a 50 yard punt pinning UF back on their own 13. UF's offense could go nowhere and UF's John James shanked a punt giving GA the ball on the UF 34. In four carries, Johnny Poulos got the ball down to the UF 1. From the one, Poulous dove over the UF defensiv line into the end zone. Braswell kicked the PAT. GA led 7-0.
Early in the second period, Buz Rosenberg returned a UF punt 36 yards down to the UF27. Lake went 14 yards on six carries. O the tenth play of the drive, Lake went over from the two and with Braswell's PAT, GA now led 14-0 with a little over nine minutes left in the half.
On their next series, UF QB Reaves, unde heavy pressure was intercepted by Mixon Robinson and returned 38 yards for the scor Braswell missed the PAT, but now GA led 20-0.
UF then drove from their own 20 to the G 9 in ten plays. Reaves then hit Jim Yancey i the corner of the end zone for UF's first score. Franco made it 20-7.
On GA's second possession of the second half, started a drive from the UF 48. In seve plays they were on the Gator's five. Ray the scored on a QB keeper. GA went for two, with Ray hitting Shirer, making the score now 28-7 in favor of the Dogs.
GA shut down the UF offense and forced another punt. GA got the ball on their own 42. In three plays, they were on the UF 38. Ray then hit Shirer for a 38-yard TD pass. Braswell's PAT was good. GA now lead 35-
GA once again held the Gators, something UF had not been able to do to GA all after-

oon. GA rushed for 52 yards on seven plays with
...ake scoring on a two-yard thrust. Braswell kicked
...is fourth PAT and GA led 42-7.

GA, after holding off the Gators again, brought in
...eir third string QB, Steve Watson. He led the Dogs
...om their own 48 to the UF 25 in just six plays. On
...e next play, Bob Burns took a Watson pass and
...ped into the end zone. Braswell's PAT made it 49-7.
...A's Defense had held Reaves to just nine comple-
...ons on 21 attempts for only 87 yards. GA ran up a
...tal offense amassing 380 yards.

GA's only loss of the year was to come the next
...eek with a 35-20 defeat by Pat Sullivan-led
...uburn. The loss sealed the SEC championship for
...labama. After beating North Carolina 7-3 in the
...ator Bowl, the 11-1 Dogs ended up ranked seventh
... one poll and eighth in another.

1972

President Nixon makes unprecedented eight-day
...sit to Communist China and meets with Mao
...edong • Britain takes over direct rule of Northern
...eland in bid for peace • Eleven Israeli athletes at
...lympic Games in Munich are killed after eight
...embers of an Arab terrorist group invades Olympic
...illage; five guerrillas and one policeman are also
...lled • Nixon orders "Christmas bombing" of North
...ietnam • Gov. George C. Wallace of Alabama is
...ot by Arthur H. Bremer at Laurel, Md., political
...lly • Five men are apprehended by police in
...tempt to bug Democratic National Committee
...eadquarters in Washington, D.C.'s Watergate com-
...lex—start of the Watergate scandal • US Supreme
...ourt rules that death penalty is unconstitutional.
...uper Bowl   Dallas d. Miami (24-3)
...orld Series   Oakland A's d. Cincinnati (4-3)
...BA Championship   LA Lakers d. New York (4-1)
...entucky Derby Champion   *Riva Ridge*
...CAA Basketball Championship **UCLA d. FSU (81-76)**
...CAA Football Champions   USC (12-0-0)
...est Picture: The French Connection
...ecord of the Year: "It's Too Late," Carole King
...lbum of the Year: Tapestry, Carole King   Song of
...e Year: "You've Got a Friend," Carole King.
...Time Inc. transmits HBO, the first pay cable net-
...ork • Women dominate the 1971 Grammy Awards,
...king all four top categories. Carole King won
...ecord, Album and Song of the Year, while Carly
...mon takes the Best New Artist award • The
...ational Institute of Mental Health and the surgeon
...neral issue a report that claims exposure to vio-
...nce on television fosters aggression in children.
...Gloria Steinem's Ms magazine debuts • M*A*S*H
...emieres on CBS • Atari introduces the arcade ver-
...on of Pong, the first video game. The home version
...mes out in 1974.
...ovies: The Godfather, Deliverance, Cabaret,
...euth, The Discreet Charm of the Bourgeoisie
...CAT (Computerized Axial Tomography) scanning
...developed in England • The compact disk is devel-
...ed by RCA • The antidepressant Prozac (fluoxe-
...e) is developed by Bryan B. Malloy and Klaus K.
...hmiegel • The video disk is introduced by Philips
...ompany • Electronic mail is introduced. Queen
...izabeth will send her first email in 1976 • Apollo
...VII, the last manned moon landing to date, returns
... Earth with 250 pounds of lunar samples.

he Game: 1972 GA-10 UF-7

Who was going to pay attention to this year's
...me with so much going on in the world?
...ho's going to really care about the football
...me being played in the Gator Bowl? Well, sur-
...isingly enough, there were around 67,000 fans
...ho had this game on their minds so much that
...ey filled the stadium. The big game in the SEC
...is weekend was supposed to be between num-
...r two Alabama and number six LSU, but
...body in Jacksonville cared what happened
...tween the "Elephants" and the "Tigers."

The pre-game match-up would be between
GA running back Jimmy Poulos and UF's junior
college transfer runner Nat Moore. Moore hadn't
played football in two years, but he had made up
for it pretty fast, scoring nine touchdowns in
UF's first six games and was the SEC's leading
rusher.

On their first drive, UF knocked the Dogs'
defense all the way back to their own 13, only to
lose the ball over to them when UF QB Chan
Gailey fumbled. That was the extent of the
offense for both teams in the first quarter.

With a little over two minutes gone in the second quarter, UF QB Dave Bowden hit Nat
Moore with a 47-yard TD pass. UF's Clifton
Aust kicked the PAT and UF led 7-0. With a
field goal missed by both teams. This score held
up through the half. The defensive struggle continued through the third quarter, with neither
team taking advantage of field position or penalties. In the final period, Dickey tried a little trickery on the Dogs. Moore was handed the ball and
he ran towards the line before pulling up and
lofting a pass downfield. GA defensive back Buz
Rosenberg intercepted the pass and returned it 11
yards to the UF 46. Instead of trying to move the
ball on the ground, QB Andy Johnson rolled out
and hit end Rex Putnal downfield with a pass.
Putnal avoided tacklers and ran into the end
zone. Kim Braswell kicked the PAT and the
game was tied at 7.

After being pinned at their own 10, UF's Vince
Kendrick ran for nine and Moore moved the ball
over the UF 22. On third down QB Bowden's
hand-off to Carey Geiger was missed and the
loose ball recovered by GA's Joe McPipkin.
There was a little over two minutes remaining in
the game and GA was down on the UF 30 yard
line. On fourth down, still needing more yardage
for a first down, Dooley decided to send in
Braswell to kick a FG. The kick was weak, but
good enough to pass through the uprights giving
GA a 10-7 win.

1973

• A ceasefire is signed, ending involvement of
American ground troops in the Vietnam War. • US
bombing of Cambodia ends, marking official halt to
12 years of combat activity in Southeast Asia
• Chile's Marxist president, Salvadore Allende, is
overthrown; Gen. Augusto Pinochet takes power
• Fourth and largest Arab-Israeli conflict begins
when Egyptian and Syrian forces attack Israel as
Jews mark Yom Kippur, holiest day in their calen-
dar. Egypt and Israel sign US-sponsored cease-fire
accord • Organization of Petroleum Exporting
Countries (OPEC) hikes oil prices tremendously in
retaliation for Western countries' involvement in
Yom Kippur War • Nixon, on national TV, accepts
responsibility, but not blame, for Watergate; accepts
resignations of H. R. Haldeman and John D.
Ehrlichman, fires John W. Dean III as counsel
• Spiro T. Agnew resigns as Vice President and then
pleads no contest to charges of evasion of income
taxes while Governor of Maryland • In the
"Saturday Night Massacre," Nixon fires special
Watergate prosecutor Archibald Cox and Deputy
Attorney General William D. Ruckelshaus; Attorney
General Elliot D. Richardson resigns
• US Supreme Court rules on Roe v. Wade.
Super Bowl   Miami d. Washington (14-7)
World Series   Oakland A's d. NY Mets (4-3)
NBA Championship   N Y d. LA Lakers (4-1)
Kentucky Derby Champion   *Secretariat*
(also won the Triple Crown: Kentucky Derby, Preakness Stakes

and Belmont Stakes)
NCAA Basketball Championship
UCLA d. Memphis St. (87-66)
NCAA Football Champions
Notre Dame (AP, FW, NFF) (11-0-0) & Ala. (UPI) (11-1-0)
Best Picture: The Godfather Record of the Year:
"The First Time Ever I Saw Your Face," Roberta
Flack Album of the Year: The Concert for Bangla
Desh, George Harrison, Ravi Shanker, Bob Dylan,
Leon Russell, Ringo Starr, Eric Clapton and others.
Song of the Year: "The First Time Ever I Saw Your
Face" • At the 1972 Academy Awards, Sacheen
Littlefeather stands in for Marlon Brando and refus-
es his Best Actor Oscar for his role in The
Godfather, to protest the U.S. government's treat-
ment of Native Americans • The Jamaican film The
Harder They Come, starring Jimmy Cliff, launches
the popularity of reggae music in the United States.
• PBS airs the series An American Family, about the
dysfunctional Loud family.
Movies: The Harder They Come, American Graffiti,
Exorcist, The Sting, Last Tango in Paris
• Transmission Control Protocol/Internet Protocol
(TCP/IP) is designed and in 1983 it becomes the
standard for communicating between computers over
the Internet • Nuclear Magnetic Resonance (NMR),
the technology behind MRI scanning, is developed.
• Skylab, the first American space station, is launched

The Game: 1973 UF-11 GA-10

Because of the number of starters returning
to play for UF, Playboy magazine chose the
Gators to win the 1973 National Championship.
After seven games into the season, UF was 3-4.
Nat Moore had been injured and was out for the
season. GA was 4-3-1. Both teams had upset
their opponents of the week before. UF beat
Auburn and GA had beaten Tennessee.

ABC had originally scheduled this year's contest, but had reconsidered, as both teams floun-
dered during the season. The two upsets the
week before convinced ABC that it wouldn't be
fair to just let the 70,000 fans who filled the
Gator Bowl to be the only ones to enjoy the
game, so their cameras were televising it to the
southeast regional audience.

UF QB Don Gaffney was making his first
start, and in front of his hometown fans. On
UF's first series he passed to Joel Parker on a
fourth down play, and Parker rambled through
the GA secondary down to the GA 16. GA
stopped the Gators on their 11 and UF sent Larry
Williams in to kick a FG, which he did. UF 3,
GA 0.

GA found their run game and marched the
next drive down to the UF 2, but was stopped
short on fourth and goal. UF took over but could
go nowhere and had to punt. GA took over at the
UF 44 and drove down to the Gator 15 when the
officials gifted the Dogs.

QB Johnson hit receiver Richard Appleby with
a pass just outside the UF end zone and within
inches of the sideline marker. The official's arms
went up into the air, signaling a touchdown, but
the replays on tv showed that Appleby had
caught the ball out of bounds. The play stood
and Allan Leavitt kicked the PAT that gave GA
the lead, 7-3.

The third quarter belonged to the defenses.
Neither team scored, until late in the period
when GA drove near enough to allow Leavitt to
kick a 42-yard FG. It was now GA 10 UF 3.

In the fourth quarter, Gaffney led the Gators on
an 80-yard,13 play drive that culminated in a
perfect pass from Gaffney to McGriff for the
score. Dickey wanted no tie, so he instructed his
team to go for two and the win. Gaffney took the

snap, faded back and hit Hank Foldberg in the end zone for two. UF led 11-10. The Bulldogs never recovered and were stifled by UF the remainder of the game.

1974

• Encouraged by Chairman Mao Zedong, the Cultural Revolution begins in China • OPEC ends the oil embargo begun in 1973 during the Yom Kippur War • Nixon and Brezhnev meet in Moscow to discuss arms limitation agreements • Leftist revolution ends almost 50 years of dictatorial rule in Portugal • India successfully tests an atomic device, becoming the world's sixth nuclear power • Emperor Haile Selassie of Ethiopia is deposed. A collective military dictatorship assumes power • Patricia Hearst, 19-year-old daughter of publisher Randolph Hearst, kidnapped by Symbionese Liberation Army • House Judiciary Committee adopts three articles of impeachment charging President Nixon with obstruction of justice, failure to uphold laws, and refusal to produce material subpoenaed by the committee • Richard M. Nixon announces he will resign the next day, the first President to do so • Vice President Gerald R. Ford of Michigan is sworn in as 38th President of the US. • Ford grants "full, free, and absolute pardon" to ex-President Nixon.
Super Bowl Miami d. Minnesota (24-7)
World Series Oakland A's d. LA Dodgers (4-1)
NBA Championship Boston d. Milwaukee (4-3)
Kentucky Derby Champion *Cannonade*
NCAA Basketball Championship
N.C. State d. Marquette (76-64)
NCAA Football Champions
Okla. (AP) (11-0-0) & USC (UPI, FW, NFF) (10-1-1)
Best Picture: The Sting
Record of the Year: "Killing Me Softly With His Song," Roberta Flack Album of the Year: Innervisions, Stevie Wonder Song of the Year: "Killing Me Softly With His Song" • Patti Smith releases what is considered to be the first punk rock single, "Hey Joe." • People magazine debuts, with Mia Farrow gracing the cover • Premier Russian dancer Mikhail Baryshnikov defects and joins the American Ballet Theatre.
Movies: Chinatown, The Godfather Part II, Day for Night, Blazing Saddles, The Towering Inferno
• For safety reasons, the National Academy of Sciences calls for a temporary ban on some types of genetic engineering research

The Game: 1974 GA-17 UF-16

UF was ranked sixth in the nation, and having just upset Auburn could well have the invitation to play in the Sugar Bowl. UF's record was 7-1 and GA's was 5-3, but both were 3-1 in the SEC and vying to be champion.

GA QB Matt Robinson was the SEC total offense leader. UF's wishbone attack was directed by QB Don Gaffney with Jimmy DuBose and Tony Green covering the ground aspects of the attack. Lee McGriff led the SEC in receptions and had caught six TD passes. If there was a weakness with the UF team it was in its pass defense. The GA offense was averaging 34 points per game, which lead the SEC. GA started the game rushing at the Gators. When Robinson attempted a long pass, UF cornerback Randy Talbot intercepted it at the UF 2.

UF's wishbone attack picked up four first downs on their initial drive, but weathered out at the GA 24. David Posey tried a 44-yard FG, but the snap was muffed and GA got the ball back on their own 34. GA's Robinson came up big on third downs on the Dogs' ensuing drive. He hit Richard Appleby for 16 on the first one, and ran for 31 on the second. Horace King ran the final ten yards to score. Leavitt made it 7-0 with his PAT.

UF substituted Jimmy Fisher at QB early in the

second quarter. Starting from inside the UF 10, Fisher was dropped for a two-yard loss on the first play. On the next, he slipped and fell down in the end zone for a safety. GA led now 9-0.

Taking the second half kick-off, the Gators passed and ran their way down the field. Gaffney hit McGriff for 25 yards, then DuBose ran for seven, seven, and nine yards. UF had the ball on the GA 3, where Gaffney tossed a quick pass to Larry Brinson for the score. Posey made it 9-7.

On GA's next drive, Horace King broke into the clear and was heading for the end zone when he fumbled the ball deep in UF territory. Gaffney took the UF offense right down the field until the GA defense held firm at their own 30. Posey came in and kicked a FG, putting the Gators ahead 10-9. Robinson then went airborne. After hitting Mark Wilson with a 16-yard pass at the UF 29, GA ground down to the five, where King made up for his fumble, by rumbling into the end zone, putting the Dogs back on top. Dooley decided to go for two. The play were Robinson hit Appleby in the end zone was just what the coach ordered. GA now lead 17-10.

After exchanging the ball, UF started driving towards the GA goal with just over two minutes remaining in the game. Gaffney scrambled from the GA 4 into the endzone. Dickey went for the two-point conversion and the win. Gaffney's pass to DuBose was low and he couldn't hold onto the ball. The Score remained GA 17 UF 16. UF's hopes died when their on-side kick was covered by Chip Miller for the Dogs. Dooley was given a ride on the shoulders of his team across the field. It was one of the biggest upsets by any of Dooley's teams.

1975

• Pol Pot and Khmer Rouge take over Cambodia • The city of Saigon is surrendered and remaining Americans are evacuated, ending the Vietnam War • American merchant ship Mayaguez, seized by Cambodian forces, is rescued in operation by US Navy and Marines, 38 of whom are killed • Apollo and Soyuz spacecraft take off for US-Soviet link-up in space • John N. Mitchell, H. R. Haldeman, John D. Ehrlichman found guilty of Watergate cover-up ; sentenced to 30 months to 8 years in jail •President Ford escapes assassination attempt in Sacramento, Calif • President Ford escapes second assassination attempt in 17 days.
Super Bowl Pittsburgh d. Minnesota (16-6)
World Series Cincinnati d. Boston Red Sox (4-3)
NBA Championship
Golden St. Warriors d. Wash. Bullets (4-0)
Kentucky Derby Champion *Foolish Pleasure*
NCAA Basketball Championship
UCLA d. Kentucky (92-85)
NCAA Football Champions Oklahoma (11-1-0)
Best Picture: The Godfather Part II Record of the Year: "I Honestly Love You," Olivia Newton-John Album of the Year: Fulfillingness' First Finale, Stevie Wonder Song of the Year: "The Way We Were"
• ABC, CBS and NBC agree to create a "family hour," an early evening time slot that is free of violence and sex. • Saturday Night Live premieres on NBC. George Carlin hosts the first show • One Flew Over the Cuckoo's Nest sweeps the top Oscars, winning Best Picture, Director, Actor, and Actress.
Movies: One Flew Over the Cuckoo's Nest, Jaws, Nashville, Dog Day Afternoon, Barry Lyndon
• Home videotape systems (VCRs) are developed in Japan by Sony (Betamax) and Matsushita (VHS) • The Altair home computer kit allows consumers to build and program their own personal computers.

The Game: 1975 GA-10 UF-17

The showers that had fallen on Jacksonville the

night before were expected to continue on Saturday. UF was fighting for the SEC crown. They had a six game win streak and were a touchdown plus favorites against the 6-2 Bulldogs. UF's DuBose was one of the top rushers in the league. The wishbone was now called the "broken bone" because of the passing options Dickey had added to the attack. GA counted on Glynn Harrison, a first-team All-SEC rusher and scoring star Kevin McLee to lead them in their attack on the Gators. GA Defensive guhru Erk Russell had nicknamed his defensive unit "the Junkyard Dogs," and the fans just loved it!

GA's Harrison ran for nine yards on the first play but because of the soggy turf injured his knee and had to leave the game. GA fumbled at their own 4 and the Gators, behind DuBose and Larry Brinson were soon camped on the GA17. Gaffney hit Alvin Darby at the 2. On fourth down, Gaffney handed off to Tony Green for a Gator TD. Posey's PAT made it 7-0.

GA took the next UF punt at their own 45. Gene Washington took a screen pass from Goff and wen 22 yards to the UF 33. Harrison, then back in the game, ran for 22 yards down to the UF 16. The Dogs made it to the UF 4, but could go no further. Leavitt kicked a 21-yard FG to put GA on the scoreboard. UF 7 GA 3.

Early in the second half, UF drove down to the GA 18. On fourth and one, Green was stood up and dropped short of a first down, stopping the Gator drive, a very pivital play in the game.

The defenses ruled until late in the fourth quarte The GA coaching staff decided a little trickery wa in order. Appleby, who had gained good yardage on an end-around earlier in the game, would be called upon to pass instead of run.

Appleby had thrown only one other pass in his college career and Vandy had intercepted it. Here' how the play went: the ball was snapped to Robinson; Appleby ran back into the backfield and took the handoff. He then ran towards the line as i he was going to run again. At the last minute, he pulled up and lofted a pass over the defenders' out stretched arms to Washington. Washington caught the ball on the UF 30 and ran untouched into the end zone. Leavitt's PAT made it 10-7 in favor of the Dogs.

Washington later told the Atlanta Journal and Constitution, "I watched the ball come right into hands, and Richard must have done a great job of faking the run, because there wasn't a single UF defensive back around me."

With under two minutes left, UF made its last threat. After driving to the GA 21, and time running out, Gator kicker Posey came onto the field to kick a game-winning FG. The snap was low an the kick was no no better. GA had held and upset the Gators once again.

1976

• Khmer Rouge leader Pol Pot becomes prime minister of Cambodia after Prince Sihanouk steps dow • Israeli airborne commandos attack Uganda's Entebbe Airport and free 103 hostages held by pro-Palestinian hijackers of Air France plane; one Israel and several Ugandan soldiers killed in raid • 19-month civil war ends in Lebanon after threatening escalate to global level • US Supreme Court rules that blacks and other minorities are entitled to retroactive job seniority • Ford signs Federal Election Campaign Act • US Supreme Court rules that death penalty is not inherently cruel or unusual and is a constitutionally acceptable form of punishment • Nation celebrates Bicentennial • Mysterious disease strikes American Legion convention in Philadelphia, eventually claiming 29 lives • Jimmy Carter elected US President
Super Bowl Pittsburgh d. Dallas (21-17)

World Series   Cincinnati d. NY Yankees (4-0)
BA Championship   Boston d. Phoenix (4-2)
entucky Derby Champion   *Bold Forbes*
CAA Basketball Championship Ind. d. Mich. (86-68)
CAA Football Champions   Pittsburgh (12-0-0)
est Picture: One Flew Over the Cuckoo's Nest
ecord of the Year: "Love Will Keep Us Together,"
aptain and Tennille   Album of the Year: Still Crazy
fter All These Years, Paul Simon   Song of the
ear: "Send in the Clowns"
The Steadicam is used for the first time in Rocky.
NBC broadcasts Gone with the Wind and scores
cord-breaking ratings.
Movies: Rocky, Taxi Driver, Network, All the
esident's Men
Air France and British Airways begin the first regu-
rly scheduled commercial supersonic transport
ST) flights • Viking I lands on Mars. • The US
avy tests the Tomahawk cruise missile.
Richard Leakey discovers a 1.5 million year old
omo erectus skull in Kenya. • Cosmic string theory
st postulated by Thomas Kibble.

The Game: 1976 GA-41 UF-27

As the crowd of over 70,000 was warming up
e Gator Bowl for this year's clash, new
esident Carter was just over an hour away,
sting on St. Simons after his successful cam-
ign. Speaking of successful campaigns…
ickey's Gators were 4-0 in the conference and
1 overall. GA was 7-1 overall and 3-1 in SEC.
e Gators had Wes Chandler, while the Dogs
atured Kevin McLee.
The Goff-led Dogs marched down the field
ter receiving the opening kick-off. From their
vn 25, the Dogs ran five plays and found them-
lves on the UF 23. Four more plays brought
em to the UF 9. On the tenth play of the drive,
off ran the option into the end zone. Leavitt
cked the PAT and the Dogs led 7-0.
The Gators started their drive on their own 29.
F behind QB Jimmy Fisher headed downfield
e same as GA had. After 13 plays, UF was on
e GA 13. A pass interference call gave UF a
st down on the 6. Fisher then hit Chandler in
corner for the TD. Posey's PAT was good
d the game was tied.
On UF's next possession, they rushed for sev-
ty yards from their own 25 to the GA 5. On
e last play of the first quarter, Fisher fell into
e end zone. Posey's kick made it 14-7.
A, combining the short pass and the option
n, moved from their own 18 to the UF 8 in 13
ays. Goff then hit Ulysses Norris with a TD
ss. Leavitt's PAT was blocked and UF main-
ned the 14-13 lead.
UF took advantage of a nick in the "Junkyard
ogs'" armor. With Carr and Wilder leading the
ay, they ran at will at the left side of the GA
e. Fisher hit Chandler with a 24 yard pass. On
cond down, Carr ran right, crossing up the
ogs who were waiting for a run at their left.
rr went all the way into the end zone. GA's
cky Clark blocked Posey's PAT. UF led 20-13
th a little over six minutes remaining in the
st half.
Dooley replaced an inefficient Goff with Matt
binson at QB. Robinson led the Dogs near the
goal before the end of the first half. Spotting
orris wide open, Robinson let a pass rip to him,
ly to have UF's Terry LeCount intercept in the
d zone and run it all the way to the GA 43.
was not content to just run the clock out.
her hit TE Jimmy Stephens for a 34-yard
mpletion with the ball placed on the GA 9. On
next play GA's Johnny Henderson tripped in
end zone, leaving Chandler wide open to
ch Fisher's TD pass. Posey's PAT made it 27-

13 as the clock ran out.
In the second half, GA started a drive on their
own 20. McLee ran for 32 yards, followed by
Goff for 26. A six-yard pass to Norris completed
the eighty yard drive. Leavitt kicked the PAT and
GA narrowed the score to 27-20.
UF started at their own 20 and after three
plays, gained nine yards. It was fourth and inch-
es on their own 29. Dickey decided to gamble
and go for the first down deep in their own terri-
tory. The play called was a wide-sweep with
Carr running the ball. GA safety Johnny
Henderson read the play all the way and stopped
Carr for no-gain and the Dogs took over.
This would be the "Play of the Game."
Carr said, after the game, "When I was running
the play, I was asking myself why in the world
we were running this play."
GA reached the UF 2 in five plays. FB Al
Pollard blew into the end zone from there.
Leavitt's kick tied it at 27-all.
Late in the third quarter, GA began a drive
from their own 30. Runs by McLee, Pollard, and
Goff ate up the clock and moved the Dogs down
near the UF goal. Goff ran an option into the end
zone. Leavitt kicked the PAT and GA led 34-27.
After holding UF, GA got the ball back on
their own 20 with ten minutes left in the game.
Once again GA followed the running of McLee,
Pollard, and Goff on a 16-play drive that emp-
tied the clock and ended when Goff sneaked into
the end zone from the one. Leavitt kicked the
PAT and GA now led 41-27 and time was up
again for the Gators.
GA held UF (the fifth-leading offense in the
country) to just 65 yards in the second half.

1977

• Deng Xiaoping, purged Chinese leader, restored to
power as Gang of Four is expelled from Communist
Party • South African activist Steve Biko dies in
police custody • Nuclear-proliferation pact, curbing
spread of nuclear weapons, is signed by 15 countries, including US and USSR • First woman
Episcopal priest ordained • Scientists identify previously unknown bacterium as cause of mysterious
"legionnaire's disease" • Carter pardons Vietnam war
draft evaders • Supreme Court rules that states are
not required to spend Medicaid funds on elective
abortions.
Super Bowl   Oakland d. Minnesota (32-14)
World Series   NY Yankees d. LA Dodgers (4-2)
NBA Championship   Portland d. Phil. 76ers (4-2)
Kentucky Derby Champion   *Seattle Slew*
NCAA Basketball Championship
Marquette d. North Carolina (67-59)
NCAA Football Champions   Notre Dame (11-1-0)
Best Picture: Rocky   Record of the Year: "This
Masquerade," George Benson   Album of the Year:
Songs in the Key of Life, Stevie Wonder
Song of the Year: "I Write the Songs"
• The TV miniseries Roots draws an audience of 130
million • Star Wars hits theaters--for the first time--
and will go on to be the second highest-grossing film
of all time • Saturday Night Fever sparks the disco
inferno and the popularity of movie soundtracks.
• Elvis Presley dies at Graceland, his Memphis,
Tenn. home. He was 42.
Movies: Saturday Night Fever, Star Wars, Annie
Hall, Close Encounters of the Third Kind, Julia
• The neutron bomb is developed. Background:
nuclear weapons • The space shuttle Enterprise
makes its first test glide, from the back of a 747
• Lasers are first used to initiate a fusion reaction.

The Game: 1977 UF-22 GA-17

This wasn't a national spotlight year for either
club. UF was 3-2-1 and GA was 5-3. No SEC

crown for either team this year, and neither team
was ranked in the national polls. Nevertheless,
over 70,000 were in the stands, and as had come
to expected, the game was televised nationally.
An early punt by UF's Alan Williams rolled
out of bounds on the GA 6. On their first play,
GA's Willie McClendon ran through right tackle
for 53 yards to the UF 41. GA QB Jeff Pyburn
threw to Jesse Murray for a first down on the UF
14. In four plays, GA was on the UF 2. Pyburn
pitched to McClendon, who rammed it into the
end zone. Rex Robinson kicked the PAT and Ga
led 7-0 with just minutes left in the first quarter.
First play of the second quarter found Pyburn
running for 11 yards down to the UF 37. Pyburn
was injured on the play and Steve Rogers
replaced him at QB. Rogers fumbled on his first
play and UF's Flournoy came up with the ball
on the UF 31.
The "JY" Dogs held UF on their next series
forcing them to punt. Rogers was back in as QB.
On third down, at his own 24, Rogers was hit by
UF's Hutchinson and again fumbled back to the
GA 12 where UF's Sylvester King came up with
the ball. On their second play from there, UF QB
Terry LeCount threw to Wes Chandler in the end
zone. Berj Yepremian kicked the PAT and the
game was tied with just over 11 minutes remaining in the first half.
GA charged back in less than a minute. Rogers
rushed for six yards, and held onto the ball! On
the next play he faked a run into the line and
pitched back to McClendon, who was at a full
head of steam. With a terrific block downfield by
Ulysses Norris, McClendon only stopped after
running over the goal line, some 74 yards downfield. Robinson kicked the PAT and GA now led
14-7.
UF took the kick-off and moved right back
downfield. LeCount threw towards a routing
end, but GA's Jim Griffith intercepted at his own
37. As he ran towards the UF 42, Griffith
attempted a lateral to Bill Krug, but the toss was
wild and UF's Tony Green fell on the ball near
the sideline. UF continued driving down to the
GA 26 where the GA defense constructed a brick
wall. Yepremian came in and booted a 43-yard
FG to bring UF closer with a 14-10 score.
When UF got the ball back, LeCount was
intercepted by Billy Woods at the UF 32. In
seven plays GA was on the UF 12. With only
seconds left in the half, Robinson kicked a 29-
yard FG, giving the Dogs a 17-10 halftime lead.
On their second series of the second half, UF's
LeCount ran for 48 yards to the GA 26. On third
down, from the GA 18, Chandler lined up in the
backfield and got the ball. Faster than the "JY"
Dogs reaction, Chandler was spiking the ball in
the end zone. The PAT was missed when holder
Alan Williams bobbled the snap and tried to run
with the ball. GA's Krug crushed Williams
behind the line. GA 17 UF 16.
UF's defense was starting to completely handle the GA offense. After a GA punt to UF's 27,
the Gators moved to the GA 38 before Green's
fumble was picked off in mid-air by Krug.
Dooley brought in Randy Cook at QB, but he
wasn't any more able to ward off the UF rush as
his two predecessors.
UF got the ball back on their own 43. This
drive snapped along to the GA 27 where
Yepremian calmly kicked the ball into the goalposts, killing UF's opportunity of taking the lead.
On their first play from the 20, McLee ran for
five, then fumbled the ball over to UF's Brantley.
Less than ten minutes remained in the game, and
UF knew it was now or never. In seven plays,

UF was on the GA 1. Chandler ran over left guard for the score. UF tried a two-point conversion, but LeCount was buried behind the line.

GA got the ball one more time, but once again, UF's defense was there to play. Rogers moved the Dogs into UF territory, the first time in the second half. Then he lost five yards. On the next play, UF sealed their win by throwing Rogers for a 17-yard loss and recovering his fumble all on the same play. There had been eight GA fumbles in this game. They lost five of them.

1978

• US Senate approves Panama Canal neutrality treaty; votes treaty to turn canal over to Panama by year 2000 • Former Italian Premier Aldo Moro kidnapped by left wing terrorists, who kill five bodyguards; he is found slain • Pope Paul VI , dead at 80, mourned; new Pope, John Paul I, 65, dies unexpectedly after 34 days in office; succeeded by Karol Cardinal Wojtyla of Poland as John Paul II
• "Framework for Peace" in Middle East signed by Egypt's President Anwar Sadat and Israeli Premier Menachem Begin after 13-day conference at Camp David led by President Jimmy Carter • Jim Jones's followers commit mass suicide in Jonestown, Guyana • President Carter chooses Federal Appeals Court Judge William H. Webster as F.B.I. director
• US Supreme Court in Bakke case, bars quota systems in college admissions but affirms constitutionality of programs giving advantage to minorities .
Super Bowl   Dallas d. Denver (27-10)
World Series   NY Yankees d. LA Dodgers (4-2)
NBA Championship   Wash. Bullets d. Seattle (4-3)
Kentucky Derby Champion   *Affirmed*
NCAA Basketball Championship
Kentucky d. Duke (94-88)
NCAA Football Champions
Alabama (AP, FW, NFF) (11-1-0) & USC (UPI) (12-1-0)
Best Picture: Annie Hall   Record of the Year "Hotel California," Eagles   Album of the Year: Rumours, Fleetwood Mac   Song of the Year: "Love Theme From A Star Is Born" (Evergreen), Barbra Streisand
Movies: The Deer Hunter, Midnight Express, Heaven Can Wait, Coming Home
• Sony introduces the Walkman, the first portable stereo • Balloon anigoplasty is developed to treat coronary artery disease • Louise Brown, the first test-tube baby, is born at Oldham Hostpital in London • Recombinant DNA techniques are used to produce human insulin

The Game: 1978 GA 24 UF 22

An overcast day, turned to sunshine, but UF Coach Dickey would still be under fire by disgruntled UF fans, who were calliing for his dismisal. UF was 3-4, after a surprise upset of Auburn. GA was after another SEC crown and a probable berth in the Sugar Bowl. GA's McClendon was leading the SEC in rushing, averaging 139 yards a game. But he would be playing this game with a fractured left hand and a strained left knee. UF was led by QB John Brantley and E Chris Collinsworth. Collinsworth was second in the SEC, averaging 183 yards a game, while catching 10 TD passes.

On its opening possession, GA's Lindsay Scott (you'll hear more from him) caught a pass from Pyburn, but fumbled the ball over to UF's Dave Little on the GA 29.

Collinsworth caught a pass from Brantley that put the Gators on the GA 13, but the "JY" Dogs held fast. Yepremian kicked a 30-yard FG. UF 3, GA 0.

GA marched 88 yards after receiving the kick-off. McClendon, James Womack and Ronnie Stewart did most of the groundwork. Pyburn completed passes of 15 and 24 yards to Antony Arnold. McClendon went the final three yards into the end zone. Robinson kicked the PAT and GA led 7-3.

Another drive by GA and a 32-yard FG by Robinson gave GA a 10-3 lead. It was early in the second period when UF took the GA kick-off and began a drive that was capped by Collinsworth catching a 33-yard pass from Brantley for a TD. Yepremian tied the game with his PAT.

GA's Womack ran back the Gator kick-off 32 yards. GA's backs rushed the next 55 yards down to the UF 3. Pyburn then stepped back and hit Mark Hodge in the back of the end zone for a TD. Robinson's PAT gave the lead back to GA, 17-10.

On UF's first play after the GA kick-off, a Brantley pass was intercepted by GA's Welton at the UF 44. On the next play, GA's Arnold took what appeared to be an end-around. Arnold, a former HS QB, tossed to Lindsay Scott for a 44-yard TD. Robinson kicked the PAT and GA now led 24-10. GA had scored 14 points in 26 seconds.

UF then drove 82 yards to the GA 2, where after being stopped on a third down incompletion, brought Yepremian in to kick a 19-yard FG. The score was now 24-13.

The third quarter was filled with fumbles and interceptions. GA's Scott Woerner ran back a UF punt 63 yards, but GA could not capitalize on it.

In the fourth period, UF drove to a first and goal at the GA 6. On third down, Brantley was thrown for a yard loss. Yepremian came in and kicked a 20-yard FG. The score was now GA 24, UF 16.

After stopping GA, UF got the ball back on its own 12, and in just eight plays were on the GA 35. Brantley fired a 20-yard lateral to Collinsworth, who fired the ball downfield, over the GA defenders heads to a wide-open Enclade, catching the ball at the five and rumbling in for the score. UF elected to go for two points. Brantley's pass was deflected and picked off by GA's Chris Welton, with a little more than six minutes remaining to play.

On GA's next series, UF couldn't stop the clock, nor could they stop the bevy of GA running backs. GA ran to the UF 18 with about a minute and a half left in the game. On a fourth and one, Dooley tossed the dice and went for the first down, which if made, would ice the game. GA's Stewart plunged to the UF 16 for the first down. Now all GA had to do was kill the clock, which they did. Dickey had made the mistake of once suggesting, during the scouting of players, that Womack and Stewart, GA running backs, were not big enough nor good enough to play football for Florida. This was Dickey's last GA-UF game.

1979

•Vietnam and Vietnam-backed Cambodian insurgents announce fall of Cambodian capital Phnom Penh and collapse of Pol Pot regime • Shah leaves Iran after year of turmoil ; revolutionary forces under Muslim leader, Ayatollah Ruhollah Khomeini, take over • Conservatives win British election; Margaret Thatcher becomes new prime minister • Carter and Brezhnev sign SALT II agreement • Nicaraguan President General Anastasio Somoza Debayle resigns and flees to Miami ; Sandinistas form government • Iranian militants seize US embassy in Teheran and hold hostages • Soviet invasion of Afghanistan stirs world protests • Ohio agrees to pay $675,000 to families of dead and injured in Kent State University shootings • Nuclear power plant accident at Three Mile Island, Pa., releases radiation
Super Bowl   Pittsburgh d. Dallas (35-31)
World Series   Pittsburgh d. Baltimore (4-3)
NBA Championship   Seattle d. Wash. Bullets (4-1)
Kentucky Derby Champion   *Spectacular Bid*
NCAA Basketball Championship Mich. St. d. Ind St. (75-64)
NCAA Football Champions   Alabama (12-0-0)
Best Picture: The Deer Hunter
Record of the Year: "Just the Way You Are," Billy Joel Album of the Year: Saturday Night Fever, Bee Gees Song of the Year: "Just the Way You Are," Billy Joel, songwriter

• The Sugar Hill Gang releases the first commercial rap hit, "Rapper's Delight," bringing rap off the New York streets and into the popular music scene. Movies: Apocalypse Now, All That Jazz, Kramer vs. Kramer, Breaking Away
• The first human-powered aircraft flies across the English Channel: Bryan Allen pilots the Gossamer Albatross from Folkestone, England, to Cap Gris-Nez, France • The accidental release of anthrax spores at a Soviet bioweapons facility in Sverdlovsk kills several hundred.

The Game: 1979 GA-33 UF -10

UF's new coach Charley Pell came into the GA game with a record of 0-6-1. GA was 4-4, but were unbeaten in the SEC, so the crown could still be theirs. As far as the fans were concerned, the emphasis in this year's game was on the "world's largest outdoor cocktail party." One sportswriter sai "the more spirits, the better." The Atlanta Constitution was quoted as saying, "The 'Wonderdogs' perform in league competition, while the 'Blunderdogs' are 0-4 in non-conference play." Only 69,000 attended the Gator Bowl game on a windy afternoon. UF won the toss and chose to receive rather than have the wind at their backs. The decision quickly came back to bite the Gators. GA stuffed the UF offense deep in their own territory. A UF punt only went 28 yards and GA was in business at the UF 38. Failing to make a first down GA's Rex Robinson, with the wind at his back, kicked a 48-yard FG to give GA the lead, 3-0.

On the first play after the kick-off, UF's Terry Williams fumbled and GA's Gordon Terry fell on the ball at the UF 31. GA QB Buck Belue tossed to Lindsay Scott for 14 yards. He then hit Carnie Nor for ten. Then Belue handed off to Norris who ran around the right end for the score. Robinson kicked his 61st consecutive PAT, tying him with Alan Leavitt for the conference record. Now GA led 10-0

UF wasn't content to sit on the ball, nor were the content to hold on to the ball. On a nine-yard pass play from QB Ochab, Curt Garrett lost the ball to GA's Pat Collins on the UF 37. GA's Matt Simon rushed for nine and fifteen yards to give GA the ba on the UF 8. On the next play Belue, under heavy pressure, found flanker Carmon Prince in the end zone for a 6-yard TD. Robinson kicked his 62nd consecutive PAT and GA now led 20-0 with over 1 minutes remaining in the first half.

Ochab finally got the Gators moving and holding on to the ball. They drove for 15 plays to get to the GA 13. On third and eight, Ochab threw to a Gator open in the end zone, but the ball was tipped away UF's TE Chris Faulkner caught the deflection for t score. Brian Clark booted the PAT and UF was on the board. GA 20, UF 7.

GA started its next drive on the GA 24, and in seven plays were on the UF 40. Belue hit Scott wi a pass across the middle. Scott avoided one tackler and proceeded to run to the UF goal line. GA wen for two and Belue's pass fell incomplete. GA now led 26-7.

On their second play after the kick-off, UF FB John Whittaker fumbled and GA's Tim Parks recovered the ball on the UF 20. Simon rushed for seven and then to the three. Belue then hit Norris Brown for the score. Robinson kicked the PAT and GA led 33-7.

UF, with 22 seconds left in the half, went for broke. Darrell Jones ran the kick-off back 27 yards Ochab threw 11 yards to Williams. Two facemask penalties against GA moved the ball close enough for UF's Clark to kick a 47-yard FG. GA 33 UF

The second half was full of second and third stringers for GA and interceptions by Ochab (3). T "JY" Dogs had held UF to 40 yards rushing and 1 yards passing. GA's Frank Ros had 12 tackles. Six Gator turnovers pretty much dictated how this gam would turn out.

gators

UNIVERSITY OF FLORIDA / OFFICIAL FOOTBALL MAGAZINE

FLORIDA VS UNIVERSITY OF GEORGIA · NOVEMBER 7, 1970 · ONE DOLLAR

1970 · UFL 24 UGA 17

GEORGIA

vs Florida

JACKSONVILLE, FLA. / THE GATOR BOWL / NOVEMBER 6, 1971 / ONE DOLLAR

1971 · UGA 49 UFL 7

gators

UNIVERSITY OF FLORIDA / OFFICIAL FOOTBALL MAGAZINE

FLORIDA VS. UNIVERSITY OF GEORGIA • NOVEMBER 11, 1972 • ONE DOLLAR

1972 · UGA 10 UFL 7

GEORGIA

vs **Florida**

JACKSONVILLE, FLA. / THE GATOR BOWL / NOVEMBER 10, 1973 / ONE DOLLAR

1973 • UFL 11 UGA 10

FLORIDA  FOOTBALL

FLORIDA VS. UNIVERSITY OF GEORGIA • NOVEMBER 9, 1974 • ONE DOLLAR

1974 · UFL 16 UGA 17

vs **Florida**

JACKSONVILLE, FLA./THE GATOR BOWL/NOVEMBER 8, 1975/ONE DOLLAR

1975 · UFL-17 UGA-10

1976 · UGA 41 UFL 27

GEORGIA

Vs. FLORIDA Jacksonville, Fla. / The Gator Bowl / November 5, 1977 / One Dollar

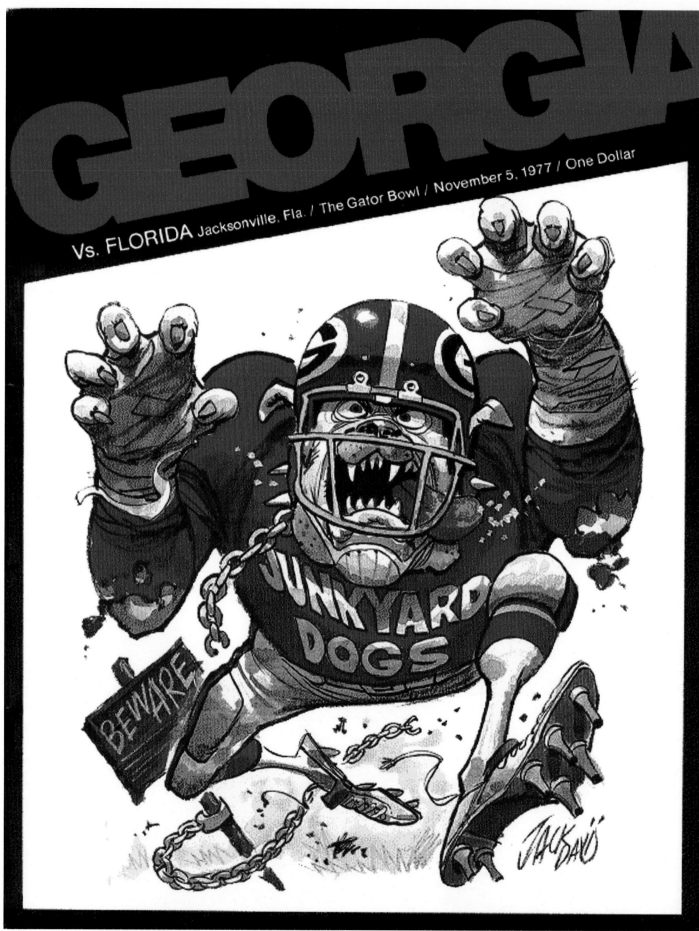

1977 · UFL 22 UGA 17

Nov. 11, 1978
$1.00

GATORS

**FLORIDA
VS.
GEORGIA
JACKSONVILLE**

1978 · UGA 24   UFL 22

GEORGIA

Vs. Florida/Jacksonville, Fla./Gator Bowl/Nov. 10, 1979

$1.50

26

1979 · UGA 33 UFL 10

The 1980s

1980

- American hostages in Teheran
- Anastasio Somoza Debayle, ousted Nicaraguan ruler, and two aides are assassinated in Paraguayan capital of Asunción • Iraqi troops hold 90 square miles of Iran after invasion; 8-year Iran-Iraq War begins • Three US nuns and a lay worker are found shot in El Salvador
- F.B.I.'s undercover operation "Abscam" (for Arab scam) implicates public officials • US Supreme Court upholds limits on federal aid for abortions • Ronald Reagan elected president in Republican sweep.

Super Bowl Pittsburgh d. La Rams (31-19)
World Series
Phil. Phillies d. Kansas City (4-2)
NBA Championship
LA Lakers d. Phil. 76ers (4-2)
Kentucky Derby Champion
Genuine Risk
NCAA Basketball Championship
Louisville d. UCLA (59-54)
NCAA Football Champions
Georgia (12-0-0)
Best Picture: Kramer vs. Kramer
Record of the Year: "What a Fool Believes," Doobie Brothers
Album of the Year: 52nd Street, Billy Joel Song of the Year: "What a Fool Believes." Kenny Loggins and Michael McDonald.
- John Lennon of the Beatles shot dead in New York City • Ted Turner launches CNN, the first all-news network
Movies: Raging Bull, Ordinary People, Coal Miner's Daughter, The Elephant Man, Tess
- Janice Brown, a 98-lb. former teacher, makes the first long-distance solar-powered flight in the Solar Challenger • Voyager I reaches Saturn, returning data on its 14 moons as well as its more than 1,000 rings • In Diamond v. Shakrabarty, the US Supreme Court rules that genetically engineered organisms may be patented.

The Game:
1980 GA-26 UF -21

Before this magical season had begun, GA Coach Dooley had decided to return to the team wearing silver pants, last worn by Wally Butts' teams. Finally, GA fans could yell, "Go you silver britches" again!

GA was unbeaten after 8 games (4-0 in the SEC) and ranked 2nd in the polls. UF was 6-1 (3-1 in SEC) and ranked number 20. UF had a new QB and leader in freshman Wayne Peace. GA had successfully recruited a freshman star of their own, a running back from Wrightsville, GA named Herschel Walker. Walker was averaging 137 yards rushing per game, almost six yards a carry, and had 1,096 yards for the season so far.

Herschel wasted no time in making his mark in this game. On GA's fourth play, at their own 28, Walker broke through the UF line and into the open. 40 yards downfield,

Walker got a great block from Lindsay Scott, knocking away the last UF defender. Just another 72-yard run for Walker, and a TD for GA. Robinson kicked the PAT (his 91st consecutive PAT) and GA led 7-0 with only a little over a minute gone in the game.

On UF's next series, Peace was intercepted by GA's Fisher at the UF 41. With a first down on the UF 30, Belue hit Amp Arnold for nine yards. In his effort to stretch the play out, Arnold fumbled the ball. UF's Kyle Knight fell on it on the UF 21.

Peace's "Run and Gun Gators" drove down the field with their next possession. When the GA defense held, UF's Clark booted a 40-yard FG. GA 7 UF 3.

GA started at its own 23. Belue hit Kay for eight, then Scott for 21. The ball was now on UF's 45. Belue ran for ten and was tackled out-of-bounds. The penalty moved the ball down to the UF 20. Belue rolled to his left, setting up a pitch to Walker who was right behind him, but instead hit Ronnie Stewart, who had gotten open at the UF 3. Stewart carried the ball across the goal line. Robinson made it 14-3 with just two minutes passed in the second quarter.

UF's second play after the kick-off found Peace being tackled for a six-yard loss and fumbling the ball to GA's Eddie "Meat Cleaver" Weaver on the UF 23. GA drove to the UF 16, but Belue was intercepted by UF's Ivory Curry who returned the ball back to the UF 29.

After an incompleted pass from a faked punt by UF, GA got the ball back, but GA's Walker fumbled the ball for the first time, and UF had the ball back. Peace hit Collinsworth for 12 to the GA 34. He then hit FB James Jones for 12 more. Peace hit Collinsworth again for 13 down to the GA 9. On the next pass, Collinsworth beat Woerner and gathered in the pass for a score. Clark's PAT closed the gap at the half, GA 14 UF 10.

Starting the second half, Walker ran twice for 15-yards per pop. Before they realized it, GA was on the UF 12. A 3rd down pass by Belue fell to the ground, and Robinson kicked a FG, taking GA ahead by 17-10.

GA held UF once again, and a poor punt gave GA the ball on their own 47. Walker gained 13 to the UF 40. Womack ran for seven, and a facemask violation moved GA further down the field, placing the ball on the UF 18. Walker gained 14 on the first play, and added another two yards on two tough rushes placing the ball on the UF 2. Belue lost two on third down. Dooley sent in Robinson to boot the short FG, putting GA ahead 20-10. There were only around four minutes remaining in the third quarter.

After swapping the ball back and forth, UF started their next drive from their own 19. Peace hit Tyrone Young for 11 yards. He then hit Jones for five. Peace again found Young in the clear over the middle and hit him with a pass. Young blasted away from several defenders and rambled 54 yards to the GA 11. Jones then ran through right guard for the score. Peace hit Young in the end zone for the two-point conversion. It was now 20-18 with just over 14 minutes remaining to play.

UF held the Dogs and forced a punt. From their own 24, UF went on a 10-play drive that took over five minutes off the clock. Running out of steam at the GA 24, UF's Clark kicked a 40-yard FG, and UF led for the first time in the game, 21-20.

UF's defense stiffened and held GA and forced another punt. UF then drove from their own 31 to the GA 36. On fourth down, Pell decided to pin GA deep in their own territory, instead of risking a long FG. Punter Mark Dickert punted out of bounds on the GA 8 with just a little over a minute left on the clock. GA just wanted to get close enough to allow Robinson to kick a game-winning FG. If they can just get the ball into UF territory, they felt Robinson would do the rest. With only one time-out remaining, GA had to use the clock wisely. And, so they did!
1st down- Belue ran around in the backfield, looking for an open receiver. The blocking broke down and

he was thrown for a yard loss. The clock ticked on. 2nd down- Belue attempted a pass, but it fell to the ground. The clock stopped, but just briefly.
3rd down-With the UF players chiding, "It's over!" and with a pretty good bit of landscape between them and the UF goal, Belue tried to calm his huddled team. GA broke the huddle. The ball was snapped to Belue, who went back to pass. The rushing Gators forced him to the right side of the field. Out of the corner of his eye, Belue noticed that Lindsay Scott had broken into the open around the GA 25. Running a perfect pattern, Scott jumped and caught the pass in the middle of the field, then raced towards the sidelines, running right past Gator safety Tim Groves. With Coach Dooley running along the sideline, Scott zipped past him on his way to the most famous 93-yard TD in GA history. It was Scott's first TD catch of the year. He was mobbed in the end zone by teamates and fans, flooding out onto the field.

Larry Munson, GA Radio Announcing Legend's audio of the TD was instantly a legend.
His description of the play: "Florida in a standup-5 They may or may not blitz. They won't. Buck back, third down on the 7. In trouble.........Gonna pick up a block behind him......Gonna throw on the run, complete to the 25. Lindsay Scott, 35,40, Lindsay Scott, 45, 50! Run Lindsay!! 25, 20, 15, 10, 5.........Lindsay Scott! Lindsay Scott!! Lindsay Scott!!!" Munson was so excited in the press box calling the play that he broke his chair while jumping around, calling the play. Ga went for two, but Belue's pass was knocked down.

UF had 1:03 left to try to get back in the game, bu Peace's first pass was picked off by GA Cornerback Mike Fisher. GA then ran out the clock.

Peace had passed for 286 yards in the losing effort Walker had rushed for 237. With Ga. Tech tying No 1 Notre Dame in Atlanta, GA was now in the top position in the rankings.

1981

- US-Iran agreement frees 52 hostages held in Teheran since 1979• Pope John Paul II wounded by gunman • Israel annexes the disputed Golan Heights territory • Egyptian president Anwar el-Sadat is assassinated by Islamic extremists during a military parade in Cairo • President Hilla Limann is overthrown in Ghana as Jerry J. Rawlings seizes power. Ronald Reagan takes oath as 40th President • President Reagan wounded by gunman, with press secretary and two law-enforcement officers • US Supreme Court rules, 4-4, that former President Nixon and three top aides may be required to pay damages for wiretap of home telephone of former national security aide • Reagan nominates Judge Sandra Day O'Connor, 51, of Arizona, as first woman on US Supreme Court • Air controllers strike, disrupting flights; government dismisses strikers.

Super Bowl Oakland d. Philadelphia (27-10)
World Series LA Dodgers d. NY Yankees (4-2)
NBA Championship Boston d. Houston (4-2)
Kentucky Derby Champion *Pleasant Colony*
NCAA Basketball Championship Ind. d. NC (63-50
NCAA Football Champions Clemson (12-0-0)
Best Picture: Ordinary People Record of the Year: "Sailing," Christopher Cross Album of the Year: Christopher Cross, Christopher Cross
Song of the Year: "Sailing," Christopher Cross
- MTV goes on the air running around the clock music videos, debuting with "Video Killed the Rad Star" • The Supreme Court rules to allow television cameras in the courtroom • Pacman-mania sweeps the country.
Movies: Raiders of the Lost Ark, Chariots of Fire, On Golden Pond, Reds, Atlantic City
- AIDS is first identified • IBM introduces its first personal computer, running the Microsoft Disk Operating System (MS-DOS) • The 236-m.p.h. TGV, Europe's first high-speed passenger train, begins operating out of Lyons, France • The FDA

proves the use of the artificial sweetener aspar-
ne (Nutrasweet).

The Game: 1981 GA-26 UF -21

No. 4 GA was 7-1. UF was 5-3. 70,000 attended
e affair to see what the Gators had in mind for the
gs after last year's historic loss. UF's Pell thought
 would inspire his team by outfitting them in
ange pants, not worn since 1940. It inflamed the
tors and their fans. For a second, it seemed to
rk. Peace hit Miller for 20 yards and after a penal-
against GA, UF was on the GA 19. The "JY"
gs, without Erk Russell who was now GA.
uthern's new coach, came out of their slumbers
d threw Peace for three straight losses totaling 21
rds. After a UF punt, GA found the same crazed
fense facing them. Targeting Walker, the UF line
ld GA from advancing the ball.
The game was pure defense, until the six minute
ark of the second period, when Peace hit Miller
wn the sidelines for a 54-yard TD. Clark made it 7-

The kick-off bounced past Walker and GA took
er at their own 2. GA's Ronnie Stewart fumbled to
F linebacker Fernando Jackson at the GA 5. Four
F rushes, the last by QB James Jones gave the
tors their second score. Clark made it 14-0.
GA's offense woke up on its next possession. Belue
 Scott Williams with a 34-yard pass. From the UF
, Belue passed to Walker who left the entire Gator
m in his dust as he glided into the end zone. Kevin
tler kicked the PAT and it was now 14-7.
Savannah Morning News report described Walker
e this, *"Imagine a jet-propelled, supersonic tank
t turns like a Ferrari and you will begin to get the
ture."*
Late in the third quarter, GA churned out a 12-play
ve, using more than five minutes off the clock.
lue hit Norris Brown for 19. Then he hit Scott for
. Then one to Stewart for another 15. Belue was
ting the Gators up! He then tossed a short pass
er the middle to Walker. Walker churned towards
 UF goal. UF's Ivory Curry came up to stop the
ay and was literally "run-over" by Walker. Herschel
n't stop until he could hand the ball to the referee
the end zone. Butler's PAT tied the game at 14.
GA stuffed the Gators on their next possession,
cing a punt. In four plays, GA went from the UF
 to the UF 4 with Walker carrying the load. He
en carried a pitchout into the endzone. Butler's PAT
s no good, but the dogs led, 20-14.
Peace then took to the air, hitting passes of 21, 12,
 and 21 yards as he moved the Gators to the GA
. Miller gained 10 to the 4. Then Peace hit Spencer
ckson for the score. Clark's PAT gave the lead back
UF, 21-20.
GA started at their own five, trailing 21-20...sound
miliar? This year, they had more time to work with.
ith Belue's passing and Walker's pounding of the
F defensive line, the Dogs moved 95 yards in 17
ys. Walker dove over from the one with just over
o minutes reamaining to play. A two-point conver-
n attempt was missed, but GA led now 26-21.
UF got the ball twice more, but could not move
th it. GA had won the battle in Jacksonville and
o one the SEC once again, and were going into the
wl season ranked NO. 2, behind the only team
ey had lost to this year, Clemson.

982

British overcome Argentina in Falklands war
srael invades Lebanon in attack on PLO • Princess
ace, 52, dies of injuries when car plunges off
untain road; daughter Stephanie, 17, suffers seri-
s injuries • Lebanese Christian Phalangists kill hun-
ds of people in two Palestinian refugee camps in
est Beirut • Leonid I. Brezhnev, Soviet leader, dies
75. Yuri V. Andropov, 68, chosen as successor.
ohn W. Hinckley, Jr. found not guilty because of
sanity in shooting of President Reagan • Alexander
. Haig, Jr., resigns as Secretary of State • Equal
ghts Amendment fails ratification

Super Bowl   San Francisco d. Cincinnati (26-21)
World Series   St. L Cardinals d. Mil. Brewers (4-3)
NBA Championship   LA Lakers d. Phil. 76ers (4-2)
Kentucky Derby Champion *Gato Del Sol*
NCAA Basketball Championship
North Carolina d. Georgetown (63-62)
NCAA Football Champions   Penn St. (11-1-0)
Best Picture: Chariots of Fire
Record of the Year: "Bette Davis Eyes," Kim Carnes
Album of the Year: Double Fantasy, John Lennon
and Yoko Ono Song of the Year: "Bette Davis Eyes"
• Michael Jackson releases Thriller, which sells more
than 25 million copies, becoming the biggest-selling
album in history •John Belushi dies of a drug over-
dose at age 33 • Cats opens on Broadway. Becomes
Broadway's longest-running play.
Movies: E.T. – the Extra-Terrestrial, Tootsie, Gandhi,
The Verdict
• A permanent artificial heart is implanted in a human
for first time in Dr. Barney B. Clark, 61, at University
of Utah Medical Center in Salt Lake City • The
space shuttle Columbia makes its first mission,
deploying two communications satellites • MRI
(magnetic resonance imaging) diagnostic machines
are introduced in Britain • Washington University in
St. Louis develops the Flavr Savr tomato, the first
genetically-engineered plant approved for sale.

The Game: 1982 GA-44 UF -0

The Gator Bowl would now hold more than
80,000, and hold it would because Herschel Walker
had the Bulldogs not only fighting for a national
championship, but Walker was also in the fight for
the Heisman Trophy.
It was Dooley's 19th year as GA coach and this
year's edition was 8-0 and ranked second in the UPI
and third in the AP and on top of the SEC rankings.
UF was 5-2, with losses to LSU and Vandy, were
out of the SEC race. Peace was the leading passer in
the nation, completing 75% of his passes. He was
expected to pass Spurrier and move into number two
in the UF career passing record books, behind John
Reaves.
GA's Walker owned eight NCAA rushing records
and needed only 15 yards to become the NCAA's
fifth all-time leading rusher. GA relied on a strong
offensive blocking line because their new QB John
Lastinger was rated last in passing in the SEC.
UF not only had Peace, but they rushing weapons
such as James Jones, John L. Williams, and Lorenzo
Hampton.
On GA's first drive, they marched 31 yards before
Lastinger threw an interception. UF countered with a
Peace fumble on the UF 37. Walker ran for seven,
and on the next play went 30 yards into the end zone.
Butler kicked the PAT and with only 2:23 gone in the
game, GA led 7-0.
UF followed the rushes of Jones and Hampton on a
drive from their 20 to the GA 17. The drive ended
with GA's Jeff Sanchez intercepting a Peace pass.
GA started at their 20 and went on a 15 play, six first-
down drive to the UF 1. From there, Walker leaped
over the UF line into the endzone. Butler kicked the
PAT and the rout was on.
UF's next possession saw them perform their best
drive of the day. Peace passed 33-yards to Hampton.
On the ground, Hampton and Jones rushed the
Gators down to the GA 5. Going for the score on
fourth down, the Dogs stopped Hampton inches from
the goal.
The only other scoring of the first half came on a
32-yard FG by Kevin Butler. Walker had rushed for
162 yards in the first half.
Taking the second half kick-off, GA drove to the
UF 12 where Butler kicked another FG. It was now
20-0. Moments later GA fell on a Peace fumble. GA
drove 80 quick yards to the UF 1. Lastinger was
going for a QB sneak, but lost the handle on the ball.
Walker grabbed the ball out of the air and bulled into
the end zone, scoring his third TD of the game.
Butler's kick made it 27-0.
Substitutions became the order of the day for GA.

Walker was through after rushing for 219 yards on 35
carries and three scores. While GA was pummeling
UF, news came out that Number one Pittsburgh had
been upset by Notre Dame, meaning there was a
good chance that GA would be ranked tops in the
nation by next week.
GA's second string QB Todd Williams led the Dogs
on a 63-yard drive that ended with Carnie Norris
scoring from the one. Butler made it 34-0.
Butler added another 30-yard FG before Williams
drove the dogs 64 yards, allowing Tron Jackson to
score from the 20. Butler's PAT made it 44-0.

1983

• Pope John Paul II signs new Roman Catholic code
incorporating changes brought about by Second
Vatican Council • South Korean Boeing 747 jetliner
bound for Seoul apparently strays into Soviet air-
space and is shot down by a Soviet SU-15 fighter
after it had tracked the airliner for two hours; all 269
aboard are killed • Terrorist explosion kills 237 US
Marines in Beirut • US invades Grenada • Second
space shuttle, Challenger, makes successful maiden
voyage, which includes the first US space walk in
nine years • Sally K. Ride, 32, first US woman astro-
naut in space as a crew member aboard space shuttle
Challenger • US admits shielding former Nazi
Gestapo chief Klaus Barbie, 69, the "butcher of
Lyon," wanted in France for war crimes
Super Bowl   Washington d. Miami (27-17)
World Series   Baltimore d. Phil. Phillies (4-1)
NBA Championship   Phil. 76ers d. LA Lakers (4-0)
Kentucky Derby Champion   *Sunny's Halo*
NCAA Basketball Championship
N.C. St. d. Houston (54-52)
NCAA Football Champions   Miami-FL (11-1-0)
Best Picture: Gandhi
Record of the Year: "Rosanna," Toto Album of the
Year: Toto IV, Toto   Song of the Year: "Always on
My Mind" • With the introduction of noise-free com-
pact discs, the vinyl record begins a steep decline •
Harvey Fierstein's Torch Song Trilogy wins the New
York Drama Critics' Circle Award and Tony Award
for best play, marking the acceptance of gay theater •
Singer Karen Carpenter dies of complications from
anorexia nervosa at age 32 • More than 125 million
viewers tune in to the last episode of M*A*S*H.
Movies: The Big Chill, Terms of Endearment, Fanny
& Alexander, The Right Stuff • "Crack" cocaine is
developed in the Bahamas, and soon appears in the
United States • The FCC authorizes Motorola to
begin testing cellular phone service in Chicago.
•The El Nino phenomenon disrupts global weather
patterns.

The Game: 1983 GA-10 UF -9

Coming into this game, UF was 6-1-1 and ranked
ninth in the nation. GA was 7-0-1 with an offense
built around running backs Keith Montgomery, Barry
Young, and David McCluskey.
The Atlanta Constitution wrote, "In this war between
the states, the weapons, before kickoff are beer bot-
tles and the goal is to conquer sobriety. It doesn't
matter if you win or lose, it's how you have a good
time."
With all that was on the line for this game, over
82,000 packed the Gator Bowl for this year's contest.
On the third play of the game, Peace threw 50-
yards to Hampton down to the GA 15. GA held and
UF had to settle for a Bobby Raymond FG of 21
yards. UF led 3-0.
GA's first offensive series ended up with a
Lastinger pass being intercepted by Bruce Vaughan at
the GA 47, running it back 32 yards to the GA 15.
UF made it down to the GA 8, but that was as far as
they could go. Raymond kicked another FG from the
25. UF now led 6-0.
Lastinger brought the GA offense to life, leading
them on a 12-play, 44 yard drive to the UF 34.
Stalling there, GA brought in Butler to kick a 51-yard
FG. It was now 6-3.

GA's punter, Chip Andrews kept the Gators backed up by averaging 46.2 yards per punt. Before half-time, Peace led the Gators from their own 43 down to the GA 7. Raymond kicked another FG from 32 yards out. Florida now led 9-3. Early in the third quarter, UF drove deep in GA territory. Raymond missed a 41-yard FG attempt.

UF had outplayed GA the entire game, but only led by six points. GA got the ball on its own 1. Lastinger plunged for 2. Then he surprised everyone by running for 16 yards. UF linebacker Marshall was penalized 15 yards for a personal foul, moving the ball even further out. In three plays, GA was on the UF 22. On fourth and two, Dooley decided to go for the first down and not for the field goal. Lastinger went for four yards and a first down. GA's Barry Young blasted in for GA's lone TD. Butler kicked the PAT and GA led 10-9. The 16-play is considered to be one of the great offensive series in the rivalry's history.

Peace directed the UF offense right back down the field. When they were stalled, Raymond came in to hit a "chip shot" FG that would put UF on top. The kick was wide to the right. GA held on to the lead.

Holding GA once again, UF with another possession, had a chance to get back in the game, but on 3rd down, GA's Gilbert brought Peace down behind the line on the UF 11 yard line. With only a minute remaining in the game, UF went for the first down and continued possession of the ball. Gilbert was all over Peace, causing him to throw wildly incomplete. UF could only look back on the six drives inside the GA 25 that netted only three field goals. There was also a 51-yard touchdown run by Williams called back by the officials because the whistle had blown before the score.

GA lost the next weekend in Athens against Auburn 13-7, losing the SEC crown. But after beating Ga. Tech 27-24, GA was selected to play top-ranked Texas in the Cotton Bowl. GA shocked the Longhorns 10-9 and finished with a 10-1-1 record, good enough to be ranked fourth in the UPI and AP polls.

1984

• Syria frees captured US Navy pilot, Lieut. Robert C. Goodman, Jr. • US and Vatican exchange diplomats after 116-year hiatus • Reagan orders US Marines withdrawn from Beirut international peacekeeping force • Yuri V. Andropov dies at 69; Konstantin U. Chernenko, 72, named Soviet leader • Italy and Vatican agree to end Roman Catholicism as state religion • Soviet Union withdraws from summer Olympic games in US, and other bloc nations follow • Jose Napoleon Duarte, moderate, elected president of El Salvador • Three hundred slain as Indian Army occupies Sikh Golden Temple in Amritsar • Indian Prime Minister Indira Gandhi assassinated by two Sikh bodyguards; 1,000 killed in anti-Sikh riots; son Rajiv succeeds her • Toxic gas leaks from Union Carbide plant in Bhopal, India, killing 2,000 and injuring 150,000 • Bell System broken up • Congress rebukes President Reagan on use of federal funds for mining Nicaraguan harbors • Thirty-ninth Democratic National Convention, nominates Walter F. Mondale and Geraldine A. Ferraro • Thirty-third Republican National Convention renominates President Reagan and Vice President Bush • President Reagan re-elected in landslide with 59% of vote
Super Bowl   LA Raiders d. Washington (38-9)
World Series   Detroit d. San Diego (4-1)
NBA Championship   Boston d. LA Lakers (4-3)
Kentucky Derby Champion   *Swale*
NCAA Basketball Championship
Georgetown d. Houston (84-75)
NCAA Football Champions   BYU (13-0-0)
Academy Award, Best Picture: Terms of Endearment,
Record of the Year: "Beat It," Michael Jackson
Album of the Year: Thriller, Michael Jackson   Song of the Year: "Every Breath You Take," Sting
• The Cosby Show debuts on NBC. The sitcom is

widely considered the most popular show of the 1980s • The Supreme Court rules that taping television shows at home on VCRs does not violate copyright law.
• Led by Bob Geldof, the band Band Aid releases "Do They Know It's Christmas," with proceeds of the single going to feed the starving in Africa.
Movies: Amadeus, The Killing Fields, A Passage to India, The Pope of Greenwich Village
• Joe W. Kittinger makes the first solo transatlantic balloon flight in the helium-filled Rosie O'Grady's Balloon of Peace. He travels 3,535 miles from Caribou, Maine to Savona, Italy • Apple introduces the user-friendly Macintosh personal computer.

The Game: 1984 UF-27 GA-0

UF opened the year with their Head Coach Charley Pell being forced to resign because of NCAA violations in recruiting high school players. Galen Hall, an assistant, became the interim coach. UF was 6-1-1 and ranked 10th, heading into the "big game" against number eight (7-1) Bulldogs. GA was led by redshirt-freshman David Dukes and running backs Lars Tate, Cleveland Gary and Andre Smith.

The Gators relied on their rushing core of Neal Anderson, Lorenzo Hampton, and John L. Williams. UF had a red-shirted freshman QB named Kerwin Bell.

On UF's second possession, Bell completed passes of 17 and 12 yards to Hampton. The Gators were on the GA 26. On third and one, Williams dove to the 25. Bell then hit Hampton for a 25-yard score. Raymond added the PAT and UF led 7-0.

After holding UF and forcing a punt, GA's Tony Flack fumbled the punt to the Gators on the GA 8. After a short rush and an incomplete pass, GA was called for pass interference, giving UF a first down on the GA 2. Two plays later, Anderson dove over the goal. Raymond made the PAT and the Gators were ahead 14-0.

In the third quarter, the only scoring was a 34-yard FG by Raymond. UF led 17-0.

Late in the third quarter, starting from their own 30, GA's Smith rushed 3 times for 38 yards. Todd Williams, the new GA QB, then hit Cassius Osborn for 18 yards. David McCluskey ran for 10 more. After two offside penalties, GA was on the UF 2. Smith pushed to the one. Gary was hit in the backfield for no gain. Tony Mangram rushed for the goal and was leveled behind the line. The Gators seemed to be in the backfield before the GA backs were even handed the ball. GA tried one more play, Williams handed off to Smith…he never made it back to the line.

UF had successfully made one of the series' finest goal line stands. Now, they found themselves trying to get out of their own end zone. After pushing the ball out to the four, Bell hit Nattiel, who had run by all GA defenders, for a 96-yard touchdown pass. Raymond's PAT was good and UF now led 27-0.

UF went on to beat Kentucky and win the SEC crown. They beat FSU in their final game to end the year 9-1-1, but NCAA sanctions made the Gators ineligible for postseason play and SEC members voted to strip UF of its first-ever conference crown.

1985

•Soviet leader Chernenko dies at 73 and is replaced by Mikhail Gorbachev, 54. Under the slogans of glasnost and Perestroika, Gorbachev initiates a broad program of reform and liberalization • Two Shi'ite Muslim gunmen capture TWA airliner with 133 aboard, 104 of them Americans; 39 remaining hostages freed in Beirut • PLO terrorists hijack Achille Lauro, Italian cruise ship, with 80 passengers, plus crew; American, Leon Klinghoffer, killed; Italian government toppled by political crisis over hijacking • Reagan and Gorbachev meet at summit; agree to step up arms control talks and renew cultural contacts • Terrorists seize Egyptian Boeing 737 airliner after takeoff from Athens; 59 dead as Egyptian forces storm plane on Malta • Ronald Reagan, 73, takes

oath for second term as 40th President • General Westmoreland settles libel action against CBS • US Supreme Court, 5-4, bars public school teachers from parochial schools • Arthur James Walker, 50, retired naval officer, convicted by federal judge of participating in Soviet spy ring operated by his brother, John Walker • US budget-balancing bill enacted.
Super Bowl   San Francisco d. Miami (38-16)
World Series   KC d. St. Louis Cardinals (4-3)
NBA Championship   LA Lakers d. Boston (4-2)
Kentucky Derby Champion   *Spend A Buck*
NCAA Basketball Championship
Villanova d. Georgetown (66-64)
NCAA Football Champions   Oklahoma (11-1-0)
Academy Award, Best Picture: Amadeus
Record of the Year: "What's Love Got to Do With It,"
Tina Turner Album of the Year: Can't Slow Down,
Lionel Richie Song of the Year: "What's Love Got to Do With It"
• Rock Hudson dies of AIDS at age 59. He's the first major star to fall victim to the disease • Madonna launches her first road show, the Virgin Tour •Dozens of top-name musicians and bands perform at the Live Aid concerts in Philadelphia and London. The shows benefit African famine victims • With the availability of relatively inexpensive laser printers and computers, tools for desktop publishing begin to be commonly used.
Movies: Kiss of the Spider Woman, Out of Africa, Prizzi's Honor, The Color Purple
• British scientists report the opening of an enormous hole in the earth's ozone layer over Antarctica.
• Researchers at IBM develop the scanning tunneling microscope, which can visualize images on an atomic scale • Coca-Cola attempts to change its 99-year-old formula in an effort to attract younger drinkers. "New" Coke is poorly received, and the company soon reintroduces the original, "Classic" beverage.

The Game: 1985 GA-24 UF-3

My how things change in time. UF was ranked NO 1 in the nation with a 7-0-1 record. They had an 18 game winning streak going into the GA game. They were in the process of serving two years' NCAA probation; no live television, loss of scholarships, and no conference title or postseason bowl game. UF followed Kerwin Bell, and they well should. He was leading an offense that was averaging 392 yards per game. Running Backs Neal Anderson and John L. Williams had rushed for a combined 1364 yards, and All-American linebacker Alonzo Johnson led the Gator defense, ranked seventh in the nation.

The Bulldogs followed QB James Jackson, the MVP of the 1984 Citrus Bowl. The Bulldog running backs included Lars Tate, Keith Henderson, and Tim Worley.

GA took the fight to the Gators. On his first rush of the game, FB Keith Henderson went 76 yards for the score. Crumley kicked the PAT, and GA was on its way.

GA held the touted UF offense in check. GA's next posession saw Worley running for 16 yards to the UF 32. Henderson took the ball through the UF defense and dove over the flag in the corner of the end zone for his second TD. Crumley's PAT made it 14-0. UF drove with a series of short Bell passes into GA territory, but when the GA defense stiffened, Dawson's FG attempt went wide right.

It wasn't until Nattiel returned a Carpenter punt 3 yards to the GA 30 that Dawson finally broke the ice and connected on a 46-yard FG. Now the scoreboard read, GA 14 UF 3.

GA started their next drive from their own 8 late in the second quarter. Tate was handed the ball and he promptly broke through the UF line and scampered 40 yards. The new GA QB Johnson then hit Fred Lane for another 17 yards. With seconds left in the half, Crumley kicked a 32-yard FG to give GA a lead of 17-3 at the half.

No GA team had ever beaten a top-ranked team before, and now they only had one more half to complete to do so.

GA stopped the UF rushers and Bell passed almost every play. Even with his completions, UF could not get in scoring range. GA rested on the superb punting of Carpenter to keep UF pinned deep in their own territory.

With around seven minutes left in the game, Bell drove the Gators inside the GA 10, but the drive died when Williams fumbled at the GA 8 and Steve Boswell gathered it up.

At the five minute mark, a second down run by Tim Worley broke the Gator's back. Worley took a pitchout and swept to the right, following his blocking. UF was bunched up in a short-yardage defense and could only watch as Worley broke free and ran 49 yards to score. Crumley's PAT made it 24-3. UF's hopes for a national championship was going out with the tide.

Chris Weaver, or as UF students knew him, "Albert the Alligator," the UF mascot was beaten by a mob of Georgia students and had his costume ripped off.

GA's rushing totaled 344 yards, while UF was held to 28. Bell completed 33 or 49 passes for 408 yards, but it was not enough to lift the Gators to victory.

crown. They beat FSU in their final game to end the year 9-1-1, but NCAA sanctions made the Gators ineligible for postseason play and SEC members voted to strip UF of its first-ever conference crown.

1986

Spain and Portugal join European Economic Community • President Reagan freezes Libyan assets in US. US planes attack Libyan "terrorist centers" • Haitian President Jean-Claude Duvalier flees to France • President Ferdinand Marcos flees Philippines after ruling for 20 years; newly elected Corazon Aquino succeeds him • Union Carbide agrees to settlement with victims of Bhopal gas leak in India • Major nuclear accident at Soviet Union's Chernobyl power station alarms world • Ex-Navy analyst, Jonathan Jay Pollard, 31, guilty as spy for Israel • World Court rules US broke international law by mining Nicaraguan waters • US Supreme Court bars racial bias in trial jury selection • Space shuttle Challenger explodes after launch at Cape Canaveral, Fla., killing all seven aboard • US Supreme Court reaffirms abortion rights • Senate Judiciary Committee approves William H. Rehnquist as Chief Justice of US Supreme Court • House votes arms appropriations bill rejecting Administration's "star wars" policy • Secret initiative to send arms to Iran revealed; Reagan denies exchanging arms for hostages and halts arms sales; diversion of funds from arms sales to Nicaraguan Contras revealed.
Super Bowl Chicago d. New England (46-10)
World Series NY Mets d. Boston Red Sox (4-3)
NBA Championship Boston d. Houston (4-2)
Kentucky Derby Champion *Ferdinand*
NCAA Basketball Championship L'ville d. Duke (72-69)
NCAA Football Champions Penn St. (12-0-0)
Best Picture: Out of Africa
Record of the Year: "We Are the World," USA for Africa Album of the Year: No Jacket Required, Phil Collins Song of the Year: "We Are the World"
• Barry Diller, head of News Corp., creates Fox, the fourth television network. Fox offers 10 hours of prime-time programming a week. • The Television Bureau of Advertising announces that the average American household watches television for more than seven hours a day • The Oprah Winfrey Show gets national television • The Academic American Encyclopedia is available on CD-ROM. It is the first reference work published in this medium. • Nintendo video games introduced in U.S.
Movies: Platoon, Hannah and Her Sisters, The Color of Money, The Mission
• Dick Rutan and Jeana Yeager make the first non-stop flight around the world without refueling. The Voyager flew around the world (24,986 miles) from Edwards AFB, California, returning in 216 hours, 3 minutes, and 44 seconds • The first genetically-engineered vaccine, for hepatitis B, gains FDA approval.

• The Voyager 2 probe passes Uranus in January, returning images and data on its moon, rings, atmosphere, interior, and magnetic field.
• Halley's comet yields information on return visit.

The Game: 1986 UF-31 GA-19

It was the year of Jan Kemp, a coordinator in GA's developmental studies program and the suit she had filed claiming her dismissal from school resulted from her protesting preferential treatment being received of some students over others, namely athletes. She was awarded $2.57 million in damages as well as being reinstated at the university. GA along with many other universities began reassessing their academic standards for student athletes.

The other main concern with this year's game was that of the injured players. UF's Bell had been out of action for the past month with a sprained knee. GA running backs Tim Worley and Keith Henderson were expected to miss this year's game with knee injuries. GA was relying on QB James Jackson, who had tossed for 1353 yards so far this season and Lars Tate to be the ground workhorse. Besides Bell, UF was concerned with an injury to Ricky Nattiel, who had separated his shoulder against Auburn.

GA was 3-1 in the SEC and trying for another crown, while UF was sitting near the bottom with a 1-3 record.

Because of the celebrating by GA fans after last year's game, there were around 400 law enforcement types assigned to the stadium and surrounding parking lots. With the stricter enforcing of the alcoholic beverage ban in the stadium, many considered the game changed from the "world's largest outdoor cocktail party" to the "North Florida Milk and Cookie Festival." So the stands were filled with 82,000 fairly sober fans.

GA began the game with a 13-play drive starting at their own 32. Tate carried eight time. Jackson tossed to John Thomas for 15 yards, then hit Troy Sadowski for another 12. Tate scored on a sweep right. Crumley kicked the PAT and GA led 7-0.

GA held UF to three and out and began another drive down the field. After 11 plays, they were at the UF 7 yard line, but could move no further. Crumley came in and kicked a 24-yard FG. GA now led 10-0. UF then drove from its own 26 on 11 plays down to the GA 6. When the push stalled, Dawson kicked a 23-yard FG. UF was on the board. 10-3.

GA used eight plays to get to the UF 19. Crumley was called on again and he booted a 35-yard FG, stretching GA's lead to 13-3.

Miles Smith intercepted a Bell pass on the UF 34, killing the Gators' next drive. Crumley then kicked a 45-yard FG and GA led 16-3.

Bell answered with an assortment of passes that moved the Gators down to the GA 8. Nattiel, who had just entered the game, beat GA's cornerback Williams for an 8 yard TD. Dawson's PAT cut GA's lead to 16-10.

Late in the third quarter, GA marched 47 yards. Crumley was called on again. His 43 yard FG made the score 19-10.

Bell began to thin out the GA defense. GA was going to live or die by the blitz. Bell would make them die. He steered the Gators from their own 23 down to the GA 9. Nattiel again psyched the man-on-man coverage and caught his second TD pass. GA 19 UF 17.

After a 35 yard kick-off return by Henderson, Tate was leveled by UF linebacker Arthur White and fumbled the ball away to the Gators at the GA 41. In five plays, UF was on the GA 3. On the first play of the fourth quarter, UF's James Massey slid through and over the goal line, giving UF their first lead of the game. Dawson made it 24-19.

At the seven minute mark, UF began driving from their own 33. In four plays the ball was on the GA 42. Nattiel caught the next pass and didn't quit running till he was out of field. Dawson's PAT made the score UF 31 GA 19

1987

• William Buckley, American hostage in Lebanon, reported slain • Iraqi missiles kill 37 in attack on US frigate Stark in Persian Gulf ; Iraqi president Hussein apologizes • Prime Minister Thatcher wins rare third term in Britain • Klaus Barbie, 73, Gestapo wartime chief in Lyon, sentenced to life by French court for war crimes • US Supreme Court rules Rotary Clubs must admit women • US Supreme Court Justice Lewis F. Powell, Jr., retires • Oliver North, Jr., tells Congressional inquiry higher officials approved his secret Iran-Contra operations • Admiral John M. Poindexter, former National Security Adviser, testifies he authorized use of Iran arms sale profits to aid Contras • George P. Shultz testifies he was deceived repeatedly on Iran-Contra affair • Defense Secretary Caspar W. Weinberger tells inquiry of official deception and intrigue • Reagan says Iran arms-Contra policy went astray and accepts responsibility • Senate, 58-42, rejects Robert H. Bork as US Supreme Court Justice
Super Bowl NY Giants d. Denver (39-20)
World Series Minnesota d. St. Louis Cardinals (4-3)
NBA Championship LA Lakers d. Boston (4-2)
Kentucky Derby Champion *Alysheba*
NCAA Basketball Championship
Indiana d. Syracuse (74-73)
NCAA Football Champions Miami-FL (12-0-0)
Best Picture: Platoon Record of the Year: "Higher Love," Steve Winwood Album of the Year: Graceland, Paul Simon Song of the Year: "That's What Friends Are For"
• Though African, Latin American and other genres of international music have been around for centuries, a group of small, London-based labels coin the term "world music," which helps record sellers find rack space for the eclectic music • thirtysomething debuts on ABC and departs from typical dramas, featuring analytical, self-absorbed baby-boomer characters.
Movies: Moonstruck, Wall Street, The Last Emperor, Fatal Attraction
• Prozac released for use in US by Eli Lilly & Company • AZT wins FDA approval for use in the treatment of AIDS • An international treaty signed in Montreal calls for a 50% reduction in the use of CFCs by the year 2000 • Richard Branson and Per Lindstrand make the first transatlantic hot-air balloon flight. 2,790 miles from Sugarloaf Mountain, Maine, to Ireland Virgin Atlantic Flyer.

The Game: 1987 GA-23 UF-10

82,000 crammed the Gator Bowl for the WTBS-nationally televised game. Ocean breezes could play havoc with the passing and kicking games. UF QB Kerwin Bell was a pre-season Heisman favorite, but freshman RB Emmitt Smith was getting all the news-play this year.

In just his seventh game, Smith surpassed the 1,000 yard mark, earlier than any other freshman in college football history.

GA relied on Lars Tate and freshman Rodney Hampton to carry their multi-quarterback line up. QB James Johnson could run, but could not run the offensive machine. Wayne Johnson, his back-up was seeing more and more playing time.

GA was 6-2 and tied with Clemson in the No. 10 spot. In the SEC, they were 3-1 and had the top rushing game in the conference, averaging 290 yards a game. UF (5-3) was ranked No.17 in the nation and carried a 2-2 SEC record. UF's defense ranked near the top in the SEC allowing less than 100 yards a game rushing and under 12 points scored on them.

On the Gators' first possession, moved to the GA 42 in five plays, but their drive stalled there. With the wind at their backs, Coach Hall called on Robert McGinty to kick a 52-yard FG. Early on UF led 3-0. Later in the first quarter, having their drive stall, GA's David Dukes dropped a punt into the "coffin corner," pinning UF in on their own 2. GA kept the Gators right there, forcing UF's Jamie McAndrews to punt. A 29-yard punt gave GA a first down on the UF 34.

Behind the running of Hampton and Tate, and a face mask penalty, GA was deep in the UF portion of the field. Tate ran through four defenders and ended up near the goal line. He then shoved his way into the end zone. John Kasay's PAT was good and GA led 7-3.

GA shut down Smith and forced Bell to pass. Here's where the wind comes in. A Bell pass thrown into that wind was intercepted by GA's Ben Smith at the GA 29. A 10-play drive featuring runs by Tate, Hampton, and Johnson got the Dogs down to the UF 34. With the wind at his back, Crumley came on and kicked a 51-yard FG, the longest of his career. GA now led 10-3. As the half ended, the GA defense walked the tallest off the field. Emmitt Smith had been held to 26 yards rushing for the first half. Bell had been sacked three times, and was rushed on every play.

In the third period, Bell had successfully, behind the running of Smith and Wayne Williams, driven the Gators down to the GA 29. There he attempted a pass that Ben Smith intercepted on the GA 22. GA drove to the Gator 19 on the running of Hampton and Tate. Kasay kicked a 35-yard FG into the wind, to make the score, 13-3.

After a UF fumble on their own 34, GA drove to the UF 1. A delay of game backed them up to the six, where Crumley kicked a 21-yard FG to make the score 16-3. UF was to have the ball only three minutes in the fourth period.

GA drove 44-yards to the UF 1. This time, Tate broke through for the score. With Kasay's PAT, GA now led 23-3 with just over two minutes left in the game.

On the kick-off, UF's Wayne Williams returned it 70 yards. Bell then hit Stacey Simmons for 17 yards and the score. McGinty's PAT made it 23-10.

Hampton ran for 103 yards. Tate for 89. UF's Smith was held to 46 yards on 13 attempts. Bell was sacked four times for lossese totalling 41 yards and was intercepted twice.

1988

• US and Canada reach free trade agreement
• Terrorists kill nine tourists on Aegean cruise
• Benazir Bhutto, first Islamic woman prime minister, chosen to lead Pakistan • Pan-Am 747 explodes from terrorist bomb and crashes in Lockerbie, Scotland, killing all 259 aboard and 11 on ground
• Robert C. McFarlane, former National Security Adviser, pleads guilty in Iran-Contra case • US Navy ship shoots down Iranian airliner in Persian Gulf, mistaking it for jet fighter; 290 killed • Democratic convention nominates Gov. Michael Dukakis of Massachusetts for President and Texas Senator Lloyd Bentsen for Vice President • Republican convention nominates George Bush for President and Indiana Senator Dan Quayle for Vice President
• Republicans sweep 40 states in election, and Bush beats Dukakis
Super Bowl   Washington d. Denver (42-10)
World Series   LA Dodgers d. Oakland A's (4-1)
NBA Championship   LA Lakers d. Detroit Pistons (4-3)
Kentucky Derby Champion   *Winning Colors*
NCAA Basketball Championship
Kansas d. Oklahoma (83-79)
NCAA Football Champions   Notre Dame (12-0-0)
Best Picture: The Last Emperor
Record of the Year: "Graceland," Paul Simon
Album of the Year: Joshua Tree, U2
Song of the Year: "Somewhere Out There" • Ninety-eight percent of U.S. households have at least one television set • CDs outsell vinyl records for the first time • Ted Turner starts Turner Network Television (TNT) and buys MGM's film library.
Movies: Rain Man, Mississippi Burning, A Fish Called Wanda, Bull Durham
• France and China permit first use of "morning-after" birth-control drug RU486 (Mifepristone) • NASA scientist James Hansen warns congress of the dangers of the global warming and the greenhouse effect.

The Game: 1988 GA-26 UF-3

It was less than a week before VP George Bush and challenger Michael Dukakis would face off for the presidency. Thunderstorms blanketed Jacksonville the night before the game, but the sun came out an hour before kick-off. 82,000 were there to see the game in person and many more content to watch it on WTBS.

Anyone entering the stadium was searched for alcoholic beverages. "obscene" bumper stickers were not allowed. One reported stated, "Despite the best efforts to control alcohol at the gate, the entire stadium had the unmistakable smell of bourbon."

UF, after starting off 5-0, was now 5-3, dropping out of national ranking. GA was 6-2 and tied with Auburn at 4-1 for the SEC crown. The UF defense was nicknamed "the Great Wall," ranked second in the nation, giving up only 226 yards per game. GA, behind Worley and Hampton, averaged close to 425 yards in offense and led the SEC in rushing.

In the first quarter, UF stopped Worley and GA stopped Smith. GA did drive down to the UF 37, where Kasay kicked a 47-yard FG. GA led 3-0.

In the second quarter, UF QB Morris was intercepted by GA's Demetrius Douglas, returning the ball to the UF 35. In four plays, GA was on the UF 22. QB Wayne Johnson then hit John Thomas with a 22-yard TD pass. Kasay kicked the PAT and GA led 10-0. Late in the third quater, UF drove to the GA 27. When the drive petered out, J.D. Francis kicked a 44-yard FG to put UF on the board. The score was now 10-3.

After a short kick-off, GA drove down the field. Johnson passed for 11 yards to Henderson. Hampton rumbled for 17 yards. Johnson ran for 11 to the UF 5. On the first play of the fourth quarter, Worley broke the plane of the goal line. Kasay missed the PAT and the score was now 16-3, GA.

A UF pass hit the intended receiver Mark McGriff in the helmet and was caught on the rebound by GA's Douglas at the UF 38. Three plays later, Kasay hit a 45-yard FG. GA was now up 19-3.

After the kickoff, UF drove near mid-field, where Morris fumbled with GA's Wycliffe Lovelace recovering. On GA's third play in this series, Worley ran 51 yards for his second TD. Kasay's PAT made it 26-3.

Dooley described the game as the most complete game the team had played all year. Emmitt Smith was held to 68 yards rushing. Worley had rushed for 135 yards and had scored two TDs. GA lost the next week to Auburn, losing the SEC crown, but beat GA. Tech, giving Coach Dooley his 200th victory.

This would be Vince Dooley's last GA-UF game. He would retire at the end of this season and would name Ray Goff as the new head coach.

1989

• US planes shoot down two Libyan fighters over international waters in Mediterranean • Iran's Ayatollah Khomeini declares author SalmanRushdie's book The Satanic Verses offensive and sentences him to death • Tens of thousands of Chinese students take over Beijing's Tiananmen Square in rally for democracy. More than one million in Beijing demonstrate for democracy; chaos spreads across nation. Thousands killed in Tiananmen Square as Chinese leaders take hard line toward demonstrators.
• Mikhail S. Gorbachev named Soviet President
• P. W. Botha quits as South Africa's President
• Deng Xiaoping resigns from China's leadership
• After 28 years, Berlin Wall is open to West • Czech Parliament ends Communists' dominant role
• Romanian uprising overthrows Communist government; President Ceausescu and wife executed • US troops invade Panama, seeking capture of General Manuel Noriega • George Herbert Walker Bush inaugurated as 41st US President • Ruptured tanker Exxon Valdez sends 11 million gallons of crude oil into Alaska's Prince William Sound • US jury convicts Oliver North in Iran-Contra affair • Army Gen. Colin R. Powell is first black Chairman of Joint

Chiefs of Staff
Super Bowl   San Francisco d. Cincinnati (20-16)
World Series   Oakland A's d. SF Giants (4-0)
NBA Championship Detroit Pistons d. LA Lakers (4-0)
Kentucky Derby Champion   *Sunday Silence*
NCAA Basketball Championship
Michigan d. Seton Hall (80-79 OT)
NCAA Football Champions   Miami-FL (11-1-0)
Best Picture: Rain Man
Record of the Year: "Don't Worry Be Happy," Bobby McFerrin   Album of the Year: Faith, George Michael
Song of the Year: "Don't Worry Be Happy," Bobby McFerrin
• America's beloved comedienne Lucille Ball dies at age 87 • Visionary Jaron Lanier coins the term virtual reality and produces the equipment to experience it. Movies: Glory, Born on the Fourth of July, My Left Foot, Sex, Lies, and Videotape, Field of Dreams
• Human gene transfer developed by Steven Rosenberg, R. Michael Blaese, and W. French Anderson • First World Wide Web server and browser developed by Tim Berners-Lee while working at CERN • Peter Deutsch of McGill University who devlops Archie, an archive of FTP sites, the first effort to index the Internet. Another indexing system WAIS (Wide Area Information Server), is developed by Brewster Kahle of Thinking Machines Corp.
• Voyager 2 speeds by Neptune after making startling discoveries about the planet and its moons

The Game: 1989 GA-17 UF-10

UF was 6-2, but Galen Hall resigned due to the investigation by the NCAA and a grand jury into illegal payments made to assistant coaches and arranging that money be given to a player to help make child support payments. Many felt the NCAA would impose penalties on the school. No one knew how extreme the penalties might be. Ray Goff had GA at 5-3 and was trying to live up to Dooley's traditions. UF's Gary Darnell was just trying to hold the UF team together.

81,500 + fans filled the Gator Bowl. It was a Sunny Saturday. Avid fans were tossing toy bulldogs and to alligators at each other. Just another day on the ol' gridiron.

UF's Douglas and GA's Talley were harassed by the opposing defenses for the first period.

GA broke out in the second period, driving to the UF 26, where Kasay kicked a FG. GA 3 UF 0.

In the closing minutes of the first half, UF's Douglas hit Ernie Mills for a 37-yard gain. Four plays later, they were on the GA 19, were Douglas again found Mills in the end zone. With Francis's PAT, UF led 7-3.

GA held Smith. UF picked off Talley. UF fumbled a pass back to GA. Starting at their own 24, GA behind a sweeping Hampton moved to the 47. On a third and inches play, Talley's intended pass dribbled off his hand, towards Hampton in the GA backfield. He caught it and ran the ball down to the UF 15. Two plays later, Hampton drove the ball into the end zone. Kasay's PAT gave GA a 10-7 lead.

UF's Douglas was intercepted on the next drive by GA's Ben Smith at the UF 37. Talley hit Kevin Maxwell for 15 yards. A personal foul penalty and rushes by Hampton gave GA another TD. Kasay made it 17-7.

Late in the fourth quarter, Lex Smith came in to QB UF. He quickly completed six passes for 66 yards, and had the Gators on the GA 8. From there, Francis kicked a FG, narrowing the score to 17-10.

Hampton outgained Smith 121 to 106. The other GA rushers accounted for a minus 18 yards.

Emmitt Smith was named SEC Player of the Year and First-Team All-American. GA finished 6-6. UF finished at 7-5.

Gators 80

NOV. 8, 1980
FLORIDA VS. GEORGIA
$1.50

1980 · UGA 26 UFL 21

Vs. Florida/Jacksonville, Fl./Gator Bowl/Nov. 7, 1981 $1⁵⁰

1981 · UGA 26   UFL 21

GATOR BOWL   NOVEMBER 6, 1982 $2.00

FLORIDA
GEORGIA

1982 · UGA 44 UFL 0

$2.00

GEORGIA

THE FLORIDA GAME

Nov. 5, 1983
Gator Bowl
Jacksonville, FL

1983 · UGA 10 UFL 9

GATOR!

THE GEORGIA GAME

GATOR BOWL   NOVEMBER 10, 1984 $2

1984 • UFL 27 UGA 0

GEORGIA vs FLORIDA

GATOR BOWL • JACKSONVILLE, FLORIDA • NOVEMBER 9, 1985 • $2.00

1985 • UGA 24 UFL 3

FLORIDA VS. GEORGIA

GATOR BOWL · JACKSONVILLE
NOVEMBER 8 1986 $2.50

1986 · UFL 31 UGA 19

GEORGIA vs FLORIDA

NOVEMBER 7, 1987 / MAZDA GATOR BOWL STADIUM / JACKSONVILLE, FLORIDA

$2.00

WE ♥ JACKSONVILLE

1987 · UGA 23 UFL 10

FLORIDA

THE GEORGIA GAME

1988 • UGA 26 UFL 3

$3.00

THE GEORGIA-FLORIDA GAME

November 11, 1989 / The Gator Bowl / Jacksonville, Florida

1989 • UGA 17 UFL 10

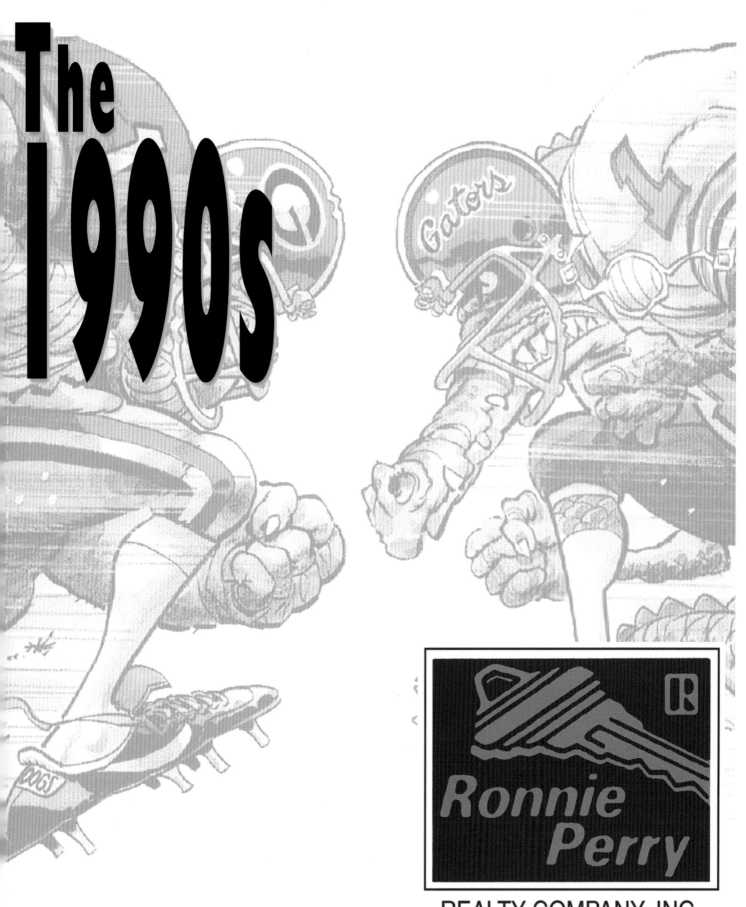

The 1990s

Ronnie Perry
REALTY COMPANY, INC.
912-267-0006 fax 912-265-3350

1990

• General Manuel Noriega surrenders in Panama • Yugoslav Communists end 45-year monopoly of power • Communist Party relinquish sole power in Soviet government • South Africa frees Nelson Mandela, imprisoned 27 years • US-Soviet summit reaches accord on armaments • Western Alliance ends Cold War and proposes joint action with Soviet Union and Eastern Europe • Iraqi troops invade Kuwait, setting off the Persian Gulf War • East and West Germany reunited • Margaret Thatcher resigns as British Prime Minister; John Major succeeds her • Lech Walesa wins Poland's runoff Presidential election • US Supreme Court upsets law banning flag burning • US Appeals Court overturns Oliver North's Iran-Contra conviction • Republicans set back in midterm elections
Super Bowl   San Franc. d. Denver (55-10)
World Series   Cincinnati d. Oakland A's (4-0)
NBA Championship   Detroit d. Portland (4-1)
Kentucky Derby Champion   *Unbridled*
NCAA Basketball Championship
UNLV d. Duke (103-73)
NCAA Football Champions
Colorado (AP, FW, NFF) (11-1-1)
& Georgia Tech (UPI) (11-0-1)
Academy Award, Best Picture: Driving Miss Daisy Record of the Year: "Wind Beneath My Wings," Bette Midler
Album of the Year: Nick of Time, B. Raitt
Song of the Year: "Wind Beneath My Wings"
•The X rating is replaced by NC-17 (no children under 17) • Ninety-nine percent of U.S. households have at least one radio, with the average owning five • The Simpsons debuts on Fox and becomes an instant hit • Euro dance band Milli Vanilli admits to lip-synching hits such as "Girl You Know Its True," and has its Grammy award revoked.
• Seinfeld debuts on NBC • Entertainment Weekly hits newsstands.
Movies: Dances with Wolves, GoodFellas, Henry and June, Reversal of Fortune
• The Hubble Space Telescope is launched
• President Bush signs the Clean Air Act, mandating a variety of pollution-reducing changes in the automobile and fuel industries
• The FDA approves use of the surgically-implanted contraceptive Norplant.

The Game: 1990 UF-38 GA-7

81,259 fans braved winds bringing the temperature down to a cold 44 degrees. Troops had been sent to the Middle East and a "war" with Iraq seemed on the way.

It was Steve Spurrier's first year as Head Coach of UF and the Gators were ranked NO.10.

UF was 7-1 with the second ranked defense in the country. The NCAA had given the Gators a one-year probation, keeping them from going to a bowl game or winning the conference.

GA was 4-4 and faced oddsmakers giving an 18-point spread favoring the Gators in this year's game.

UF drove the opening kick-off to the GA 17 before a fumble by McClendon gave the Dogs the ball. On GA's second play, Alphonso Ellis fumbled the ball back to UF on the GA 15. After three rushes towards the goal, McClendon held onto the ball and fell into the end zone. Arden Czyzewski kicked the PAT and UF led 7-0.

In their next series, GA's Talley threw to Sean Hummings at the GA 36. The ball hit him in the shoulder pads and was intercepted by UF's Tim Paulk, who ran it back into the end zone. Czyzewski kicked the PAT and UF now led 14-0.

After stuffing the Dogs, UF drove to the GA 1, where QB Matthews fumbled, giving the ball back to GA. On a seven-play drive, Talley hit Maxwell for 22 yards, Chris Broom for 25 yards, and after a 15-yard pass interference call, hit Andre Hastings for the final 23 yards and the score. Kasay made it 14-7.

Matthews then threw UF 67 yards down the field with passes to Kirkpatrick and McClendon. From the GA 23, Czyzewski kicked a FG. UF now led 17-7.

After a bungled kickoff, GA had the ball at their own 6. Talley tried a short pass, but the wind caught the ball and UF's Richard Fain intercepted it and stepped out of bounds inside the GA 6.

Two plays and Matthews hit Ernie Mills for a TD. Czyzewski's PAT put UF ahead 24-7. GA couldn't get a first down in the third quarter. In that period, UF ran a flea-flicker where Matthews pitched to Rhett who handed he ball back to Matthews who passed to Barber all alone at the GA 5 who easily scored. Czyzewski's PAT made it 31-7.

Late in the third period, UF started on its own 46. Matthews passed to Duncan for 17 and to Kirkpatrick for 12. Then Matthews hit Mills for a 16-yard TD. Czyzewski kicked the PAT and UF now led 38-7.

Matthews threw for 344 yards with three touchdowns. He was named 1990 SEC Player of the Year.

1991

• Cease-fire ends Persian Gulf War; UN forces are victorious • Europeans end sanctions on South Africa. South African Parliament repeals apartheid laws • France agrees to sign 1968 treaty banning spread of atomic weapons. China accepts nuclear nonproliferation treaty. Bush-Gorbachev summit negotiates strategic arms reduction treaty • Communist Government of Albania resigns • Warsaw Pact dissolved • Boris Yeltsin becomes first freely elected president of Russian Republic. Yeltsin's stock increases when he takes a prominent role in suppressing an anti-Gorbachev coup by communist hardliners • Lithuania, Estonia, and Latvia win independence from USSR; US recognizes them • Haitian troops seize president in uprising. US suspends assistance to Haiti • US indicts two Libyans in 1988 bombing of Pan Am Flight 103 over Lockerbie, Scotland • Soviet Union breaks up after President Gorbachev's resignation; constituent republics form Commonwealth of Independent States • US Supreme Court limits death row appeals • William H. Webster retires as Director of CIA; Robert H. Gates succeeds him • Professor Anita Hill accuses Judge Clarence Thomas of sexual harassment; Senate, 52-48, confirms Thomas for US Supreme Court after stormy hearings.
Super Bowl   NY Giants d. Buffalo (20-19)
World Series   Minn. d. Atlanta Braves (4-3)
NBA Championship   Chic. d. LA Lakers (4-1)
Kentucky Derby Champion   *Strike the Gold*
NCAA Basketball Championship
Duke d. Kansas (72-65)

NCAA Football Champions
Miami-FL (AP) (12-0-0) &
Washington (USA, FW, NFF) (12-0-0)
Best Picture: Dances With Wolves
Record of the Year: "Another Day in Paradise, Phil Collins Album of the Year: Back on the Block, Quincy Jones (Qwest/Warner Bros.)
Song of the Year: "From a Distance" • Fox Broadcasting is the first network to permit con dom advertising on television • Seattle band Nirvana releases the song "Smells Like Teen Spirit" on the LP Nevermind and enjoys natio al success. With Nirvana's hit comes the grung movement, which is characterized by distorted guitars, dispirited vocals and lots of flannel.
• Paul Reubens (aka Pee Wee Herman) is arrested in a Florida movie theater for indecen exposure.
Movies: The Silence of the Lambs, Beauty an the Beast, JFK, Thelma & Louise
• Yugoslav Federation broken up. US recognizes three former Yugoslav republics. UN expels Serbian-dominated Yugoslavia • Bush and Yeltsin proclaim a formal end to the Cold War • US lifts trade sanctions against China • General Manuel Noriega, former leader of Panama, convicted in US court and sentenced to 40 years on drug charges • Russian Parliament approves START treaty • US force leave Philippines, ending nearly a century of American military presence • Czechoslovak Parliament approves separation into two natio • UN approves US-led force to guard food for Somalia • North American Free Trade Agreement (NAFTA) signed.

The Game: 1991 UF-45 GA-1:

Kick-off time for this year's game had bee moved by ESPN to 4PM and the 82,000 fans sat through one of the coldest games on reco with wind chill in the twenties.

UF's "Fun and Gun" offense had them at 7 1 and 5-0 in the SEC and ranked NO. 6 in th country. GA was 6-2 and 3-2 in the SEC. They were ranked NO. 23. Eric Zeier had replaced Tallery at QB and had responded with GA's first 300-yard passing game since 1963. The main weakness in this year's UF team was its pass defense. The strength was the passing of Matthews and the running of Rhett, McClendon, and Dexter McNabb.

UF took the kick-off and drove 75 yards v running by Rhett and Matthews passing to Jackson, Houston, and even to Rhett. Matthews hit Jackson in the corner of the end zone from the five. Czyzewski's PAT made i 7-0, right off the bat.

GA, behind Zeier, drove to the UF 25. Zeier's first pass of the day went to Andre Hastings, moving the ball and the chains to the UF 35. Hearst gained some ground, but Zeier was thrown for a loss. On fourth down Kanon Parkman kicked a 41-yard FG to put GA on the board. 7-3.

After exchanging punts, UF got the ball back on their own 29. Matthews hit McNabl over the middle and sped down to the GA 4. Duncan caught a first down pass at the 26. Matthews hit Sullivan for another first down on the 13. Rhett blasted it into the end zone the next play.

Czyzewski's PAT made the score 14-3 wit only 27 seconds gone in the second period. UF started next on their own 30. Matthews Sullivan for 13. Five plays later, he hit FB Randolph down on the GA 37. Matthews the hit Houston in the rear of the end zone for a TD.

Czyzewski's PAT extended UF's lead to 21-3. After holding GA, UF started off from their own 4. Rhett [ra]n to the 16. Rhett's running and short passes by [M]atthews brought the Gators out to their 39. [M]atthews then hit Sullivan, open on the sideline, who [t]hen raced untouched into GA's end zone for a 61-[y]ard TD. Czyzewski's PAT made it 28-3 with just [o]ver two minutes left in the second period.

In the final two minutes of the first half, GA drove [fr]om their 38 down to the UF 8, where the drive [st]alled. Parkman then kicked a 25-yard FG as time [r]an out. UF28 GA 6

GA's Hastings ran the second half kickoff back to [th]e GA 41. Zeier was bumped and fumbled the ball [o]ver to UF on the UF 49. Matthews, through runs [a]nd passes, moved the Gators to the GA 8, but the [D]ogs would not allow UF in the end zone. [C]zyzewski then kicked a 25-yard FG. UF now led [3]1-6.

GA started on their own 36 for what would be their [b]est drive of the day. On second down, Hearst caught [a] shovel pass from Zeier and ran 22 yards. Zeier [th]en passed to Marshall at the UF 19. After extending [th]e drive with penalties, Zeier hit Hastings in the end [z]one. Peterson's PAT made the score 31-13.

A missed UF FG after a sustained drive and a short [u]nsuccessful GA series gave UF the ball on the GA [3]7. On three rushes, McNabb got the Gators down to [th]e GA 24. Rhett ran the draw play down to the [G]A10. Matthews then hit Willie Jackson for a TD. [C]zyzewski's PAT was good. UF now led 38-13.

UF replacements filled the field. Brian Fox [re]placed Matthews and immediately steered the [G]ators into the GA end zone for a sixth time with a [p]ass to Jackson. Czyzewski's PAT was good and the [s]coreboard now read 45-13.

Matthews completed 22 of 32 attempts for 303 [y]ards and four touchdowns. Zeier was 18 of 35 for [3]95 yards and one touchdown.

1992

Four officers acquitted in Los Angeles beating of [R]odney King; violence erupts in Los Angeles [•] Caspar W. Weinberger indicted in Iran-Contra affair [•] US Supreme Court reaffirms right to abortion [•] Democratic convention nominates Bill Clinton and [A]l Gore • Court clears Exxon Valdez skipper (July [9]). Background: Oil Spills • Four police officers [in]dicted in Rodney King beating • Republicans [n]ominate Bush and Quayle • Senate ratifies second [st]rategic Arms Limitation Treaty • Bill Clinton elect-[e]d President, Al Gore Vice President; Democrats [ke]ep control of Congress•Bush pardons former [R]eagan Administration officials involved in Iran-[C]ontra affair.
[S]uper Bowl   Washington d. Buffalo (37-24)
[W]orld Series   Toronto d. Atlanta Braves (4-2)
[N]BA Championship Chicago d. Portland (4-2)
[K]entucky Derby Champion Lil E. Tee
[N]CAA Basketball Championship
[D]uke d. Michigan (71-51)
[N]CAA Football Champions Alabama (13-0-0)
[B]est Picture: The Silence of the Lambs
[R]ecord of the Year: "Unforgettable" Natalie Cole [w]ith Nat King Cole Album of the Year:Unforgettable, [N]atalie Cole with Nat King Cole   Song of the Year: [U]nforgettable"
[C]ompact discs surpass cassette tapes as the pre-[fe]rred medium for recorded music •There are 900 [m]illion television sets in use around the world; 201 [m]illion are in the United States • Woody Allen and [M]ia Farrow engage in a very public and nasty cus-[to]dy battle over their three children. Allen's affair [w]ith Farrow's adopted daughter, Soon-Yi Previn, [m]arked the feud • Johnny Carson hosts The Tonight [Sh]ow for the last time. He had ruled late-night televi-[si]on for 20 years.

Movies: Unforgiven, The Crying Game, Howards End, Glengarry Glen Ross, The Player

The Game: 1992 UF-26 GA-24

Halloween of '92 was to bring many tricks and treats. UF and GA had already experienced a year of "halloween" surprises. Coning in to the game, GA was 7-1 and ranked seventh in the nation behind the running of Garrison Hearst. Hearst was leading the nation in rushing and was running up number better than Herschel's.

UF, who had been expected to win the SEC crown again this year in an expanded field of competitors (South Carolina and Arkansas having been added to the SEC ranks and there would be a western and an eastern division of the conference whose leaders would play for the championship) came into the game at 4-2.

UF wasted no time going for the throat in this game. On their second play, Matthews threw 41 yards to Willie Jackson. UF drove to the GA 8 but had to settle for a Bart Edmiston FG. UF led 3-0.

UG wasted even less time with a little "treat" of their own. Zeier handed off to Frank Harvey who ran for 80 yards and a TD. Peterson's PAT gave the Dogs a 7-3 lead.

On GA's next possession, the Gators partially blocked a Scot Armstrong punt, knocking the ball out of bounds on the GA 39. Matthews, through a couple of pass completions, plus a face mask call against the dogs, and the running of Rhett, were soon back ahead, 10-3 after Rhett's plunge and Edminston's PAT.

GA was held on its next drive, UF wasn't. From their own 27, UF followed Matthews and Rhett back down the field again, ending when the UF QB hit Jack Jackson open for 9-yards and a TD. Edmiston missed the PAT and UF now led 16-7 with over eleven minutes remaining in the first half.

UF pressured and sacked Zeier the next GA series. Monty Duncan returned an Armstrong punt to the GA 38 and the Gators were in business again. Matthews hit Kevin Randolph for 12 and Rhett ran for eight before a pass was lofted to Willie Jackson in the end zone for another Gator score. Edmiston made it 23-7.

The GA offense now seemed to come to life. From the 20, Hearst ran out to the 31. Zeier hit Ha'son Graham for 18 more. A couple of runs and a couple of penalties moved the ball down to the UF 36. Zeier ended the brief offensive with an interception into the arms of UF's Ed Robinson. The fired up Dog Defense held the Gators and started their next drive from their own 38. Zeier found Hastings open across the middle on a screen pass down to the UF 37. Damon Evans caught Zeier's next pass on the UF 18. Zeier then hit Graham for the score. Peterson's PAT made the score UF 23, GA 14.

With just over three minutes left before half, GA wanted more. They held the Gators and Matthews and Rhett in check, causing a Gator punt. From their own 27, Zeier hit Hastings for 19 yards. Hearst was the target, catching the pass and running down to the UF 32 with 13 seconds remaining. Peterson then nailed a 49-yard FG to bring GA back within a TD. UF 23, GA 17.

On their first possession of the second half, UF drove from their 45 down to the GA 9, but a Rhett fumble, recoverd by GA's Greg Jackson stopped the UF drive. UF held GA and got the ball back. From his own 20, Matthews handed off to Rhett for 13 yards, then hit Chris Bilkie at the GA 41. Then he hit Hill for 17 more and Jackson for six more, down to the GA 18. Ga stiffened and Edmiston hit a 34-yard FG to make the score 26-17.

After ball exchanges and thwarted drives by both teams, GA got the ball back with just over five min-utes left on the clock. Zeier hit Hastings for 25 yards.

He then hit Hearst at the UF 45, Garrison streaked down the sidelines to the UF 24. Zeier then hit an outstretched Brian Bohannon in the end zone. With Peterson's PAT, GA trailed 26-24 with just over four minutes left to play. Now all the Dogs had to do was stop the Gators.

Matthews had other ideas. He drove his team against the fired up GA defense. After nudging the line and completing the necessary passes, UF watched GA call its final time out with just over two minutes left. Matthews then surprised the defense with a quarterback draw up the middle to achieve UF's final needed first down, allowing them to run out the clock.

Florida players, who taunted GA fans, found them-selves in the middle of a hale-storm of ice, cups and boos in the Georgia fans side of the end zone. Spurrier later said, "What our players did was just uncalled for. There is a lot of jawing in football games between players…but when players taunt the opposing team's fans, that's wrong."

UF's defense had held Hearst to 41 yards on 14 carries. Matthews completed 28 of 45 passes for 301 yards and two touchdowns. Zeier was 15 of 28 for 238 yards, two touchdowns, and two interceptions. UF (8-3) faced Alabama in the SEC's first conference championship game. Alabama won 28-21.

Tony Stastny of Savannah Newspress wrote. "Hearst may have left the Heisman on the floor of the Gator Bowl in late October. Playing the Gators, Hearst not only needed a big game personally, but Georgia needed a big game from him. Neither got what they wanted."

1993

• Vaclav Havel elected Czech President • British House of Commons approves European unity pact. Maastricht Treaty takes effect, creating European Union • Twenty-two UN troops killed in Somalia • Israeli-Palestinian accord reached • Yeltsin's forces crush revolt in Russian Parliament • China breaks nuclear test moratorium • South Africa adopts majori-ty rule constitution • Clinton agrees to compromise on military's ban on homosexuals • Federal agents besiege Texas Branch Davidian religious cult after six are killed in raid. Fire kills 72 as cult standoff in Texas ends with federal assault • Five arrested, sixth sought in bombing of World Trade Center in New York • Two police officers convicted in Los Angeles on civil rights charges in Rodney King beating • Ruth Bader Ginsburg appointed to Supreme Court • US agents blamed in Waco, Tex., siege • House of Representatives approves North American Free Trade Agreement ; Senate follows • Clinton signs Brady bill regulating firearms purchases .
Super Bowl   Dallas d. Buffalo (52-17)
World Series   Toronto d. Philadelphia Phillies (4-2)
NBA Championship   Chicago d. Phoenix (4-2)
Kentucky Derby Champion   Sea Hero
NCAA Basketball Championship NC d. Michigan (77-71)
NCAA Football Champions   Florida St. (12-1-0)
Best Picture: Unforgiven, Clint Eastwood
Record of the Year: "Tears in Heaven," Eric Clapton
Album of the Year: Unplugged, Eric Clapton
Song of the Year: "Tears in Heaven" Eric Clapton
•A 13-year-old Los Angeles boy accuses Michael Jackson of fondling him. Jackson vehemently denies the charge. The two parties reach an out-of-court set-tlement. • River Phoenix dies of a drug overdose on Halloween. He was 23 • Lost in Yonkers is edited on an Avid Media Composer system, the first non-linear editing system to allow viewing at film's required "real-time"-viewing rate of 24 frames per second. By converting film into digital bits, film can now be cut on a computer.
Movies: Schindler's List, The Piano, Philadelphia, Six Degrees of Separation, In the Name of the Father • Mosaic is developed by Marc Andreeson at the

National Center for Supercomputing Applications (NCSA). It becomes the dominant navigating system for the World Wide Web, which at this time accounts for only 1% of all Internet traffic • According to the World Health Organization (WHO), tuberculosis threatens to kill more than 30 million in the next decade. Background: Global Health Trends • The FDA approves the use of the synthetic hormone BST (bovine somatotropin) to increase milk production in dairy cows • First humans cloned. Cells taken from defective human embryos that were to be discarded in infertility clinic are grown in vitro and develop up to 32-cell stage and then are destroyed.

The Game: 1993 UF-33 GA-26

A rain-drenched crowd of 80,392 at the Gator Bowl watched Errict Rhett splash his way to 183 yards on a UF school-record 41 carries and a determined UF defense hold GA out of the endzone in the waning moments of the game as 10th ranked UF won their fourth in a row over GA.

In the first quarter, UF's Judd Davis hit a 29-yard FG after the Gators had driven 26 yards in seven plays. GA then drove 21 yards in five plays and Parkman hit a 22-yard FG.

UF's Rhett scored from nine yards out after the Gators drove 49 yards in 3 plays. Davis kicked the PAT. UF 10 GA 3. UF's Davis added another FG from 27 yards out after a 6 play, 26 yard drive with just 37 seconds remaining in the first quarter. UF 13 GA 3.

In the second quarter, GA behind Zeier drove 83 yards in 8 plays. Zeier then hit Hunter with a 2-yard TD pass. Parkman kicked the PAT. UF 13 GA 10.

GA held UF then began to drive again. This time they went 17 yards in five plays ending with a 6-yard TD pass from Zeier to Mitchell. Parkman kicked the PAT. UF 13 GA 17.

Once again GA held and drove again. The Dogs went 48 yards in 12 plays. When the drive stalled, Parkman kicked a 27-yard FG. UF 13 GA 20

UF drove 45 yards in ten plays with Davis kicking a 36-yard FG. UF 16 GA 20

With a little over minute remaining in the first half, T. Dean hit Houston with a 35-yard TD pass. Davis kicked the PAT and UF led, 23-20 at halftime.

In the third quarter UF scored on the longest drive of the game… a 21-play 80 yard drive with Rhett scoring from one yard out. Davis kicked the PAT and UF now led 30-20.

GA bounces back with a 10-play, 49 yard drive of its own ending up with a Parkman FG from 21 yards out. UF 30 GA 23.

UF drives 42 yards in 11 plays and Davis kicks a FG from 31 yards out. UF 33 GA 23.
GA added another field goal with 5:06 left in the game, then got the ball back at their own 36 with 1:36 on the clock and no time outs. UF 33 GA 26.

The Dogs drove to UF's 12 with five seconds to play. The Gators called a timeout, which they claim is just prior to the snap. The play goes through and Zeier hits Jerry Jerman in the endzone for an apparent TD, but the referees call the play back, saying time had been called by UF. The fans just go nuts…at least the GA fans.

At the two and with no time left on the clock, Zeier spots receiver Jeff Thomas in the endzone. His pass is slightly behind Thomas and the ball bounces off his hands as the game ends. Zeier set a GA single-game record with 36 completions out of 65 attempts. His total passing yardage was 386 yards. GA was held to 44 total rushing yards.

1994

• Serbs' heavy weapons pound Sarajevo • Thousands dead in Rwanda massacre • South Africa holds first interracial national election; Nelson Mandela elected President • Israel signs accord with Palestinians,

peace treaty with Jordan • IRA declares cease-fire in Northern Ireland • Ulster Protestants declare cease-fire • Aristide returns to Haiti, forms Government with Prime Minister and full Cabinet • US sends forces to Persian Gulf • Russians attack secessionist Republic of Chechnya • Olympic figure skater Nancy Kerrigan attacked; three arrested in attack • Aldrich Ames, high C.I.A. official, charged with spying for Soviets • Four convicted in World Trade Center bombing • Clinton accused of sexual harassment while Governor of Arkansas • O. J. Simpson arrested in killings of wife, Nicole Brown Simpson, and friend, Ronald Goldman • US Supreme Court approves limit on abortion protests • Senate confirms Stephen G. Breyer for Supreme Court • Major league baseball players strike • Newt Gingrich named House Speaker Super Bowl Dallas d. Buffalo (30-13) NBA Championship Houston d. New York (4-3) Kentucky Derby Champion *Go For Gin* NCAA Basketball Championship Ark. d. Duke (76-72) NCAA Football Champions Nebraska (13-0-0) Best Picture: Schindler's List Record of the Year: "I Will Always Love You," Whitney Houston   Album of the Year: The Bodyguard…Original Soundtrack Album, Whitney Houston Song of the Year: "A Whole New World" (Theme From Aladdin)
• Kurt Cobain kills himself. He was 27 • Ninety-five million viewers watch O. J. Simpson and Al Cowlings drive along Los Angeles freeways in history's most exciting low-speed chase • Steven Spielberg wins his first directing Oscar for Schindler's List • Woodstock '94 commemorates the original weekend-long concert. Green Day and Nine Inch Nails join Woodstock veterans Bob Dylan and the Allman Brothers • For the first time in history, chain bookstores outsell independent stores, signaling what many fear to be the death of smaller booksellers at the hands of superstores • Tom Hanks wins his second consecutive Best Actor Oscar. He won in 1993 for his role in Philadelphia and in 1994 for Forrest Gump • ER and Friends debut on NBC, establishing NBC's dominance of the Thursday-night lineup Movies: Forrest Gump, Pulp Fiction, The Shawshank Redemption, Quiz Show, Nobody's Fool
• White House launches Web page. Initial commerce sites are established and mass marketing campaigns are launched via email, introducing the term "spamming" to the Internet vocabulary.
• Dr. Ned First (US) clones calves from cells of early embryos • The FDA approves the Flavr Savr tomato, the first genetically-engineered food product

The Game: 1994 UF-52 GA-14

For the first time in 63 years, UF faced GA in Gainesville. 85,604 fans filled the Swamp to watch the number 5 ranked Gators take on the Dogs. The Gator defense was the winner in this game. They forced five turnovers and held GA to 31 yards rushing and a season low 14 points.

UF jumped to a 14-0 lead on a pair of first quarter TD passes from Dann Wuerfel to Chris Doering, one for 15 yards, the other for 25 yards. UF added a 19-yard FG by Davis in the second period for a 17-0 lead.

GA made its drive of the day, going 83 yards in 9 plays with Terrell Davis scoring from the one. Parkman's PAT made it 17-7.

UF took control of the game in the final 95 seconds of the first half as Ben Hanks forced a fumble after a pass completion to GA's Larry Bowie with Michael Gilmore picking up the loose ball and running 59 yards for the score. Davis kicked the PAT. UF 24 GA 7.

With GA driving, Darren Hambrick picked of a Zeier pass and ran 81 yards for the score in the final play of the first half. Davis kicked the PAT and UF led 31 to 7.

In the third period, GA drove 73 yards in 8 plays, with Zeier scoring from the three. Parkman kicked the PAT. UF 31 GA 14.

GA held UF, then deep in their own territory, Zeier is intercepted by James Bates who runs the ball in 9 yards for the TD. Davis kicked the PAT and UF led 38-14.

UF scored again after a 26-yard drive with Williams going the final yard. Davis' PAT made it 45-14.

In the fourth quarter, UF drove 51 yards in 11 plays with Taylor carrying it the final four yards for the score. Davis' PAT made it 52-14.

UF scored 3 defensive touchdowns a new school record. Zeier threw four interceptions.

1995

• US rescues Mexico's economy with $20-billion aid program • Russian space station Mir greets first Americans. US shuttle docks with station • Nerve gas attack in Tokyo subway kills eight and injures thousands. The Aum Shinrikyo ("Supreme Truth") cult is to blame • Death toll 2,000 in Rwanda massacre • Fighting escalates in Bosnia and Croatia. Warring parties agree on cease-fire; sign peace treaty • France explodes nuclear device in Pacific; wide protests ensue • Israelis and Palestinians agree on transferring West Bank to Arabs. Israeli Prime Minister Yitzhak Rabin slain by Jewish extremist at peace rally
• Criminal trial of O. J. Simpson opens in California • Scores killed as terrorist's car bomb blows up block long Oklahoma City federal building; Timothy McVeigh, 27, arrested as suspect; authorities seek second suspect, link right-wing paramilitary groups t bombing • Los Angeles jury finds O. J. Simpson not guilty of murder charges • Pope John Paul II visits US on whirlwind tour • Million Man March draws hundreds of thousands of black men to capital Super Bowl San Francisco d. San Diego (49-26) World Series Atlanta Braves d. Cleveland (4-2) NBA Championship Houston d. Orlando (4-0) Kentucky Derby Champion *Thunder Gulch* NCAA Basketball Championship UCLA d. Arkansas (89-78) NCAA Football Champions Nebraska (12-0-0) Academy Award, Best Picture: Forrest Gump Record of the Year: "All I Wanna Do," Sheryl Crow Album of the Year: MTV Unplugged Song of the Year: "Streets of Philadelphia," Bruce Springsteen • The Rock and Roll Hall of Fame Museum opens in Cleveland. Renowned architect I. M. Pei designed the ultra-modern, 150,000 square foot building • Grateful Dead frontman Jerry Garcia dies • An estimated 150 million people watch as the not guilty verdict is read in the O. J. Simpson verdict • The Metropolitan Opera installs screens on audience seats that display captions, to attract a wider audience.
Movies: Babe, Braveheart, Leaving Las Vegas, The Usual Suspects, Dead Man Walking
• First solo transpacific balloon flight. Steve Fossett made a flight of more than 5,430 mi. from Seoul, South Korea, to Leader, Saskatchewan, Canada, in a helium-filled balloon. Also set record for distance • Drs. Ian Wilmut and Keith Campbell (UK) create the world's first cloned sheep, Megan and Morag, from embryo cells.

The Game: 1995 UF-52 GA-17

This was the first win by UF over GA in Athens i five tries. The last time the two met in Athens i 1932. 86,117 fans filled Sanford Stadium to watch the Dogs and the Gators. All they really saw was the Gators. It was one of the most complete efforts of th year by the UF offense. Uf threw for seven TD pass es, the most ever by a league team in an SEC game.

nd totals 542 yards on the day (229 rushing and 313 assing). The Gator defense forces six GA fumbles, f which three were recovered by UF. GA is held to 5 yards rushing.

In the first quarter UF scored on three Wuerffel sses. One to Hilliard for 14 yards and twice to oering, a 2-yard and a 24-yard pass. Edmiston kicks l three PATs.

In the second quarter Wuerffel hits Doering again or an 11-yard TD pass after the Gators had driven 70 ards in 8 plays. Edmiston kicks the PAT. The score now 28-0.

GA drives 64 yards in 11 plays, but has to settle on 25-yard Parkman FG. 28-3

In the third quarter, Wuerffel hits R. Anthony on a 9-yard TD pass, after a 11 play, 64 yard drive. dmiston kicks the PAT. UF 35 GA 3.

UF adds a FG by Edmiston from 47 yards out. UF 8 GA 3.

In the fourth quarter, GA drives 80 yards in 7 plays ith Hunter catcing a 2-yard TD pass from Hines ard. Parkman kicks the PAT. UF 38 GA 10.

UF then drives 80 yards in 6 plays, with Kresser tting Hilliard for 7-yards and a score. Edmiston cks the PAT. UF 45 GA 10.

GA's Tolbert recovers a UF fumble and runs 10 rds for the score. Parkman kicks the PAT. F 45 GA 17.

UF then drives 76 yards in 8 plays and scores when resser hits McGriff from eight yards out. Edmiston cks the PAT. Final score UF 52 GA 17.

996

Chechens capture 2,000 Russians • Chechnya peace aty signed • France agrees to end nuclear testing. Britain alarmed by an outbreak of "mad cow" dis-se • UN tribunal charges war crimes by Bosnian uslims and Croats • Nations pledge $1.23 billion in d to rebuild Bosnia • South Africa gets new consti-tion • Israel elects Benjamin Netanyahu as prime inister • Iraqis strike at Kurdish enclave; after warn-g, US attacks Iraq's southern air defenses • Militant liban leaders seize Afghan capital of Kabul. Ethnic violence breaks out in Zairian refugee mps; Clinton approves plan for UN-backed relief ssion for 1.2 million Hutu refugees starving in stern Zaire. Hundreds of thousands return to wanda • US budget crisis in fourth month • Clinton pproves resumption of many government operations Bob Dole sweeps primaries • F.B.I. arrests suspect- Unabomber (AClinton signs line-item veto bill President blocks ban on late-term abortions • Valujet ashes in Everglades; all 110 aboard killed • 747 air-er crashes in Atlantic off Long Island, N.Y.; all 230 oard perish • Congress passes welfare reform bill; proved by Clinton Aug. 22 • Republican conven-n nominates Bob Dole and Jack Kemp;Democratic nvention nominates incumbents Clinton and Gore, no win the national election • Clinton appoints adeleine Albright as first female US secretary of te

per Bowl   Dallas d. Pittsburgh (27-17)
orld Series   N Y Yankees d. Atl. Braves (4-2)
BA Championship   Chicago d. Seattle (4-2)
entucky Derby Champion   *Grindstone*
CAA Basketball Championship
entucky d. Syracuse (76-67)
CAA Football Champions Florida (12-1)
st Picture: Braveheart, Mel Gibson
cord of the Year: "Kiss From a Rose," Seal
bum of the Year: Jagged Little Pill, Alanis
orissette Song of the Year: "Kiss From a Rose,"
al. • President Bill Clinton signs legislation that
nificantly deregulates telecommunications, creat-
z almost limitless opportunities for broadcasters
d cable companies. Pressured by the Federal
ommunications Commission, television broadcast-

ers agree to include three hours a week of educational children's programming into their schedules.
• Janet Jackson becomes the highest paid musician in history when she signs an $80-million deal with Virgin Records • Jazz great Ella Fitzgerald dies.
• Broadcasters and television and PC manufacturers agree on a standard for HDTV (high-definition digital television) • Gangsta rapper Tupac Shakur is shot four times in a drive-by shooting. He dies six days later at age 25.
Movies: The English Patient, Fargo, Jerry Maguire, The People vs. Larry Flynt, Shine, Sling Blade
• Approximately 45 million people are using the Internet, with roughly 30 million of those in North America (United States and Canada), 9 million in Europe, and 6 million in Asia/Pacific (Australia, Japan, etc.). 43.2 million (44%) of US households own a personal computer, and 14 million of them are online • Global warming climbs to record
• Scientists analyzing a Martian meteorite claim that it may provide evidence for the existence of ancient life on Mars • Dr. Ian Wilmut and his team clone the world's first sheep from adult cells. The lamb born in July 1996 is named Dolly.

The Game: 1996 UF-47 GA-7

After two years of alternating home field games, the UF-GA contest returned to a record 84,103 fans in the Jacksonville Municipal Stadium.

UF came in undefeated and remained that way through this blow-out. UF failed to score on their ini-tial drive, something they had not done all year, but put 20 points on the scoreboard in the the first 12 minutes, to safely put the game out of reach for GA. Danny Wuerffel was 10 for 14 passes for 175 yards in the first quarter alone. He ended the day 16 of 23 for 279 yards with 4 TDs and 1 INT.

GA is held to a single fourth quarter score and ends the day with 272 total offensive yards (166 rushing and 106 passing). The UF defense forced three turnovers leading to 20 points.In the first quarter UF went 48 yards in three plays with Taylor running the final 2yds for the score. Edminston kicked the PAT. UF then scored on a 20-yard pass from Wuerffel to Anthony. The PAT was blocked. Wuerffel hit Anthony again for a 21-yard score, still in the first quarter. Edminston kicked the PAT. UF 20 GA 0

In the second quarter Wuerffel hit Allend for a 19-yard TD pass after a 10 play, 92 yard drive. Edminston kicked the PAT. Wuerffel then hit Green with an 11-yard TD pass, after having to drive only 28 yards to score. Edminston kicked the PAT. UF 34 GA 0

There was no scoring in the third quarter, but a flur-ry in the fourth. Edminston kicked a 27-yard FG after an 8 play, 48 yard drive. GA then got their only score of the game on a 9-yard Pass run. The PAT was good. Edminston kicked a 23-yard FG after a 9 play, 63 yard UF drive. The final score of the day came on a 14-yard TD pass from Johnson to Ross. Edminston kicked the PAT. Final score UF 47 GA 7.

1997

• Hebron agreement signed; Israel gives up large part of West Bank city of Hebron. Israeli government approves establishment of Jewish settlement in East Jerusalem, a setback in Middle East peace process
• US, UK, and France agree to freeze Nazis' gold loot
• Hong Kong returns to Chinese rule • Khmer Rouge hold trial of longtime leader Pol Pot • Swiss plan first payment to Holocaust victims • European Union plans to admit six nations • US shuttle joins Russian space station • O. J. Simpson found liable in civil suit
• Heaven's Gate cult members commit mass suicide in California • US Appeals Court upholds California ban on affirmative action • Clinton exercises new

line-item veto • Timothy J. McVeigh sentenced to death for Oklahoma City bombing • Two convicted in New York Trade Center bombing
Super Bowl   Green Bay d. New England (35-21)
World Series   Florida Marlins d. Cleveland (4-3)
NBA Championship   Chicago d. Utah (4-2)
Kentucky Derby Champion   *Silver Charm*
NCAA Basketball Championship
 Arizona d. Kentucky (84-79 OT)
NCAA Football Champions   Michigan (AP) (12-0) & Nebraska (ESPN/USA) (13-0)
Best Picture: The English Patient
Record of the Year: "Change the World," Eric Clapton Album of the Year: Falling Into You, Celine Dion Song of the Year: "Change the World"
• The controversial television ratings system debuts on cable stations and broadcast networks. The ratings, TV-Y, TV-G, TV-Y7, TV-PG, TV-14 and TV-M, appear for 15 seconds in the upper left-hand corner of the screen at the beginning of each show, except news and sports programs, which are not rated.
• Titanic crashes into theaters. It is the most expen-sive film of all time, costing between $250 and $300 million to produce and market • Ellen DeGeneres outs herself. She becomes the first openly gay woman to have her own sitcom • The Prince of Pop is born to Michael Jackson and wife Debbie Rowe. The child's name is Prince Michael Junior • J. K. Rowling's Harry Potter and the Philospher's Stone is published in the U.K. It comes to U.S. in 1998 as Harry Potter and the Sorcerer's Stone.
Movies: As Good as It Gets, The Full Monty, Good Will Hunting, The Ice Storm, L.A. Confidential, Titanic
• A team led by Drs. Ian Wilmut and Keith Campbell (UK) create the first sheep with a human gene in every cell of its body. The genetically engineered lamb is named Polly • Scientists at Oregon Regional Primate Research Center (US) create the first pri-mates …two rhesus monkeys named Net and Ditto… from DNA taken from cells of developing monkey embryos • Comet Hale-Bopp is the closest it will be to Earth until 4397 • US spacecraft begins exploration of Mars • US company launches first commercial spy satellite.

The Game: 1997 GA -37 UF-17

Back for a second consecutive year at the Gator Bowl, the Golden Isles celebrated almost as much as the Dawgs did after this game.

GA said enough was enough. Donnan's Dawgs decided they would not go through an entire decade of being beat by the Gators.

Instead of just talking about this particular game, it is important to look at the entire season GA had in 1997.
GA Coach Jim Donnan took a team that hadn't won more than six games since 1992 and turned them into a SEC title contender with a 10-2 record. The Dawgs not only beat UF who was the defending national champion, but they beat Wisconsin in the 1998 Outback Bowl, 33-6, and ended up ranked number 10 in the nation.
The 1997 Bulldogs made a remarkable turnaround from the 1996 5-6 season, not only in wins and losses but in statistical improvement. Donnan had always been known for his offense and his stamp was firmly imprinted on the 1997 Bulldogs. In SEC Stats, the '97 Dogs finished third in the league in total offense and 15th nationally (432.64 ypg); second in rushing offense, up from eighth the previous year (169.9 ypg); fifth in passing offense and 19th nationally (262.73 ypg); and fourth in scoring offense (31.55 ppg), up from eighth in '96. Georgia also finished first in the SEC in third down conversions (48%).

While Donnan was known for his offense, the Dogs were impressive improving their defense as well, finishing second in the SEC and 16th nationally in the most important category-scoring defense (17.18 ppg), up from ninth in the SEC the previous year. The '97 Bulldogs also finished first in the SEC in fewest penalties with 39-that was 28 better than the second best team- and second in the league in turnover margin. In addition, GA had defeated two of their three biggest rivals each of the past years-Auburn and Georgia Tech in '96 and Florida and Georgia Tech in '97.

So, since the Gators have enjoyed this entire decade, it is fitting that we dedicate the year, 1997, as the "Year of the Dog," as far as this rivalry is concerned. GA-37 UF-17

1998

• Serbs battle ethnic Albanians in Kosovo. Serbs renew attack on Kosovo rebels. NATO, on verge of air strikes, reaches settlement with Milosevic on Kosovo • Good Friday Accord is reached in Northern Ireland. Irish Parliament backs peace agreement • Europeans agree on single currency, the euro • India conducts three atomic tests despite worldwide disapproval. Pakistan stages five nuclear tests in response • Indonesian dictator Suharto steps down after 32 years in power • Iraq ends cooperation with UN arms inspectors. Clinton orders air strikes • US embassies in Kenya and Tanzania bombed • US cruise missiles hit suspected terrorist bases in Sudan and Afghanistan • Russia fights to avert financial collapse • Former Chilean dictator Augusto Pinochet arrested in London • Wye Mills Agreement between Netanyahu and Arafat moves Middle East peace talks forward • President accused in White House sex scandal; denies allegations of affair with White House intern, Monica Lewinsky • President outlines first balanced budget in 30 years • US Supreme Court rules line-item veto unconstitutional • Unabomber sentenced to four life terms • Life sentence meted out to Terry Nichols, convicted in Oklahoma City bombing fatal to 168 • Starr Report by independent counsel outlines case for impeachment proceedings against President • Matthew Shepard, gay Wyoming student, fatally beaten in hate crime; two arrested • House impeaches President Clinton along party lines on two charges, perjury and obstruction of justice.
Super Bowl Denver d. Green Bay (31-24)
World Series New York Yankees d. San Diego (4-0)
NBA Championship Chicago d. Utah (4-2)
Kentucky Derby Champion *Real Quiet*
NCAA Basketball Championship
Kentucky d. Utah (78-69)
Best Picture: Titanic
Record of the Year: "Sunny Came Home," Shawn Colvin Album of the Year: Time Out of Mind, Bob Dylan Song of the Year: "Sunny Came Home"
•Titanic becomes the highest-grossing film of all time, raking in more than $580 million domestically. • An estimated 76 million viewers watch the last episode of Seinfeld • Legendary crooner Frank Sinatra dies of a heart attack at age 82 • NBC agrees to fork over $13 million an episode for the next three years for broadcast rights to the top-rated series ER. The total dollar figure, $850 million, eclipses any price ever paid for a television show • Titanic captures a record-tying 11 Academy Awards, including those for Best Picture and Best Director (James Cameron) • The American Film Institute announces its list of the top 100 films of all time. Citizen Kane tops the list • Tina Brown, editor of The New Yorker sends shockwaves through the publishing world with her resignation from the venerable weekly. David Remnick is hired to replace her.
Movies: Affliction, American History X, Elizabeth, Shakespeare in Love, There's Something about Mary • The Athena probe finds frozen water on moon. Scientists say ice crystals mixed with soil could provide fuel for rockets exploring solar system • The

FDA approves the male impotence drug Viagra • Astronomers detect giant explosion, second in force only to the "Big Bang," in deep space • Dow Corning Corporation agrees on $3.2 billion settlement for tens of thousands of women claiming injury from manufacturer's silicone breast implants • 77-year-old Senator John Glenn, the first American to orbit the earth, returns to orbit in the space shuttle Discovery • The crew of the space shuttle Endeavour connects first two modules of the international space station.

The Game: 1998 UF-38 GA-7

Once again the crowd broke records for crowd size viewing a UF-GA game. 84,321 fans were on hand to watch the Gators manhandle the Bulldogs.

UF scored the first 21 points of the game. The UF defense forced turnovers on many GA drives.

UF QB Doug Johnson competed 11 of his first 13 passes. Johnson hit Travis Taylor for a 25-yard TD on UF's first possession.

On UF's next possession, Johnson hit Darrell Jackson for 25 yards and another score.

The GA offense powered for 461 yards for the day, but were stopped whenever they drove deep in Gator territory. The turning point in the game came when GA was driving with the ball. On the fourth consecutive screen play, GA split end, Tony Small appeared to be heading for a momentum-changing TD, when Tony George caught up with Small around the UF 5 yard line, and stripped him of the ball. UF recovered, having to only run-out 45 seconds off the clock before the half ended, with UF maintaining a 21-7 lead.

Scoring summary: First Quarter-UF goes 73 yards in 7 plays, with Johnson hitting Travis Taylor with a 25-yard TD pass. Chandler kicks the PAT. UF then drives 69 yards in 5 plays, with Johnson hitting Darrell Jackson on a 25-yard TD pass. Chandler kicks the PAT.

With a little over a minute left in the first quarter, UF drives 60 yards in 5 plays, with Johnson sneaking over from the 2 yard line. Chandler kicks the PAT. UF 21 GA 0

Second Quarter- GA drives 80 yards in 17 plays with Bradley scoring from the one. Hines kicks the PAT. UF 21 GA 7

Third Quarter- UF drives 72 yards in 12 plays. Jeff Chandler then boots a 24-yard FG.UF 24 GA 7

Fourth Quarter- UF drives 75 yards in 11 plays. Johnson is passed to by Travis McGriff for a 10-yard TD. Chandler kicks the PAT. UF scores next from GA 8 after a turnover late in the fourth quarter. John Capel runs it over for the score. Chandler kicks the PAT. UF 38 GA 7

1999

• Russian president Boris Yeltsin survives impeachment hearings, reshuffles his cabinet twice, and takes military action against Islamic separatists in Dagestan and Chechnya • Nelson Mandela, first black president of South Africa, steps down, and Thabo Mbeki takes over • War erupts in Kosovo after Yugoslavia's president Slobodan Milosevic clamps down on the province, massacring and deporting ethnic Albanians. NATO begins Operation Allied Force on March 24, 1999, launching air strikes against Belgrade for 78 consecutive days until Milosevic relents • Magnitude 7.4 earthquake kills more than 15,600 and leaves 600,000 homeless in Turkey • East Timor population votes for independence from Indonesia, which causes pro-Indonesian forces to massacre and uproot thousands of East Timorese • Pakistani government is overthrown in the midst of economic strife and intensified fighting with India over Kashmir • The world awaits the consequences of the Y2K bug, with more drastic millennial theorists warning of Armageddon.

• US Senate opens impeachment trial of President Clinton; Senate acquits Clinton and rejects censure move • Students Eric Harris, 18, and Dylan Klebold, 17, storm Columbine High School in Littleton , CO, killing twelve other students and a teacher, then themselves • John F. Kennedy Jr., wife Carolyn Bessette Kennedy, and her sister Lauren G. Bessette are lost at sea when a plane he was piloting disappears near Martha's Vineyard, off Mass. coast
Super Bowl Denver d. Atlanta (34-19)
World Series: N.Y. Yankees d. Atlanta Braves (4-0)
NBA Championship San Antonio d. NY (4-1)
NCAA Basketball Championship Conn d. Duke (77-74)
Best Picture: Shakespeare in Love
Record of the Year: "My Heart Will Go On," Celine Dion Album of the Year: The Miseducation of Lauryn Hill, Lauryn Hill Song of the Year: "My Heart Will Go On" • The merger of two major recording labels, Universal and Polygram, causes upheaval in the recording industry. It is estimated that the new company, Universal Music Group, controls 25% of the worldwide music market • The Blair Witch Project emerges as an instant cult classic and becomes the most profitable film of all time, grossing more than $125 million. The film cost $30,000 to make • Rev. Jerry Falwell outs Teletubby Tinky Winky and calls him a gay role model. Falwell deduced that because Tinky Winky's purple, carries purse and has a triangle on his head he's gay • Star Wars Episode I--The Phantom Menace opens and breaks a string of box office records. The film grosses $102.7 million in its debut five-day weekend.
Movies:Blair Witch Project, American Beauty, Three Kings, The Sixth Sense
• The number of Internet users worldwide reaches 150 million by the beginning of 1999. Over 50% are from the United States • The Melissa and Chernobyl viruses afflict computers worldwide, forcing several large corporations to shut down their e-mail servers. • The Liberty Bell 7 space capsule, piloted by Gus Grissom on America's second manned space flight, discovered off the Florida coast after being submerged for 38 years.

The Game: 1999 UF-30 GA-14

Another record-breaking crowd of 84,397 filled Alltel Stadium and CBS broadcast the game nationally for fans to watch Steve Spurrier win his 100th game in his first ten years and become the first major college coach to do that in the twentieth century.

The game was played in a steady rain for much of the contest. The Gators didn't pull away from the Dogs until the fourth quarter.

The UF defense held GA to just 53 yards of offense in the third and fourth periods.

Scoring summary-First Quarter- UF drives 84 yards in 9 plays with Johnson hitting Travis Taylor for an 11-yard score. Chandler kicks the PAT.

GA then drives 71 yards in 3 plays with Quincy Carter scoring from the three. H.Hines kicks the PAT. UF drives 45 yards in 6 plays with Chandler booting a 40-yard FG. UF 10 GA 7

Second Quarter- GA goes 81 yards on 13 plays with Quincy Carter running the final 16-yards for the score. Hines kicks the PAT.
UF answers, going72 yards in 10 plays with R. Gillespie scoring from two yards out. The PAT was fumbled. UF 16 GA 14

Fourth Quarter- UF drives 43 yards in 3 plays with B. Carroll scoring on a 30-yard run. Chandler kicks the PAT.

UF then scores after a turnover deep in GA territory, as Johnson scores on a 2-yard run. Chandler kicks the PAT.

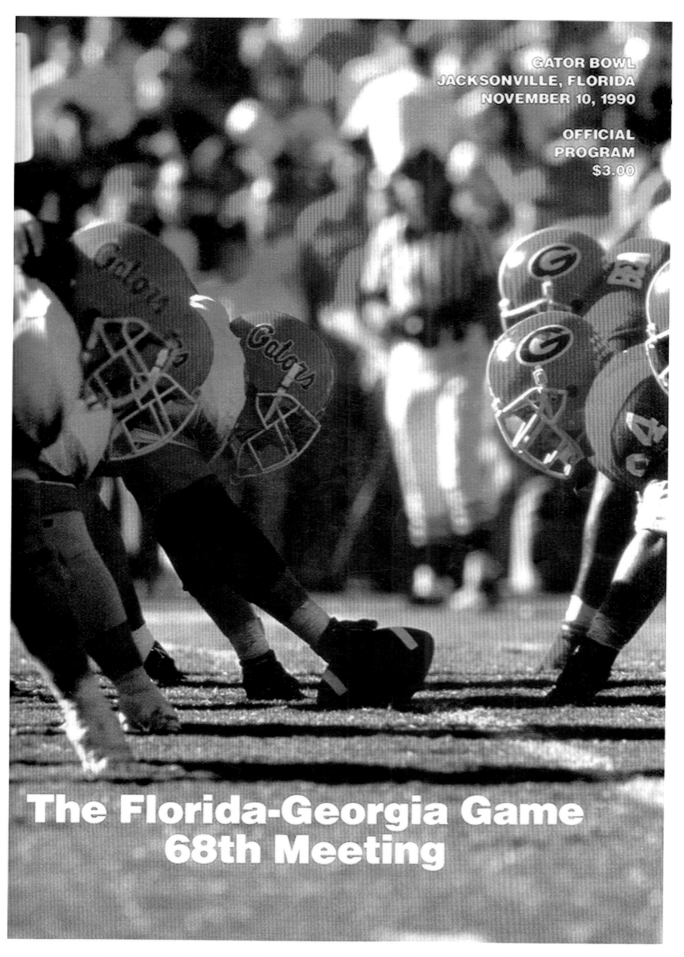

GATOR BOWL
JACKSONVILLE, FLORIDA
NOVEMBER 10, 1990

OFFICIAL
PROGRAM
$3.00

The Florida-Georgia Game
68th Meeting

1990 · UFL 38 UGA 7

$3.00

GEORGIA

**The Florida Game
The Gator Bowl**
Jacksonville, Fla.
November 9, 1991

1991 · UFL 45 UGA 13

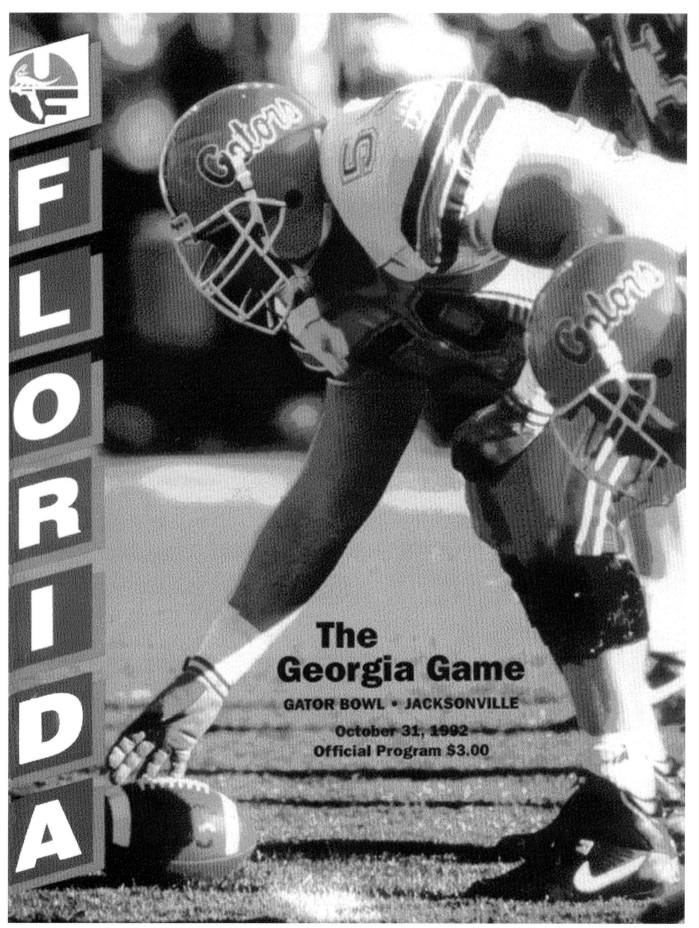

FLORIDA

The Georgia Game

GATOR BOWL • JACKSONVILLE

October 31, 1992
Official Program $3.00

1992 • UFL 26 UGA 24

GEORGIA
vs.
FLORIDA

1993 · UFL 33 UGA 26

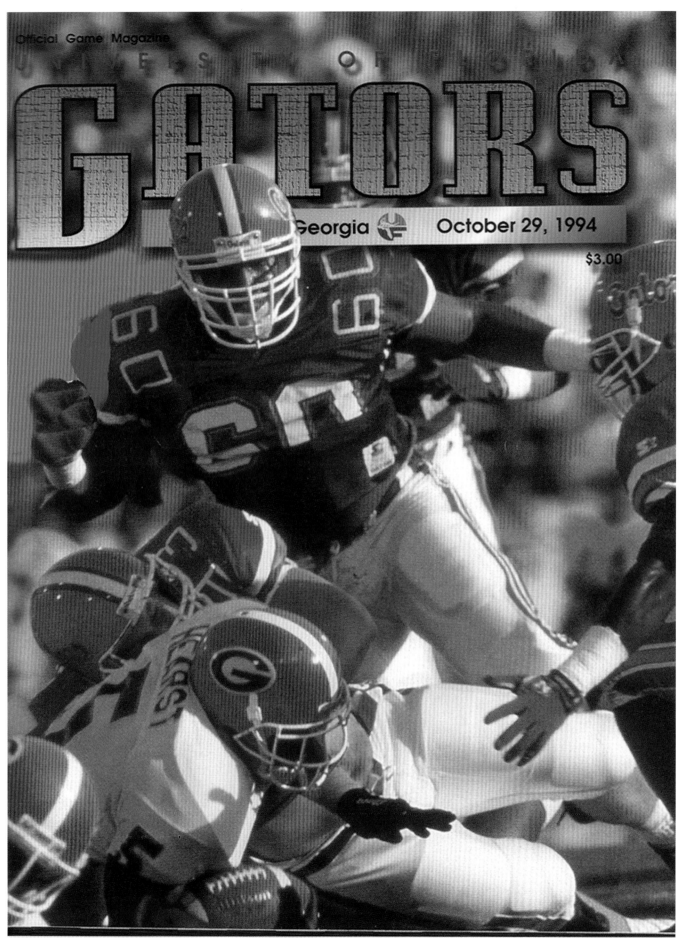

GATORS

Georgia October 29, 1994

$3.00

1994 · UFL 52 UGA 14

The Florida Game

Sanford Stadium

October 28, 1995

$5.00

1995 • UFL 52 UGA 17

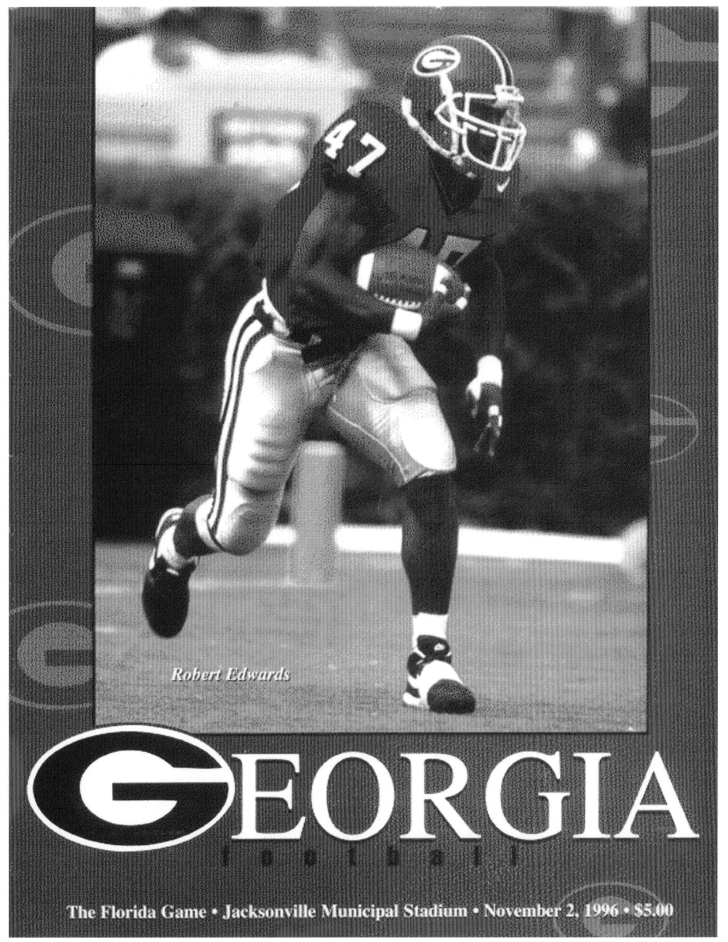

Robert Edwards

GEORGIA
football

The Florida Game • Jacksonville Municipal Stadium • November 2, 1996 • $5.00

1996 • UFL 47 UGA 7

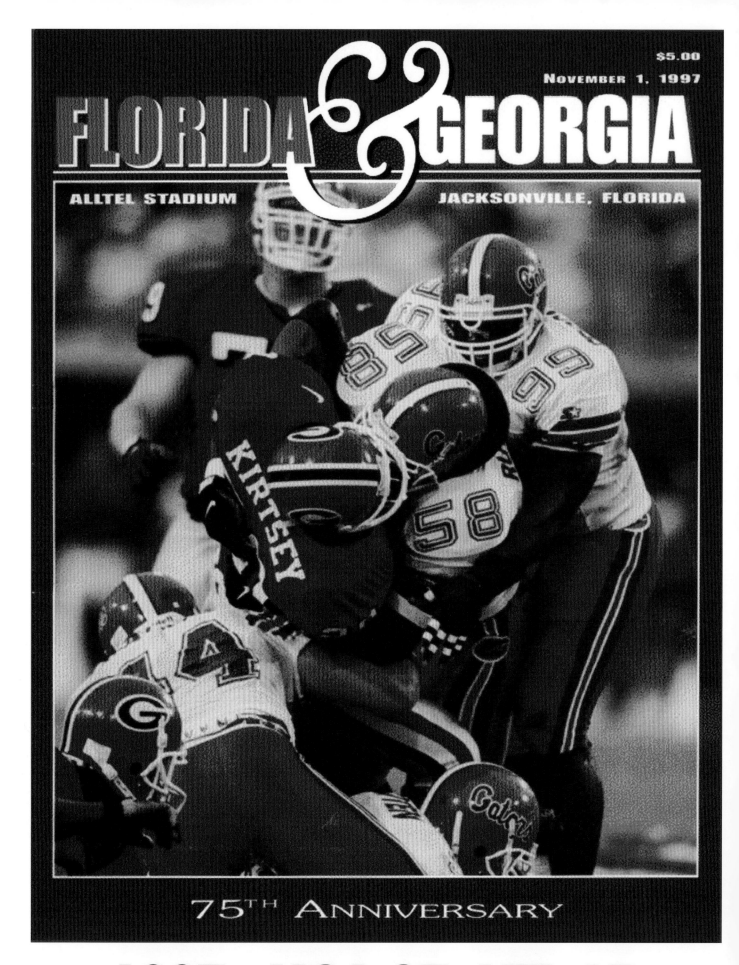

1997 • UGA 37 UFL 17

SENIOR SPLIT-END
TONY SMALL

GEORGIA
vs. FLORIDA
ALLTEL STADIUM
OCTOBER 31, 1998

$5⁰⁰

1998 · UFL 38 UGA 7

1999 · UFL 30 UGA 14

The 2000s

Oglethorpe
BANK
Brunswick-St. Simons Island, GA

2000

- Austria at center of European dispute after conservative People's Party forms coalition with the far-right Freedom Party, headed by xenophobe Jörg Haider • Reformists win control of Iranian parliament for first time since 1979 Islamic revolution • Governing of Northern Ireland passes back and forth between Britain and nascent Northern Irish parliament; major dispute over IRA's refusal to disarm • Former Indonesian president Suharto under house arrest, charged with corruption and abuse of power • Presidents of North and South Korea sign peace accord, and at least symbolically, end a half-century of antagonism • Vicente Fox Quesada elected president of Mexico, ending 71 years of one-party rule by the Institutional Revolutionary Party (PRI) • Concorde crash kills 113 near Paris • Palestinians and Israelis clash, spurred by visit of right-wing Israeli leader Ariel Sharon to a joint Jewish/Muslim holy site; "Al Aksa intifada" continues unabated • Nationwide uprising overthrows Yugoslavian president Milosevic; Vojislav Kostunica sworn in as president • U.S. sailors on Navy destroyer Cole die in Yemen terrorist explosion • Mad cow disease alarms Europe • Wary investors bring stock plunge; beginning of the end of the Internet stock boom • Cuban boy Elián Gonzállez, 6, at center of international dispute, reunited with his father after federal raid of Miami relatives' home • U.S. presidential election closest in decades; Bush's slim lead in Florida leads to automatic recount in that state. Republicans file federal suit to block manual recount of Florida presidential election ballots sought by Democrats. Florida Supreme Court rules election hand count may continue. U.S. Supreme Court orders halt to manual recount of Florida votes. Supreme Court seals Bush victory by 5-4; rules there can be no further recounting.

Super Bowl St. Louis d. Tennessee (23-16)

World Series NY Yankees d. NY Mets (4-1)

NBA Championship Los Angeles d. Indiana (4-2)

Kentucky Derby Champion

Fusaichi Pegasus

NCAA Basketball Championship Michigan State d. Florida (89-76)

NCAA Football Champions Oklahoma(13-0)

Best Picture: American Beauty

Record of the Year: "Smooth" Santana featuring Rob Thomas Album of the Year: "Supernatural" Santana Song of the Year: "Smooth" • In the biggest merger in the country's history, America Online agrees to buy Time Warner, the nation's largest traditional media company, for $165 billion. The mega-deal reflects the growing dominance of the Internet in areas including publishing, music, film, and broadcasting. It also serves to validate the Internet, proving that the Web is likely here to stay and somewhat justifying the value of Internet companies that have yet to turn a profit but are worth billions on paper • Charles Schulz, the cartoonist who created the ìPeanutsî comic strip, dies in his sleep after a battle with colon cancer. In a career that spanned nearly 50 years, Schulz drew more than 18,250 "Peanuts" comic strips, which expressed a droll philosophy through the precocious children. The "Peanuts" debuted in 1950 and went on to be the most widely read comic strip in the world, with an audience of 355 million in 75 countries. It ran in 2,600 newspapers and was published in 21 languages, including Serbo-Croatian, Chinese, and Tlingit • Kathie Lee Gifford announces she's calling it quits after the current season of Live! With Regis & Kathie Lee. She had been sharing hosting duties with Who Wants to Be a Millionaire's Regis Philbin for 11 years. She said she "has songs to sing, songs to write" • Stephen King's 66-page novella Riding the Bullet is available exclusively in electronic only as an ìe-book.î For $2.50 readers can download the book onto computers or personal organizers. The software prevents users from printing or copying the manuscript. More than 500,000 copies were downloaded in the first three days the book was available • Oprah Winfrey debuts O magazine. The Queen of All Media graces the cover and plans to be front and center on all issues ìfor the foreseeable future. "Winfrey labels her latest endeavor" a personal growth guide" that's targeted to the 25-to-49 demographic • The six cast members of Friends sign a two-year contract, with each actor earning $750,000 per episode, up from the $125,000 they now make • Ellen DeGeneres and Anne Heche announce their breakup. Unfortunately, we have decided to end our relationship. It is an amicable parting, and we greatly value the 3 1/2 years we have spent together,they said in a joint statement. The same day, Heche was hospitalized after wandering disoriented to a southern Fresno County, California, house. No word on what prompted the behavior • Madonna and director Guy Ritchie marry in an elegant ceremony at Scotland's Skibo Castle. Stella McCartney, who designed the brides's gown, serves as her maid of honor. Ritchie wears a Hunting Mackintosh kilt, sans undies

Movies: Chocolat • Crouching Tiger, Hidden Dragon • Erin Brockovich • Gladiator • Traffic

• NEAR spacecraft becomes first to orbit an asteroid

• "I love you" virus disrupts computers worldwide • Human genome deciphered; expected to revolutionize the practice of medicine • Abortion pill, RU-486, wins U.S. approval

The Game: 2000 UF -34 GA -23

Another year, another record crowd. This year 84,404 filled Alltel Stadium to watch a game of turnovers and big defensive plays, as UF won for the 10th time in the last 11 games."It was a different game for us," said UF Coach Steve Spurrier.

"We were able to survive four turnovers and then they had the turnovers in the second half. It was a game of capitalizing after turnovers and we did that better than they did."

Even with UF's season-high four turnovers in the first half, the score stood at 17-17 at halftime. UF got on the board when Jabar Gaffney caught a 27-yard pass from Rex Grossman for a 6-3 first quarter lead. Chandler added a 37-yard FG to put UF up by 9-3.GA stormed back and took advantage of its third intercepted pass as Mussa Smith scored from the 4 yard line. Minutes later the Dogs grabbed another Gator fumble and marched 42 yards in two plays with Smith scoring from the one. GA now lead 17-9.

Lito Sheppard turned in the game's biggest play and brought the Gators back as he intercepted a Quincy Carter pass deep in Gator territory with les than two minutes to go in the half, and twisted and turned 61 yards down the field. The play set up a 14-yard scoring pass from Jesse Palmer to Robert Gillespie with 30 seconds left in the first half. Reche Caldwell caught the two-point conversion pass and the game was tied at the half, 17-17.

UF scored first in the second half on Jeff Chandler's 54-yard FG and went up 27-17 on a 10 play, 82 yard drive, ending with a 1-yard Palmer run.

First Quarter- After a 61 yard, 12 play drive, GA's Bennett kicked a 24-yard FG. UF then went 73 yards in 4 plays ending with Grossman hitting Gaffney with a 27-yard TD pass. Chandler's PAT was no good. Chandler then kicked a 37-yard FG after a 12 play, 40 yard UF drive.UF 9 GA 3

Second Quarter- GA's Mussa Smith scored on a 4-yard run after a UF turnover deep in UF territor Bennett kicked the PAT. GA then drove 42 yards i two plays with Smith running the final yard. Bennett kicked the PAT. UF then went 26 yards in 3 plays with Palmer hitting Gillespie with a 14-yard TD pass. Caldwell then passed for the two-point conversion.UF 17 GA 17

Third Quarter-UF marched 19 yards in 6 plays with Chandler then kicking a 54-yard FG. UF then went 82 yards in 10 plays with Palmer running the final yard. Chandler kicked the PAT. UF 27 GA17

Fourth Quarter-GA drove 65 yards in 12 plays with J. Sanks scoring on a one-yard pass from Q. Carter. Bennett's PAT was no good.UF, after a turnover, went 29 yards in 2 plays with Gillespie running it in from the 2 yard line. Chandler kicked the PAT. Final Score UF 34 GA 23

2001

• Congo president Laurent Kabila assassinated by bodyguard. Son Joseph Kabila takes over amid continuing civil war • Ariel Sharon wins election in Israel. Right-wing leader chosen overwhelmingly as nation's fifth prime minister in just over five years during worst Israeli-Palestinian violence in years • The long-simmering resentment of Macedonia's ethnic Albanians erupts into violence in March. The rebels seek greater autonomy within Macedonia. After six months of fighting, a peace agreement is signed. British-led NATO forces ente the country and disarm the guerrillas • U.S. spy plane and Chinese jet collide; Sino-American relations deteriorate during a standoff. The 24 crew members of the U.S. plane were detained for 11 days and released after the U.S. issued a formal statement of regret • Former Yugoslav president Slobodan Milosevic is delivered to UN tribunal in The Hague to await war-crime trial • Without U.S. 178 nations reach agreement on climate accord, which rescues, though dilutes, 1997 Kyoto Protoc • In response to Sept. 11 terrorist attacks, U.S. and

British forces launch bombing campaign on Taliban government and al-Qaeda terrorist camps in Afghanistan. Bombings continue on a daily basis • Irish Republican Army announces that it has begun to dismantle its weapons arsenal, marking a dramatic leap forward in Northern Ireland peace process • At a UN-sponsored summit in Bonn, Germany, Afghani factions meet to create a post-Taliban government. Hamid Karzai is selected as head of the transitional government • Taliban regime in Afghanistan collapses after two months of bombing by American warplanes and fighting by Northern Alliance ground troops • Israel condemns the Palestinian Authority as a "terror-supporting entity" and severs ties with leader Yasir Arafat following mounting violence against Israelis. The Israeli Army begins bombing Palestinian areas • In final days of presidency, Bill Clinton issues controversial pardons, including one for Marc Rich, billionaire fugitive financier • George W. Bush is sworn in as 43rd president • U.S. submarine Greeneville sinks Japanese fishing boat, killing 9 • FBI agent Robert Hanssen is charged with spying for Russia for 15 years • Race riots in Cincinnati continue for several days following a shooting of an unarmed black man by a white police officer • Four are declared guilty in 1998 terrorist bombings of U.S. embassies in Kenya and Tanzania • Balance of the Senate shifts after Jim Jeffords of Vermont changes his party affiliation from Republican to independent. The move strips Republicans of control of the Senate and gives Democrats the narrowest of majorities (50-49-1) • Bush signs new tax-cut law, the largest in 20 years • Oklahoma City bomber Timothy McVeigh executed • Budget surplus dwindles. The Congressional Budget Office attributes this rapid change in the nation's fortunes to the slowing economy and the Bush tax cut • Terrorists attack United States. Hijackers ram jetliners into twin towers of New York City's World Trade Center and the Pentagon. A fourth hijacked plane crashes 80 mi outside of Pittsburgh. Toll of dead and injured in thousands. Within days, Islamic militant Osama bin Laden and the al-Qaeda terrorist network are identified as the parties behind the attacks • Anthrax scare rivets nation, as anthrax-laced letters are sent to various media and government officials. Several postal workers die after handling the letters.

Super Bowl Baltimore d. NY Giants (34-7)
World Series Arizona d. NY Yankees (4-3)
NBA Championship LA Lakers d. Philadelphia (4-1)
Kentucky Derby Champion *Monarchos*
NCAA Basketball Championship Duke d. Arizona (82-72)

Best Picture: Gladiator Record of the Year: "Beautiful Day," U2
Album of the Year: Two Against Nature, Steely Dan Song of the Year: "Beautiful Day," U2 • Gladiator takes five Oscars, including those for Best Picture and Best Actor (Russell Crowe). Julia Roberts wins her gold statue for her performance in Erin Brockovich. Double nominee Steven Soderbergh defies expectations with his Best Director win for Traffic; many had expected his nominations for Traffic and Erin Brockovich to cancel each other out • Pearl Harbor, the bloated World War II epic, opens and tallies a somewhat disappointing $75 million three-day box office. The Producers cleans up at the Tony Awards, taking a record 12 trophies, including Best Musical, Best Book, Best Score, Best Director, and Best Leading Actor. Proof wins Best Play. For a full list of winners, see Tony Awards • After two postponements in the wake of the Sept. 11 terrorist attacks, the Emmy Awards are finally presented. NBC's The

West Wing takes the award for Best Drama and HBO's Sex and the City nabs the Best Comedy prize • Harry Potter and the Sorcerer's Stone opens in 8,200 theaters nationwide, about one-quarter of all those available. Lukewarm reviews didn't discourage audiences; the film took in an unprecedented $93.5 million on its opening weekend.
Movies: A.I. Artificial Intelligence • Ali • A Beautiful Mind • Bridget Jones's Diary • The Fellowship of the Ring • Harry Potter and the Sorcerer's Stone • The Majestic • Monsters, Inc. * Ocean's 11 * Pearl Harbor • Shrek • Vanilla Sky • Cloning animals results in defects. Scientists report mounting evidence of random genetic errors that threaten similar efforts to duplicate humans • New class of cancer drug announced. Researchers at San Francisco conference report new drug, Gleevec, shows promise in treating patients who do not respond to chemotherapy • Report by National Academy of Sciences announces that global warming is on the rise. Leading scientists reaffirm mainstream view that human activity is largely responsible • Artificial heart implanted in man. Surgeons in Louisville, Ky., report success of first operation for self-contained organ • Embryos created to harvest stem cells at Virginia clinic. Move breaks medical taboo and stirs national debate. Stem cells show promise in being able to regenerate human tissue of various kinds, with notable success in treating neurological diseases and conditions, such as Parkinson's disease and spinal cord damage • In address to the nation, President Bush approves the use of federal funds for studies on human embryos, but says that research with such funds must be limited to cells that have already been extracted. He declares government will not finance destruction of new embryos • Bigger supply of stem cells urged by scientists. Experts conclude that more embryonic material is needed to advance research

The Game: 2001 UF-24 GA-10

Nearly the same total of fans (84,401) filled Alltel Stadium to watch this year's battle. UF racked up 584 total yards of offense, but had needed to overcome four turnovers and 12 penalties to defeat the Dogs.

Taking advantage of an interception, GA grabbed a 3-0 first quarter lead on a Billy Bennett 42-yard FG. UF's Chandler answered with a 32-yard FG to tie the game. The Gators then went up 10-3 after driving 69 yards.

GA recovered a UF fumble and went 43 yards to tie again. UF answered with their own drive, highlighted by a 21-yard Taylor Jacobs reverse. UF's defense registered several big plays in the second half.

UF stopped GA on a fourth-and-two play at UF's 6-yard line. A Lito Sheppard tackle stopped Fred Gibson one yard short of a first down on a fourth-and-thirteen play deep in UF territory.

Scoring Summary

First Quarter- GA goes 31 yards in 8 plays. Bennett hits a 42-yard FG. UF then drove 75 yards on 11 plays with Chandler hitting a 32-yard FG. UF then went 69 yards on 7 plays with Grossman hitting Gaffney for a 21-yard score. Chandler kicked the PAT. UF 10 GA 3

Second Quarter- GA goes 43 yards in 7 plays with Sanks running the last 3 for the score. Bennett kicks the PAT. UF then drives 79 yards in 13 plays with Grossman running the final yard. Chandler kicked the PAT. UF 17 GA 10

No scoring in the third period.

Fourth Quarter- UF drives 76 yards in 6 plays with Grossman hitting Caldwell on a 30-yard TD pass. Chandler kicked the PAT.
Final Score UF 24 GA 10.

2002

• Former Yugoslav leader Slobodan Milosevic's trial on charges of crimes against humanity opens at The Hague • Tamil Tigers and Sri Lankan government sign a cease-fire agreement, ending 19 years of civil war • India's worst Hindu-Muslim violence in a decade rocked the state of Gujarat after a Muslim mob fire-bombed a train, killing Hindu activists. Hindus retaliated, and more than 1,000 died in the bloodshed
• U.S. and Afghan troops launch Operation Anaconda against remaining al-Qaeda and Taliban fighters in Afghanistan • Israeli tanks and warplanes attack West Bank towns of Nablus, Jenin, Bethlehem, and others in response to string of Palestinian suicide attacks. In the first three months of 2002, 14 suicide bombers kill dozens of Israeli civilians, and wounded hundreds • International Criminal Court wins UN ratification; U.S. refuses to ratify • Venezuelan president Hugo Chavez ousted in coup, then reinstated • U.S. and Russia reach landmark arms agreement to cut both countries' nuclear arsenals by up to two-thirds over the next 10 years • East Timor becomes a new nation • Terrorist bomb in Bali kills hundreds • Government suspended in Northern Ireland in protest of suspected IRA spy ring • North Korea admits to developing nuclear arms in defiance of treaty • Chechen rebels take 763 hostages in Moscow theater. Russian authorities release a gas into theater, killing 116 hostages and freeing remainder • China's Jiang Zemin officially retires as general secretary; Hu Jintao named as his successor
• UN Security Council passes unanimous resolution calling on Iraq to disarm or else face "serious consequences." • UN arms inspectors return to Iraq • President Bush's first State of the Union address vows to expand the fight on terrorism and labels Iran, Iraq, and North Korea "an axis of evil" • Kenneth L. Lay, chairman of bankrupt energy trader Enron, resigns; company under federal investigation for hiding debt and misrepresenting earnings • U.S. withdraws from International Court treaty • FBI lawyer Coleen Rowley criticizes FBI for thwarting terrorist efforts in a letter to the FBI director • U.S. abandons 31-year-old Antiballistic Missile treaty • Bush announces change in Middle East policy: U.S. will not recognize an independent Palestinian state until Yasir Arafat is replaced • Bush signs corporate reform bill (July 30) in response to a spate of corporate scandals: Enron, Arthur Andersen, Tyco, Qwest, Global Crossing, ImClone, and Adelphia, among others, were convicted or placed under federal investigation for various misadventures in fraud and crooked accounting • Pennsylvania miners rescued after spending 77 hours in a dark, flooded mine shaft • Bush addresses United Nations, calling for a "regime change" in Iraq • Snipers prey upon DC suburbs, killing ten and wounding others. Police arrest two sniper suspects, John Allen Muhammad and John Lee Malvo
• Republicans retake the Senate in midterm elections; gain additional House seats • Bush signs legislation creating cabinet-level Department of Homeland Security • Boston archbishop Cardinal Bernard Law resigns as a result of the Catholic Church's sexual abuse scandals and cover-up of priest-child molestation.
Super Bowl New England d. St. Louis (20-17)
World Series Anaheim d. SF Giants (4-3)
NBA Championship LA Lakers d. New Jersey (4-0)
Kentucky Derby Champion *War Emblem*
NCAA Basketball Championship Maryland d.

Indiana (64-52)

Best Picture: A Beautiful Mind, Brian Grazer and Ron Howard

Record of the Year: "Walk On," U2 Album of the Year: O Brother, Where Art Thou? Song of the Year: "Fallin'," Alicia Keys

• The soundtrack to the film O Brother Where Art Thou recording wins five Grammy awards, including album of the year award and best country vocal. Newcomer Alicia Keys also nets five awards • The MTV reality show The Osbournes debuts. It follows the daily events of aging heavy metallist Ozzy Osbourne and his family. The offbeat and often bizarre show became an instant hit, delivering about six million viewers a week to MTV, its largest audience in history. The Osbournes won an Emmy Award in September for best reality series • Black actors won top Oscars. Denzel Washington and Halle Berry honored for Training Day and Monster's Ball, respectively • The movie Spider-Man was the year's box-office blockbuster, grossing more than $406 million. In all, Americans spent $9.3 billion on about 1.6 billion movie tickets in 2002óa 10% increase over 2001 figures

Movies: Harry Potter and the Chamber of Secrets •Lord of the Rings: The Two Towers • My Big Fat Greek Wedding • About Schmidt • Far From Heaven • Adaptation • The Hours • Chicago • Gangs of New York • National Academy of Sciences issues report opposing human reproductive cloning, but supports therapeutic cloningóthe creation of embryonic stem cells to aid in cures for such illnesses as Parkinson's Disease and diabetes • U.S. health officials issue new guidelines on mammograms, strongly recommending that breast cancer screening beginning at age 40, instead of 50. Recommendation follows months of controversy over the effectiveness of breast cancer screening • AIDS deaths are projected to skyrocket. The UN announced that the toll could reach an additional 65 million by 2020 if preventative measures are not expanded • Hormone replacement questioned. Study finds that drug therapy for menopausal women can cause increases in rate of breast cancer, heart attacks, blood clots, and strokes • Early skull is discovered in Chad. French scientists report in the journal Nature that they have unearthed a 7-million-year-old member of the human family, Sahelanthropus tchadensis, who has been nicknamed "Toumai." Fossil combines human and chimpanzee characteristics • Scientists report a new type of black hole. Hubble Space Telescope finds evidence of a middleweight class of gravitational sink, adding to earlier identified small and super classifications • Scientists compare mouse and human genomes. The first analysis of two complete genomes reveals striking similarities. Scientists hope finding will hasten understanding of genetic diseases.

The Game: 2002 UF-20 GA-13

84,433 fans watched Rex Grossman pass for 339 yards and two touchdowns, as the 22nd ranked Gators dropped No. 5 Georgia from the ranks of the unbeaten on this Saturday night.

Trailing 13-12 early in the fourth quarter, Grossman capped a 10-play, 89-yard drive when he hit Ben Troupe with a 10-yard TD pass to put UF up 18-13. Grossman ran the two-point conversion in to give the Gators a seven-point lead they would never surrender. Marcus Oquendo-Johnson sacked GA QB David Greene on the final play of regulation to preserve victory as the Gators improved to 6-3 on the year, keeping their chances alive in the race for the SEC Eastern Crown.

J.T. Wall got GA on the board first in the open-

ing quarter, catching a 10-yard pass from Greene for a 7-0 lead. UF's Grossman then hit Aaron Walker with a 5-yard TD pass but the kick failed. Guss Scott put the Gators on top when he intercepted a J.D. Shockley pass and ran it back 47 yards for a TD.

First Quarter- GA After a 48-yard drive, Greene hit Wall with a 10-yard TD pass. Bennett's PAT was good. GA 7 UF 0

Second Quarter- UF went 58 yards in 13 plays with Walker catching a 5-yard TD pass from Grossman. Talcott's PAT was no good. UF's Scott intercepted Shockley's pass and returned it 47-yards for the score. Grossman's two-point attempt was no good. After two short drives, GA's Bennett hit on two FGs, one from 47-yards, the other from 25-yards.GA 13 UF 12

Fourth Quarter-UF, after a 10-play, 89 yard drive, Grossman hits Troupe with a 10-yard TD pass, then the UF QB runs for the two-point conversion. UF 20 GA 13

2003

• North Korea withdraws from treaty on the non-proliferation of nuclear weapons • In State of the Union address, Bush announces that he is ready to attack Iraq even without a UN mandate • Ariel Sharon elected Israeli prime minister • Nine-week general strike in Venezuela calling for President Chavez's resignation ends in defeat • U.S. Secretary of State Powell presents Iraq war rationale to UN, citing its WMD as imminent threat to world security • U.S. and Britain launch war against Iraq • Baghdad falls to U.S. troops • First Palestinian prime minister, Mahmoud Abbas, sworn in • U.S.-backed "road map" for peace proposed for Middle East • The U.S. declares official end to combat operations in Iraq • Terrorists strike in Saudi Arabia, killing 34 at Western compound; Al-Qaeda suspected • Burmese opposition leader Aung San Suu Kyi again placed under house arrest by military regime • International Atomic Energy Agency (IAEA) discovers Iran's concealed nuclear activities and calls for intensified inspections • Palestinian militant groups announce ceasefire toward Israel • Liberia's autocratic president Charles Taylor forced to leave civil-war ravaged country • NATO assumes control of peacekeeping force in Afghanistan • Libya accepts blame for 1988 bombing of flight over Lockerbie, Scotland; agrees to pay $2.7 billion to the families of the 270 victims • Suicide bombing destroys UN headquarters in Baghdad, killing 24, including top envoy Sergio Vieira de Mello (Aug. 19). • Palestinian suicide bombing in Jerusalem kills 20 Israelis, including 6 children • After Israel retaliates for suicide bombing by killing top member of Hamas, militant Palestinian groups formally withdraw from cease-fire in effect since June 29 • Palestinian Prime Minister Mahmoud Abbas resigns; "road map" to peace effectively collapses • The Bush administration reverses policy, agreeing to transfer power to an interim Iraqi government in early 2004 • Suicide bombers attack two synagogues in Istanbul, Turkey, killing 25 • Another terrorist attack in Istanbul kills 26 (Nov. 20). Al-Qaeda suspected in both • Georgian president Eduard Shevardnadze resigns after weeks of protests • Paul Martin succeeds Jean Chretien as Canadian prime minister • Saddam Hussein is captured by American troops • Libyan leader Muammar Qaddafi announces he will give up weapons program • Space shuttle Columbia explodes, killing all 7 astronauts • Bush signs ten-year, $350-billion tax cut package, the

third-largest tax cut in U.S. history • In one of the most important rulings on the issue of affirmative action in twenty-five years-the Supreme Court decisively upholds the right of affirmative action in higher education • Investigation into the loss of space shuttle Columbia cites egregious organizational problems at NASA • Congressional Budget Office predicts federal deficit of $480 billion in 2004 and $5.8 trillion by 2013

• California governor Gray Davis ousted in recall vote; actor Arnold Schwarzenegger elected in his place • President Bush signs $87.5 billion emergency package for post-war Iraq reconstruction; this supplements $79 billion approved in April • John A. Muhammad, convicted in the 2002 Washington, DC, area shootings, receives death sentence • President Bush eliminates steel tariffs after WTO says U.S. violated trade laws

Super Bowl Tampa Bay d. Oakland (48-21)
World Series Florida d. New York (4-2)
NBA Championship San Antonio d. New Jersey (4-2)
Kentucky Derby Champion *Funny Cide*
NCAA Basketball Championship Syracuse d. Kansas (81-78)
NCAA Football Champions Louisiana State and So. Calif.
Best Picture: Chicago, Martin Richards, producer
Record of the Year: "Don't Know Why," Norah Jones
Album of the Year: Come Away with Me, Norah Jones
Song of the Year: "Don't Know Why" Norah Jones

• Norah Jones dominated the Grammy Awards, picking up five trophies, including those for Best Record ("Don't Know Why"), Best Album (Come Away With Me), and Best New Artist • Harry Potter and the Order of the Phoenix, the sixth installment in the wildly popular series, hit the shelves in June and rocketed up the best-seller lists • Big-budget sequels lured fans into the megaplexes. The Lord of the Rings: The Return of the King not only dominated the 2003 box office, but it also led the way in Oscar nominations. The Matrix fans were treated to two sequels: Matrix: Reloaded and Revolutions • Johnny Depp earned a surprise Oscar nomination for his Keith Richards-inspired, swaggering swashbuckler in Pirates of the Caribbean, a Disney special effects extravaganza based on a theme park ride • The Pixar team released another animated treasure with Finding Nemo, a fish-out-of-water tale about pair of clown fish who brave dark waters and menacing aquatic creatures to be reunited. The film grossed more than $340 million.

• The Recording Industry Association of America cracked down on people who illegally swapped more than 1,000 songs over the Internet, filing lawsuits against hundreds of people, including a 12-year-old girl. Apple Computer, however, made downloading both affordable and easy with its iTune Music Store. It allows fans to download tunes for 99 cents each.

Movies: Lost in Translation • Pirates of the Caribbean •The Lord of the Rings: The Return of the King • Finding Nemo • Mystic River • Cold Mountain • Master and Commander: The Far Side of the World • Freaky Friday • House of Sand and Fog • Seabiscuit

• Scientists uncover the fossil of a new species of flying dinosaur in northeastern China thought to have existed 120 million years ago. It is the first dinosaur ever found with four wings. The Chinese team that found the dinosaur has named it Microraptor gui, after Chinese paleontologist Gu

Chiwei • A joint NASA-Princeton University satellite, the Wilkinson Microwave Anisotropy Probe (WMAP), produced a high-resolution map that captured the oldest light in the universe. It provides some of the most important cosmological discoveries in years. The age of the universe has now been accurately determined as 13.7 billion years old and the birth of stars has been pinpointed to just 200 million years after the Big Bang. The WMAP image also revealed the contents of the universe: only 4% is made up of atoms, or the physical universe as we know it. The remainder is made up of poorly understood substances: dark energy (73%) and dark matter (23%). These findings are consistent with the Big Bang and inflation theories, which assert that the universe materialized in a "big bang" and immediately began cooling and expanding • Three fossilized skulls discovered near the Ethiopian village of Herto in 1997 have now been identified as the oldest known remains of modern humans. Assigned to a new human subspecies called Homo sapiens idaltu (idaltu means elder in the Afar language of Ethiopia), the skulls are estimated to be about 160,000 years old—a good 50,000 years older than any previously discovered Homo sapiens * Scientists publish the first comprehensive analysis of the genetic code of the Y chromosome. The Y chromosome provides just 78 genes out of the estimated 30,000 in human DNA and makes few important contributions beyond determining gender (females have two X chromosomes; males have an X and a Y chromosome). Once the size of the X chromosome, which contains about 1,000 genes, the Y chromosome has been rapidly decaying over the course of human evolution, dwindling to a mere tenth of its former self • The Hubble telescope has detected the oldest known planet, and it appears to have been formed billions of years earlier than astronomers thought possible. Nicknamed Methuselah after the aged biblical patriarch, the planet is an astonishing 12.7 billion years old

The Game: 2003 UF-16 GA-13

Keeping in the same capacity neighborhood, 84,411 fans filled the stadium this year to watch the No. 23 UF Gators extend its string of victories against No. 4 GA.

A Matt Leach FG with 33 seconds left in the game gave UF the victory, this following a 66-yard, 10-play UF drive.

After going into the half tied at three, UF scored 10 unanswered points to start the third quarter. UF's defense played the "sack" game with GA running backs and QBs.

UF's Perez's 34-yard TD reception with seven minutes left in the third period on a screen pass broke a 3-3 tie and put UF up 10-3.
scoring summary

First Quarter-no scoringSecond Quarter- UF drove 73 yards in 12 plays with Leach kicking a 24-yard FG.GA then went 70 yards in 10 plays with Bennett hitting a 21-yard FG. UF 3 GA 3
Third Quarter- UF drove 65 yards in 4 plays with Perez catching a 34-yard TD pass from Leak. Leach kicked the PAT UF 10 GA 3
Fourth Quarter- UF drove 84 yards in 11 plays. Leach then hit an 18-yard FG. GA went 65 yards in 10 plays with Lumpkin running the last yard for the score. Bennett kicked the PAT.GA then drove 77 yards in 12 plays with Bennett hitting a 1-yard FG. UF then went 66 yards in 10 plays with Leach hitting a 33-yard FG with 33 seconds remaining in game.
Final Score UF 16 GA 13

2004

• About one third of Iran's Parliament steps down to protest hard-line Guardian Council's banning of more than 2,000 reformists from running in parliamentary elections • A. Q. Khan, founder of Pakistan's nuclear program, admits he sold nuclear-weapons designs to other countries, including North Korea, Iran, and Libya • Armed rebels in Haiti force President Aristide to resign and flee the country • Spain is rocked by terrorist attacks, killing more than 200. Al Qaeda takes responsibility • Spain's governing Popular Party loses election to opposition Socialists. Outcome seen as a reaction to terrorist attacks days before and Popular Party's support of the U.S.-led war in Iraq • North Atlantic Treaty Organization (NATO) formally admits 7 new countries: Bulgaria, Estonia, Latvia, Lithuania, Romania, Slovakia, and Slovenia • Israeli prime minister Sharon announces plan to unilaterally withdraw from Gaza Strip
• Greek Cypriots reject UN reunification plan with Turkish Cypriots • Sudan rebels (SPLA) and government reach accord to end 21-year civil war. However, separate war in western Darfur region between Arab militias and black Africans continues unabated • U.S. troops launch offensive in Falluja in response to killing and mutilation on March 31 of four U.S. civilian contractors • U.S. hands over power to Iraqi interim government; Iyad Allawi becomes prime minister • Security Council demands Sudanese government disarm militias in Darfur that are massacring civilians • Summer Olympics take place in Athens, Greece • Venezuelan president Hugo Chavez survives recall referendum • Chechen terrorists take about 1,200 schoolchildren and others hostage in Beslan, Russia; 340 people die when militant detonate explosives • UN Atomic Energy Agency tells Iran to stop enriching uranium; a nascent nuclear weapons program suspected • About 380 tons of explosives reported missing in Iraq • Yasir Arafat dies in Paris • U.S. troops launch attack on Falluja, stronghold of the Iraqi insurgency (Nov. 8).
• Ukraine presidential election declared fraudulent
• Hamid Karzai inaugurated as Afghanistan's first popularly elected president • Massive protests by supporters of opposition candidate Viktor Yushchenko's lead to a new Ukrainian election; Yushchenko eventually declared prime minister
• Enormous tsunami devastates Asia; 200,000 killed • Bush proposes ambitious space program that includes flights to the Moon, Mars, and beyond • John Kerry secures Democratic nomination after winning nine out of ten primaries and caucuses • U.S. media release graphic photos of American soldiers abusing and sexually humiliating Iraqi prisoners at Abu Ghraib prison. Images spark outrage around the world • Gay marriages begin in Massachusetts, the first state in the country to legalize such unions
• Senate Intelligence Committee reports that intelligence on Iraq's weapons programs was "overstated" and flawed • Sept. 11 commission harshly criticizes government's handling of terrorist attacks
• Democratic National Convention in Boston nominates John Kerry for president • Pentagon-sponsored Schlesinger report rejects idea that Abu Ghraib prison abuse was work of a few aberrant soldiers, and asserts there were "fundamental failures throughout all levels of command" •
Republican Convention in New York renominates President Bush • Florida hit by hurricanes Bonnie and Charley • U.S.'s final report on Iraq's

weapons finds no WMDs • Congress extends tax cuts due to expire at the end of 2005
• Hurricane Ivan ravages U.S. south. Hurricane Jeanne hits Florida • George W. Bush is reelected president, defeats John Kerry
Super Bowl New England d. Carolina (32-29)
World Series Boston d. St. Louis (4-0)
NBA Championship Detroit d. Los Angeles (4-1)
Kentucky Derby Champion *Smarty Jones*
NCAA Basketball Championship Connecticut d. Georgia Tech (82-73)
NCAA Football Champions Southern California
Best Picture: Million Dollar Baby, Clint Eastwood
Record of the Year: "Here We Go Again," Ray Charles & Norah Jones
Album of the Year: Genius Loves Company, Ray Charles & Various Artists
Song of the Year: "Daughters," John Mayer
• Martha Stewart, diva of domesticity, was sentenced to five months in prison in July after being found guilty on four counts of obstruction of justice and lying to federal investigators. She began serving her sentence in October. She was also fined $30,000. The charges stem from her December 2001 sale of 3,928 shares of the biotech stock ImClone. She made the trade the day before the FDA announced it had declined to review ImClone's new cancer drug-news that sent shares tumbling • Sergey Brin and Larry Page, founders of Google, the phenomenally popular search engine, became instant billionaires when the company went public in August • Dan Rather found himself at the center of a media storm in September, when he and his network, CBS, admitted that they could not definitively prove the authenticity of documents they used in a 60 Minutes segment, which suggested President Bush received preferential treatment when he joined the National Guard and later when he served in it. He announced in December that he would step down in early 2005 • Michael Moore gained an impassioned following with the release of Fahrenheit 9/11, a documentary harshly critical of President Bush, his administration, the war in Iraq, and Bush's handling of the war on terrorism. The film won the Palme d'Or (the top prize) at the Cannes International Film Festival in May. In its opening weekend in late June, Fahrenheit 9/11 took in nearly $22 million at the box office to become the highest-grossing documentary of all time
• Mel Gibson garnered intense buzz for his incendiary film, The Passion of the Christ, months before its February release. The film, in Latin and Aramaic with English subtitles, depicts the last 12 hours of Jesus's life in explicitly violent detail. Many derided the film as anti-Semitic, saying it cast blame on the Jews for Jesus Christ's crucifixion. A number of evangelical Christian and Catholic groups, however, praised the film for its portrayal of Jesus Christ's sacrifice. It ended up the third-highest grossing film of the year, taking in $370,274,604 in 2004 • Janet Jackson and Justin Timberlake created an enormous scandal when Timberlake ripped the bodice of Jackson's costume during the halftime show of February's Super Bowl XXXVIII, exposing her right breast, which was pierced and adorned with a brooch. Timberlake promptly apologized for the "wardrobe malfunction." The Federal Communications Commission fined CBS, which broadcast the Super Bowl, $550,000 for the incident • Linda Ronstadt was ejected from Las Vegas's Aladdin Hotel in July after she dedicated the song "Desperado" to Michael Moore and encouraged the audience to see his new film, Fahrenheit 9/11 • The number of songs and

albums downloaded from the Internet continues at break-neck speed. Apple's iTunes sells its 200,000,000th song. According to Nielsen SoundScan, music fans bought 5.5 million digital albums and 140 million digital songs • Sequels fared very well at the box office, with Shrek 2 and Spider-Man 2 taking the two top spots. Meet the Fockers landed at No. 4, while Harry Potter and the Prisoner of Azkaban came in at No. 6. Movies: The Aviator • Collateral • Eternal Sunshine of the Spotless Mind • Friday Night Lights • The Incredibles • Kinsey • Maria Full of Grace • Million Dollar Baby • Sideways • Spider-Man 2 • Feb. 1: Scientists created two new chemical elements, named Ununtrium (Element 113) and Ununpentium (Element 115) • Scientists in South Korea announced they had created 30 human embryos by cloning and had removed embryonic stem cells from them • NASA announced it detected signs that water had once covered a small crater on Mars • Astronomers confirmed the discovery of the most distant object ever identified in our solar system, a planetoid names Sedna. It is the largest object discovered since Pluto in 1930 • Michael Melvil pilots SpaceShipOne into space, becoming the first person to do so in a privately developed aircraft • Cosmologist Stephen Hawking reverses himself on his Black Hole theory and concludes that information can in fact be retrieved from black holes • Australian and Indonesian archaeologists have unearthed skeletons of tiny people who are being called Homo floresiensis. These 3-foot-tall people had very long arms, heads the size of grapefruit, and are believed to have disappeared only 13,000 years ago, or perhaps even more recently • 69% of Californians vote in favor of a referendum to fund embryonic stem cell research, making the state the first to approve stem cell research.

The Game: 2004 GA-31 UF-24

Coach Mark Richt and his Georgia team finally experienced what it feels like to beat Florida with an Altel Stadium-record crowd of 84,753 whooping it up. This was not just any win. This was Georgia (7-1, 5-1 SEC) beating Florida (4-4, 2-4), who had owned the Bulldogs, winning six in a row and 13 of the past 14 in the series.

"It's awesome," said quarterback David Greene, who completed 15 of 23 passes for 255 yards and three touchdowns and tied Peyton Manning for most wins by a Division I-A quarterback with 39 wins. "It's everything I thought it would be. It stinks that it took until my senior year to beat them. At least I can put that on my resume one day."

The hero was senior wide receiver Fred Gibson, whose 15-yard touchdown catch with 8:37 remaining gave Georgia a crucial score. Florida rallied from down 24-7 to pull to 24-21 and looked like they could pull off a momentous comeback for their lame-duck coach Ron Zook who was fired the prior week.

Gibson said this week he wanted to play like Superman. He about did when he snagged a pass across the middle on a slant pattern to beating strong safety Cory Bailey and cornerback Reynaldo Hill.

"I couldn't believe I caught it, to tell you the truth," Gibson said. "I can't believe the safety didn't take the ball and go back to the other end. I guess he was looking at me the whole time. They were looking at me and I just reached my hands out and caught the football."

"I thought it was a certain interception when

David threw it. When he caught it, I could hardly believe it," Coach Richt said after the game.

It was Gibson's 18th career touchdown but first ever against the Gators, the school he committed to out of Waycross before changing his mind. Gibson dropped three passes against Florida last season when he played injured and dropped a third down slant pass on Georgia's final drive of the third quarter.

Before the fourth quarter, Richt had his team huddle around him on the field and gave an animated finger-pointing lecture.

"I wanted to make sure they were staying focused," Richt said. "I don't know how good a speech it was because after they ran an option for (38 yards)."

Georgia had scored a grand total of three touchdowns against the Gators in Richt's first three games against them.

The Bulldogs needed just 18 minutes to find the end zone that many times Saturday, scoring touchdowns on its first three possessions against a Florida defense that lost star linebacker Channing Crowder to a first quarter ankle injury. Six-foot-7 tight end Leonard Pope, whose college choices came down to Georgia and Florida, had touchdown catches of 27 and 35 yards and freshman tailback Thomas Brown scored on a 5-yard run as the Bulldogs grabbed a 21-7 lead.

Georgia was on the doorstep for another touchdown with first down at the 1-yard line, but the Bulldogs fumbled when Greene couldn't handle the snap after he collided with the guard. After Chris Leak's 3-yard touchdown pass to fullback Billy Latsko, the Gators trailed just 24-21. The Bulldogs gave up a season-high 458 yards on a day when it missed a slew of tackles and All-SEC linebacker Odell Thurman often over pursued.

Ciatrick Fason rushed for 139 yards and Leak completed 22 of 34 passes for 247 yards.

"We played as poor as we've played this year," defensive coordinator Brian VanGorder said. "We missed far too many tackles. I never thought I'd see Odell play like that."

Georgia, which got 103 rushing yards from Danny Ware, responded with an 8-play, 70-yard drive to remember capped with Gibson's score. On first down, Greene improvised when he didn't see any holes in the defense and rolled out to his left and connected with Reggie Brown for a 51-yard gain. He later hooked up with Brown again for a 14-yard gain.

"Up until that point they completely had the momentum," Greene said. "Right before that drive I told Fred and Reggie we're seniors. It's time for us to step up and make some plays."

Florida coaches tried everything offensively against the Bulldogs, including a pass to Leak in the first quarter that fell incomplete. Leak was wide open on the play.

With a first down at the Georgia 45-yard line, wide receiver Andre Caldwell took a reverse handoff, sprinted right, before lofting a pass to a wide-open Leak who was 10 yards ahead of the nearest defender.

Fortunately for the Bulldogs, the throw went just over the outstretched arms of a diving Leak, and the pass fell to the turf. The Gators were eventually forced to punt, and Georgia answered with a 10-play, 80-yard drive to extend its lead to 21-7.

"I'm glad our fans can come back to the World's Largest Outdoor Cocktail Party and won't have to hear the Florida fans run their mouth next time," defensive end David Pollack said. "At least for 365 days we can say we got the better end of

Florida," linebacker Arnold Harrison said. "For the last five years I've seen Georgia teams lose to Florida and I've seen the seniors take it the worse. We didn't waste our opportunity. Now this will be with us forever."

Why the "World's Largest Outdoor Cocktail Party"?

Bill Kastelz, a Florida Times-Union sports editor and columnist first coined the phrase "World's Largest Outdoor Cocktail Party" for the annual Florida-Georgia football game.

During his 35-year career here, he developed a widespread reputation as being a journalist.

"He was just a very tenacious guy. When he came up with a story, he would stay with it until he nailed it," said George Olson, a longtime friend and the former head of the Gator Bowl Association. "He never just took 'yes' and printed it as if it was fact. He was very certain that anything he wrote was certainly the truth."

Kastelz began working at the Times-Union in 1947 and retired in 1982. As a sports columnist, he covered the University of Florida, the Super Bowl and Bear Bryant's Alabama football teams. He wrote about most sporting events in Jacksonville, including Gator Bowl games and the Greater Jacksonville Open and Tournament Players Championship golf tournaments.

While covering the annual Florida-Georgia game in the 1950s, he made up the cocktail party nickname to describe the atmosphere that has transcended time.

"Bill was an excellent writer. He was able to kind of just tell a story and write it so well that people read his story like it was the gospel," said Joe Williams, who led the Jacksonville University men's basketball team to the national title game in 1970.

"People just believed the way he wrote things. He was the voice of sports in the city."

Mr. Kastelz assigned the Times-Union's first beat writer to Florida State's new football team as an assistant sports editor in the 1950s and made sure JU's young athletics program was covered in the 1960s.

"We were a small college and not many people believed in us, but he would still put us on the front page," Williams said. "He gave us some legitimacy."

Kastelz loved to golf and fish. He was born to Austrian immigrant parents in Aurora, Minn., and never lost his Minnewegian accent. He attended several Minnesota colleges and Duke University before serving in World War II in the Coast Guard and the Navy.

After being discharged in 1946, he became sports editor at the St. Augustine Record. When he was hired at the Times-Union, he commuted to work from St. Augustine until he bought a house in Arlington in 1956.

In 1955, Mr. Kastelz was promoted to Times-Union sports editor and was appointed to the Gator Bowl Association's board of directors. He was voted Florida Sports Writer of the Year in 1960. He was the Florida Sports Writers Association's president in '59 and '61.

After he retired from the Times-Union, Mr. Kastelz continued as a special correspondent for Sports Illustrated magazine, a post he held since the magazine's inception in 1954.

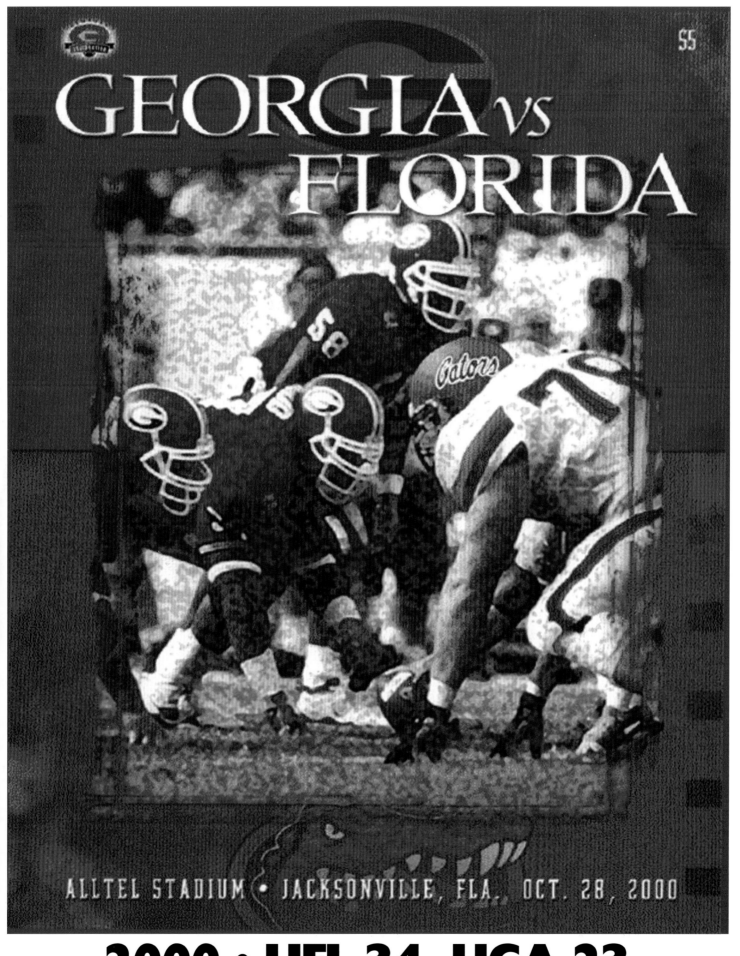

GEORGIA vs FLORIDA

55

ALLTEL STADIUM • JACKSONVILLE, FLA., OCT. 28, 2000

2000 · UFL 34 UGA 23

Florida vs. Georgia

October 27, 2001
Alltel Stadium
Jacksonville, Florida

$5.00

TALES FROM THE SWAMP

2001 · UFL 24 UGA 10

GEORGIA *vs* FLORIDA

Gator

$5⁰⁰

DAWGS

ALLTEL STADIUM
JACKSONVILLE, FLORIDA

2002 · UFL 20 UGA 13

November 1st, 2003   *Tales From The SWAMP*   Florida vs. Georgia

ALLTEL Stadium • Jacksonville, Florida

2003 • UFL 16 UGA 13

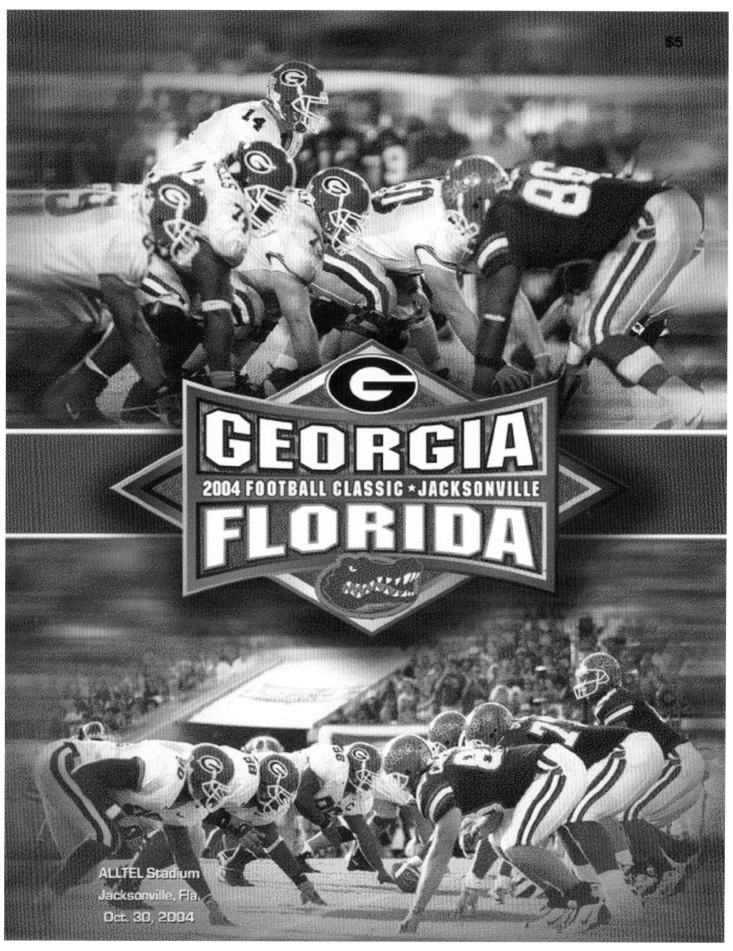

ALLTEL Stadium
Jacksonville, Fla.
Oct. 30, 2004

2004 · UGA 31 UFL 24

Comments

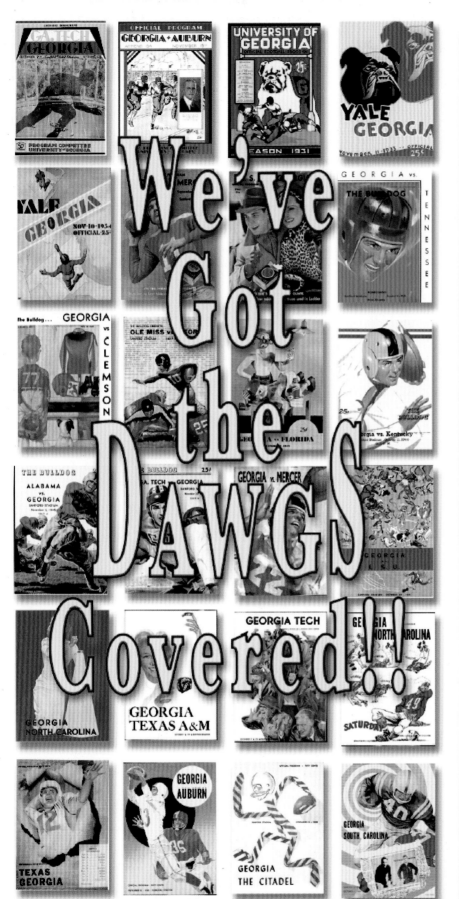
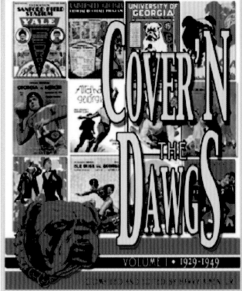
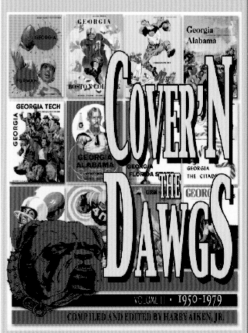